MARIE BONAPARTE

FEMALE SEXUALITY

MARIE BONAPARTE

FEMALE SEXUALITY

BF
692
B623
West

INTERNATIONAL UNIVERSITIES PRESS, INC.
NEW YORK

Copyright 1953 by International Universities Press, Inc.

All rights reserved

PRINTED IN U. S. A.

ACKNOWLEDGMENT

THE AUTHOR expresses her thanks to the Editor of the *International Journal of Psycho-Analysis* for kind permission to reprint *Passivity, Masochism and Femininity* and *Some Palaeobiological and Biopsychical Reflexions*.

I

FEMALE SEXUALITY*

* Planned 1933–4. First published as DE LA SEXUALITÉ DE LA FEMME in *Revue Française de Psychanalyse*, XIII; 1, 2, 3; 1949, and in book form by *Presses Universitaires de France*, 1951. Translated by John Rodker.

CONTENTS

I. FEMALE SEXUALITY

PART I

BISEXUALITY IN WOMAN

		PAGE
I.	WOMAN'S FREQUENT MALADAPTATION TO THE EROTIC FUNCTION	1
II.	PSYCHO-ANALYTIC AND BIOLOGICAL HYPOTHESES	5
	(a) Psycho-Analytic Findings	5
	(b) A Biological Theory of Bisexuality	7
III.	LIBIDINAL DEVELOPMENT OF THE SEXES COMPARED	13
	(a) An Embryological Note	13
	(b) Developmental Stages of the Human Libido	15
	(c) The Development of Passivity in the Girl and Boy	23
	(d) Some Divergent Analytic Theories Discussed	30
	(e) The Passive Phallus	42
IV.	DISTURBING FACTORS IN FEMININE DEVELOPMENT	46
	(a) Erotogenic Zones and Sexual Objects not necessarily Interdependent	46
	(b) Some Connections Between the Feminine Passive Oedipus Complex, the Maternal Instinct and Vaginal Function	47
	(c) Vital and Moral Dangers Inherent in the Feminine Sexual Functions	49
	(d) Infantile Masturbation, Seduction and Constitutional Cathexes of Erotogenic Zones	54

(e) Pre-Pubertal Clitoridal Orgasm and its Possible Relation to Fixation at the Phallic Stage 56
(f) The Scylla and Charybdis of the Little Girl 57
(g) A Battle of Two Males 59

PART II

THE EROTIC FUNCTION, A BIOPSYCHIC FUNCTION

I. PSYCHOLOGY, A BRANCH OF BIOLOGY . . 65

II. THE FEMALE AND HER LIBIDO 66
   (a) Poorer Libido of the Female and Basic Obstacles to Erotic Adaptation in Woman 66
   (b) The Psycho-Physiological "Vitellinism" of Woman 67
   (c) Vitellinism and Human Motherhood . 69
   (d) The Triple Stratification of the Factors that Determine Feminine Frigidity . . 70

III. ADULTS AND THE CHILD 71
   (a) Contradictory Adult Attitudes to the Sexuality of the Child 71
   (b) Sexual Ideation of the Child . . . 73

IV. ESSENTIAL FEMININE MASOCHISM . . . 76
   (a) Respective Relations of Active or Passive Oedipus Complexes to Sadism and Masochism 76
   (b) "A Child is Being Beaten" ... or a Woman 83
   (c) An Examination of Freud's "A Child is Being Beaten" 86
   (d) The Different Vicissitudes of Infantile Phantasies and of Their Instinctual Impulses 96
   (e) Affirmation of the Clitoris and Denial of the Vagina 103
   (f) Types of Women and Oedipus Complexes 109

CONTENTS

V. THE MALE'S CONSTRUCTIVE ROLE IN FEMALE SEXUALITY 116
   (*a*) Real and Oedipal Erotic Initiation Compared 116
   (*b*) Respective Roles of Father, Brother and Deflorator 125

VI. AN OUTLINE OF THE DEVELOPMENT OF FEMALE SEXUALITY 139

PART III

EVOLUTIONARY PERSPECTIVES

I. ALLO- AND AUTOPLASTIC ADAPTATION . . 145
   (*a*) Normality and Health 145
   (*b*) Alloplastic Adaptation: The Male as Mirror 146
   (*c*) Psycho-Analysis and Autoplastic Adaptation of the Central Nervous System . 148
   (*d*) A Peripheral Attempt at Autoplastic Adaptation: The Halban-Narjani Operation . 150

II. FEMALE MUTILATION AMONG PRIMITIVE PEOPLES AND THEIR PSYCHICAL PARALLELS IN CIVILIZATION . 153

III. NATURE AND CULTURE 162

II. PASSIVITY, MASOCHISM AND FEMININITY

I. The Pain Inherent in the Female Reproductive Functions 169
II. Erotic Pleasure in Women 170
III. The Infantile Sadistic Conception of Coitus . 171
IV. The Necessary Fundamental Distinction Between Masochism and Passivity 173
V. The Cloaca and the Phallus in Women . . 175

III. SOME PALAEOBIOLOGICAL AND BIOPSYCHICAL REFLECTIONS

I.	The Castration Complex and the Perforation Complex	181
II.	The Primitive Fear of Irruption into the Protoplasm	181
III.	Penetration and Nutrition	182
IV.	The Antagonism Between the Individual and the Species	182
V.	Penetration and Disintegration: Perforation Complex and Castration Complex	183
VI.	Libidinal Erotism and Moral Anxiety	184
VII.	Fear of Perforation the more General Fear	185
VIII.	Anxiety Always a Reaction to Objective Danger	186
IX.	Human Anxiety and the Human Brain	188

IV. NOTES ON EXCISION

Notes on Excision	191
List of works referred to in the Text	211
Index	217

PART I

BISEXUALITY IN WOMAN

I

WOMAN'S FREQUENT MALADAPTATION TO THE EROTIC FUNCTION

NATURE DOES not always succeed in adapting organisms to function perfectly in their environment as we may clearly see from the far greater frequency of defective adaptation to the purely erotic function in woman than in man. I emphasize *erotic* function, and not reproductive function, for no one doubts that countless women are capable of reproduction, and so are well adapted to the reproductive function while unadapted, nevertheless, to the purely erotic function. Frigidity and sterility are generally disparate factors.

As Freud has so well shown in his paper *Female Sexuality* (1931),[1] women, it appears, may be divided into three main types, each of which responds, in its own way, to the traumatic shock that every little girl experiences on first realizing the difference between the sexes. The first type soon succeed in substituting the desire for the penis for that of a child, and become true women: normal, vaginal, maternal. The next abandon all competition with men as feeling themselves too unequal, renounce all hope of obtaining an external love object and, socially and psychically, achieve a status among humans like that of the workers we see in the anthill or hive. Lastly, there are those who deny reality and never accept it; these cling desperately to the psychical and organic male elements innate in all women: the masculinity complex and the clitoris.

We must not forget, however, that these three types are rarely found unalloyed. Most often we find something of all three in each woman. And it is the dominance of elements of one type, over those of the other types within her, that will suffice to stamp her whole individuality.

We shall deal later with the first type and, for the moment, ignore the second, the *renouncers* who, naturally enough, often combine more characteristics of the third type, the *claimers*,

[1] *Coll. Papers*, Vol. V.

than of the first, the *acceptives*. Given the important psycho-biological problems raised by these last, it is to them we shall first turn our attention.

Women of this type cling desperately to whatever innate masculinity they may possess. A strange thing happens, however, for in them there is a split between the two factors which determine their adaptation to the feminine function. According to Freud, woman, to achieve ultimate femininity, must have changed both her dominant infantile clitoridal erotogenic zone and her original love object. The small girl's first love object is the mother, the woman, and it appears that, in the phallic phase through which we all pass, the first love object is loved with the same libidinal orientation, the same erotogenic zones, by the small girl as by the small boy. Jeanne Lampl-de Groot's valuable observations on these points are worth noting.[1]

Now, of the women who refuse to abandon their masculinity, some will neither give up their first love object, nor the phallically dominated erotogenic zone, and will become homosexual. Others again, though they succeed in passing from the mother to the father as their love object, and though they cannot even conceive of a love object so contemptible as to lack a phallus, cling tenaciously none the less to the dominantly phallic erotogenic zone and, with that organ, essentially male and inappropriate to the feminine function, will love and desire love objects that are themselves male.

Every analyst knows the difficulties that generally attend the cure of this last kind of woman. True, psycho-analysis has many a success to its credit in such cases, as we see from the number of newly-wed women enabled, or helped, by analysis, to pass from a solely clitoridal sensitivity to one essentially vaginal, i.e. to adaptation to the female erotic function. But in such cases of early analysis of a function not yet fully stabilized, it is difficult to distinguish between what the analyst accomplished and what life alone would have done for we know that, contrary to man, a certain period is almost always needed to allow the woman to adapt to her function and given that, that she often succeeds. Far more striking are those cases of clitoridal

---

[1] *The Evolution of the Oedipus Complex in Women* (1927).

women whose retarded adaptation to the vaginal function psycho-analysis sometimes enables us to observe.

Nevertheless, in many clitoridals of long date, successful analytic treatment remains difficult, since the patient manifests a surprisingly tenacious fixation to the phallic zone which will even survive analysis of the primary mother fixations. Such *partial frigidity*, though limited to *vaginal anaesthesia*, has often a poorer prognosis than that for *total frigidity*; that is, of *vaginal* and *clitoridal anaesthesia* together. Totally frigid women, even of long-standing, generally show more improvement than purely clitoridal women as a result of analysis or even, sometimes, of the passage of time, doubtless owing to the essentially hysterical nature of their inhibitions.

It will be seen that I deal here with just that problem which Helene Deutsch, in her paper on female frigidity in relation to the basic masochism normal to women[1] treats as a secondary issue, writing: "I will now pass on to discuss those forms of frigidity which bear the stamp of the masculinity-complex or penis-envy. In these cases the woman persists in the original demand for possession of a penis and refuses to abandon the phallic organization. Conversion to the feminine passive attitude, the necessary condition of vaginal sensation, does not take place."

This partial form of frigidity, in my opinion, is not only the most obdurate to treatment, but also the most frequent. The number of women so afflicted is far greater than men think, given the dissimulation women generally practise to hide their deficiencies in the erotic sphere. Also, the manner in which women endure this kind of frigidity varies greatly from one to another. Some resign themselves as to a command from on high and are content, for consolation, to remould *all* women in their own image. According to many clitoridals, those who boast of the pleasure experienced with the male must be braggarts or liars, or at least exceptions.

Other clitoridals compensate their inferiority in the sexual act, obvious though it is, by a kind of pride in their condition. They never surrender to a mutual passion and remain "inde-

[1] "The Significance of Masochism in the Mental Life of Women" (1930).

pendent" and aloof from the man; this enables them, at need, to be self-sufficient, in particular through masturbation, which is always possible to such women. Some clitoridals however, more honest with themselves, are well aware how much they suffer.

II

PSYCHO-ANALYTIC AND BIOLOGICAL HYPOTHESES

(a) *Psycho-Analytic Findings*

THE STUDY of such women, as we have indicated, confronts us with important psycho-biological problems. When the dominant female erotogenic zone, instead of becoming the vagina, remains the clitoris, we may first interpret this as an arrest in development since, thanks to Freud, we know how necessary it is, at puberty, for the centre of feminine sensitivity to transfer itself from the clitoris to the vagina. This observation alone far from exhausts the problem however, for, though many causes may have led to such a disturbance, given the innumerable factors that encourage or deter each individual's development, we must still search for laws in that very multiplicity.

We know that many psycho-analysts have already written on this subject, not in set terms, nor exactly as such, but indirectly as it were and in divers contexts though always, of course, in relation to woman's masculinity complex and the castration complex in general, both of which they invalidate or confirm. It will suffice here to note van Ophuijsen's *Contributions to the Masculinity Complex in Women* (1916–18),[1] for the light thrown on the fundamental relation between the feminine masculinity complex, urethral eroticism and clitoridal masturbation; Abraham's exhaustive and notable contribution entitled *Manifestations of the Female Castration Complex* (1921); Helene Deutsch's *Psychoanalyse der weiblichen Sexualfunktionen* (1925) and her admirable paper *The Significance of Masochism in the Mental Life of Women* (1930); Karen Horney's *On the Genesis of the Castration Complex in Women* (1923) her *The Flight from Womanhood* (1926) and her *The Denial of the Vagina* (1933); Josine Mueller's *A Contribution to the Problem of Libidinal Development in the Genital Phase in Girls* (1931); J. Lampl-de Groot's penetrating observations on the pre-history of *The Evolution of the Oedipus Complex in*

[1] *Int. J. Psycho-Anal.* **5**, 1924.

Women (1927); Melanie Klein's *Early Stages of the Oedipus Conflict* (1927) and her *The Psycho-Analysis of Children* (1932); Ernest Jones's *The Early Development of Female Sexuality* (1927) and *The Phallic Phase* (1933); Ruth Mack Brunswick's *The Analysis of a Case of Paranoia* (1928); Otto Fenichel's *The Pregenital Antecedents of the Oedipus Complex* (1930), a most rewarding contribution dealing exclusively with prephallic fixation on the mother[1] and, finally, those two most valuable contributions by Freud which round out the original and epoch-making views of his *Three Essays on the Theory of Sexuality* (1905); namely, *Some Psychological Consequences of the Anatomical Distinctions Between the Sexes* (1925) and *Female Sexuality* (1931), as also the chapter on "The Psychology of Women" in his *New Introductory Lectures on Psycho-Analysis* (1932).

Each of these works makes its own valuable contribution to the subject, though they often tend to deny, too absolutely, everything outside their own parcel of truth. I do not propose, however, to treat them in detail; those interested have but to consult these authors to see how far they agree with, or diverge from, my views. I shall only emphasize here that in treating the cardinal problem of the masculinity complex in women, psycho-analyst authors are animated by two main and opposite trends. Some, like Freud, J. Lampl-de Groot, Helene Deutsch and myself, assign it primarily biological roots, though it may be secondarily reinforced by other factors. Others, like Karen Horney, Melanie Klein and Ernest Jones, consider it stems from later and mainly psychogenic causes such as the flight from femininity, whether from fear of its dangers or a sense of oedipal or incestuous guilt, or again from a disappointed father attachment.

All these works, which mainly base their reasoning on such factors, end by deriving the female masculinity complex from what, above all, are secondary processes. True, it would be wrong to under-estimate the psychological importance of these secondary factors but, to assign them a dominant role in establishing the female masculinity complex seems to imply an anti-biological bias which tends to overlook that basic bisexuality

[1] (Note added in 1948.) See also Sándor Radó: *Fear of Castration in Women* (1933).

which we must always bear in mind. Male and female co-exist from the origin in each human being: the sex which predominates reinforces the other in greater or less degree, and it is upon this basic bisexuality which, in the full meaning of the term, remains biologically primitive, that the reactions to infantile events are built. Bisexuality is also at the very roots of the primary psychological manifestations such as penis envy and those first libidinal impulses which Freud, in his *Female Sexuality* says; "have an intensity of their own which is greater than anything that comes later and may indeed be said to be incommensurable with any other force".

In his *Three Essays on the Theory of Sexuality*, Freud had already written that "in human beings pure masculinity or femininity is not to be found either in a psychological or a biological sense. Every individual on the contrary displays a mixture of the character-traits belonging to his own and opposite sex, and he shows a combination of activity and passivity whether or not these last character-traits tally with his biological ones." No better description of our respective biological and psychological components could be given. Thus we are justified in thinking that libidinal fixation on the clitoris, in woman, when tenaciously maintained, corresponds to a basically biological masculine character incorporated in the feminine organism.

(b) *A Biological Theory of Bisexuality*

Everywhere in Nature we find bisexuality, and the elucidation of its problems in recent years has been one of the main preoccupations of psycho-analytical science and of all branches of biology.

I shall not, however, discuss all the works that deal with this subject, nor especially those that treat of bisexuality in the animal kingdom or which draw their conclusions therefrom. However important such conclusions may be in their application to man what, first and foremost, is required of the psychoanalyst, is the direct study of man.

Nevertheless, there is one author, not in the ranks of the psycho-analysts, whose work merits their attention; namely

Gregorio Marañon whose *The Evolution of Sex and Intersexual Conditions* (1930), might more justly have been called "The Evolution of Sex and Bisexual Conditions". In general, his thesis is that many years of clinical experience have led him to conclude that every human being, at birth, is endowed with the potentialities of both sexes. Later, influenced in constructive or protective fashion by the hormones—he little cares which—one sex eventually predominates without, however, completely suppressing the characters of the other.

Whereas, according to him, the male sex is *progressive*, that of the female is *regressive;* i.e. only the male will attain the full somatic development possible to the race. The general development of woman, however, will come to a stop at puberty through maturation of the organs destined for maternity; functions which absorb a large part of the energy which is used by the male in building up his whole organism. It would appear, therefore, that whereas the male usually passes through an intersexual crisis of feminoid type, *before full puberty is reached*, and before virility is fully established, the female will experience the customary intersexual crisis of viriloid type *after the menopause*, when the inhibitory influence of the ovaries disappears.

To quote Marañon, femininity, in relation to masculinity, would thus be a stage of evolution which has stopped midway between adolescence and the adult man, this last being the true terminal form of organic evolution.

This view, which is based on purely biological factors and which ignores metaphysical speculations, has naturally been debated. Against it, it is urged that the evolution of the male and female is not a question of degree, but of *essence;* that the male and female are simply *different creatures*. Such a rejoinder, I consider, does less than justice to Marañon's ideas, for he has never advanced that woman is solely an adolescent. What he says is that, in herself, juxtaposed as it were, or rather intermingled, she contains *both* an adolescent—as her more delicate physique shows—*and* a woman, whose maternal adjuncts must necessarily influence the whole of that delicate physique. Which amounts to saying, and the psycho-analyst would be unwise to dispute it, that woman is woman both by reason of her feminine organs and her maternal bias, and male by reason of her masculinity complex.

Other chapters deal with manifestations of this intersexuality in both woman and man, and other sections again with the main syndromes of bisexuality: hermaphroditism, pseudo-hermaphroditism, cryptorchism and hypospadia as well as with the various feminoid or viriloid manifestations, physical, psychological, specifically erotic or even social, that trouble the apparent unisexuality of every human being.

Worth considering is Marañon's attitude to the problem of the libido (which he interprets far more narrowly than the Freudians) and the orgasm, of which he says: "the non-indispensable" (to reproduction) "debilitated and belated orgasm of the woman is, to all appearance, a character of a viriloid, intermediate nature, as I have earlier remarked in the case of the libido", which agrees with one viewpoint of Freud's as regards the male, or at least the unitary essence of the libido.[1]

Elsewhere, Marañon says: "In the man the orgasm has its seat in a highly differentiated organ, elaborately vascularised and innervated: the penis. In the woman the corresponding organ

[1] In *Three Essays on the Theory of Sexuality* (1905), Freud wrote: "So far as the auto-erotic and masturbatory manifestations of sexuality are concerned, we might lay it down that the sexuality of little girls is of a wholly masculine character. Indeed, if we are able to give a more definite connotation to the concepts of 'masculine' and 'feminine', it would also be possible to maintain that libido is invariably and necessarily of a masculine nature, whether it occurs in men or in women and irrespectively of whether its object is a man or a woman."

In his *New Introductory Lectures on Psycho-Analysis* (1932), Freud writes: "There is only one libido which is as much in the service of the male as of the female sexual function. To it itself we can assign no sex; if in accordance with the conventional analogy between activity and masculinity, we choose to call it masculine we must not forget that it also includes impulses with passive aims. Nevertheless the phrase 'feminine libido' cannot possibly be justified. It is our impression that more violence is done to the libido when it is forced into the service of the female function; and that—to speak teleologically—this may be based on the fact that the achievement of the biological aim is entrusted to the aggressiveness of the male, and is to some extent independent of the co-operation of the female."

—the clitoris—remains in a rudimentary condition and is frequently insensitive to any excitation which is not very powerful and prolonged. On the other hand, in the woman, there is a great dispersion of the erotogenous zones towards the neighbouring mucous membrane (vulvar, anal) and throughout the skin, being sharply specialized in the breasts. For this reason, as I have said, she is more responsive to caresses than man." This is excellently observed, as every psycho-analyst must admit. But here our ways begin to part, for Marañon, though he starts with the just observation that erotic desire and, above all, the orgastic capacity of woman increase with age, nevertheless writes and often returns to the point that feminine orgasm, in addition to being slow, "*is almost always belated in its chronological appearance*. In numerous cases its spontaneous development does not become complete until the woman approaches the forties; and in some cases only appears then for the first time. . . . The true reason consists, in my opinion, *in the fact that the specific organ of the feminine orgasm—the clitoris—being of masculine affiliation, attains the maximum of its development very belatedly*, being comparable in this sense with the development of other virile characteristics which precede or accompany the female climacteric."[1] Here, the psycho-analyst can no longer follow the biologist; for the latter, in effect, seems to ignore what to the former seems quite elementary; namely, the existence of *two main* erotogenic zones in woman, zones often antagonistic, but each, in its own way, able to procure orgasm.

Every analyst knows how greatly a persistent clitoridal sensitivity hinders the establishment of vaginal function—indispensable to feminine response in normal coitus—and how much more then would it do so if increased. If our viewpoint is the overcoming of frigidity in coitus, it is not with a *so much the better* but a *so much the worse*, that we should greet the recrudescence which Marañon postulates.[2]

[1] Author's italics.

[2] In her paper *The Psychology of Women in Relation to the Functions of Reproduction* (1925) Helene Deutsch claims that she has often observed a regression of feminine erotogenic sensitivity from the vagina to the clitoris occurring after the menopause, which would thus conform to Marañon's theory of a post-menopause viriloid

In spite, therefore, of his just observations on the masculine significance of the clitoris, it would seem that, himself a male, he does not succeed in *ideating* orgasm apart from an organ of penis nature. Nevertheless, the most remarkable biological feat of the female organism is exactly that of being able to deflect this male energy—which clitoridal libido represents—and its supreme expression, the orgasm, into purely feminine channels by displacing the erotogenic centre from the clitoris, masculinely based, to the cloacal vagina. This displacement sometimes takes place so completely that the clitoris is insensitive. The female, in vaginal orgastic capacity, will often then outdo the male, for it seems that such ultra-vaginal women are just those in whom orgasm occurs most easily and intensely.

The uncompromising nature of clitoridal hypersensitivity as regards the feminine erotic function seems thus to have escaped Marañon's notice. In a sense more serious than he realizes, it is an "intersexual" manifestation bound up with human bisexuality and the masculinity complex which so profoundly disturbs femininity in woman.

This hiatus in Marañon's work, valuable as are his views and conclusions, demonstrates the extent to which psycho-analytic knowledge and, I would add, experience, are indispensable to every biologist wishing to study the problems of human sexuality.

Both disciplines are now too closely interwoven to be able to ignore each other. Henceforth the study of psycho-sexuality can never neglect the indispensable processes of psycho-analytic investigation. "The finer shades of female sexuality",

---

phase in woman, but not to that in which he hails the hyper-excitability of the clitoris as a forward step in feminine adaptation to a truly erotic function. For such women, formerly satisfied by normal coitus, were so no longer, as I was told by Helene Deutsch, and external caresses were needed to enable them to achieve orgasm. Nevertheless, generally speaking, I believe that the woman who has been able to experience vaginal orgasm during her period of full femininity will retain it after the menopause, as she then retains, as Marañon has also observed, the heterosexual choice of a love-object, despite the more or less viriloid phase on which she has entered. The repetition mechanism of the autonomic nervous system continues to make her react as before.

writes Marañon, "are part of a whole . . . impenetrable to the investigator." To the non-analyst investigator, we must add—for if it is true that the "dark continent"[1] of female psycho-sexuality, as Freud calls it, is still far from explored, the only pioneers who have made headway at all are the psycho-analysts.

[1] *The Question of Lay-Analysis* (1926).

III

LIBIDINAL DEVELOPMENT OF THE SEXES COMPARED

OF RECENT years, psycho-analytic authors have presented us with a considerable body of facts and if, to this, I add my own clinical findings, and compare both with what contemporary biology has to say, this should provide a sufficient basis on which to attempt an outline, in psycho-biological terms, of the comparative development of male and female sexuality. Later, we shall return to the specific problem of female sexuality with which we began.

(a) *An Embryological Note*

In his *A Short Study of the Development of the Libido, Viewed in the Light of Mental Disorders* (1924), Karl Abraham[1] wrote: "We have long since learned to apply the biogenetic principle of organic life to the mental (psycho-sexual) development of man. Psycho-analysis is constantly finding confirmation of the fact that the individual recapitulates the history of his species in its psychological aspects as well. A great quantity of empirical data, however, warrants us in laying down yet another law concerning man's psycho-sexual development. This is that it lags a long way behind his somatic development, like a late version or repetition of that process. The biological model upon which the developmental processes discussed in this paper are based takes place in the earliest embryonic period of the individual, whereas the psycho-sexual processes extend over a

---

[1] We know that Haeckel's biogenetic law, according to which ontogeny summarily recapitulates phylogeny, is nowadays much attacked. See, especially, G. R. de Beer's *Embryology and Evolution*, in which the author seeks to establish that it is not recapitulation but simple repetition which we find in ontogeny. Whether it be recapitulation or repetition, Abraham's physiological and psychological parallels, in my opinion, stand.

number of years of his extra-uterine life, namely, from his first year to the period of puberty.

"If we return to the field of embryology we can without difficulty recognize that there is an extensive similarity between the gradual development of man's psycho-sexual life ... and the organic development of his early embryonic life."

We shall again meet and, in due course, consider the biological parallels to which he refers, as well as others which might be added. But we shall begin by extending the biological parallel to the earliest stage of human development and recall the primary cellular differentiation of the gonads.

Originally, there would be the still almost undifferentiated germ cell—I say almost and not quite—for it seems impossible to imagine that the endocrine glands whose hormones, during the embryonic stage, and after, determine the predominance of one sex or other, do not themselves owe their existence and their function to a primary, more or less differentiated zygotic condition of the original fertilized cell.

We know from embryology that what will become the human sex gland appears very early in embryonic life as the so-called genital cord. If the organism is to develop into a male, testis cords will be organized from the diffuse epithelial mass already present at the indifferent stage of the gonad. If, on the other hand, the organism is to develop into a female, Pflüger's tubes will appear in the germinal epithelium, whence will arise properly female cells which will encroach more and more on the epithelial mass, which latter will then atrophy.

It almost seems as if the female sex, from this moment and this embryonic stage, were establishing itself in the manner in which, as Marañon maintains, it will biologically and psychologically develop later: that is, as a significant female appendage to an organism *which might have become male* but for the inhibitory influence of the contrary sex.[1]

We need not here discuss the various hypotheses propounded in the still current darkness of biology concerning a possible foundation for our basic human bisexuality. These are enumerated by Marañon in his chapter on hermaphroditism. But apart

[1] This form of embryonic evolution of the gonads seems special to vertebrates.

from observed cases of hermaphroditism showing both an ovary and testicle, may we not have, in certain instances, "outside the gonads", unsuspected traces which represent the opposite sex, in the form of accessory corpuscles or scattered cells in the *urogenital tract*? (Krabbe.) Or again, since the histological presence of both gonadal tissues is not absolutely necessary, might not some seemingly morphologically normal gonad, to some extent, recover its original bi-hormonal capacity and, by way of the interstitial tissue, secrete the two hormones which determine femininity and masculinity? (Zawandoski, Lipschütz.) The probable multiplicity of the sexual hormones, which recent research seems ever more to suggest, offers the widest horizons to our hypotheses. We find, in effect, folliculine in male blood and urine (Dohrn, Hirsch, Ashheim and others); and folliculine given to pre-pubescent male rats will maturate the genital tract. Nor must we forget the similarity, the probable unitary nature of the substances which help to maintain the libido, i.e. sexual excitation in its widest sense, in one and the other sex.

Finally, a last hypothesis derives the presence of male characteristics in a female organism, and vice versa, despite the postulated absence of any actual glandular basis for the bisexual characters they include, from the *anterior* presence of such a basis, which would disappear once the sexual characters were fixed. In this neuro-glandular coupling, the irreversible surviving nervous factor, here constituted by the whole nervous system, would suffice to carry on the subject's bisexual reactions even after the glandular factor which first conditioned them had disappeared.

(b) *Developmental Stages of the Human Libido*

Let us, however, leave the purely biological field, still so little explored, to turn to the more certain data which psychoanalytic enquiry provides.

As our foundation, we shall take the general outline of the development of the libido as traced by Freud, and elaborated in certain respects by Abraham, and seek to elucidate this in line with the latest findings of psycho-analysis. Thus, the basic bisexuality which governs human development may be revealed more clearly, perhaps, than we have so far been able to do.

We know that the tiny human, its libido based on the great vital and organic needs, starts life dominated by oral erotism (Freud). The mother is then its first object so to speak, for, to the suckling, the mother is originally pre-objectal and it is fixated on her without distinguishing her from itself.

In this first autoerotic phase, characterized by the urge to *suck*, there still appears no difference of behaviour in girl or boy.

The second oral phase, distinguished by Abraham from the first, and well-termed *cannibalistic*, is still centred on the mother, whom the nursling, with its newly appearing teeth, tends to want to bite and devour. In this phase, which roughly corresponds, so far as object love is concerned, to narcissism, the babe already possesses a clearer psychical awareness of the mother as a distinct object, an awareness which the adult mind is doubtless unable to picture but which, nevertheless, must exist. In this phase, the nursling loves the mother object narcissistically, as an appendage to itself, and to this cannibalistic phase corresponds its urge towards physical incorporation of that object. In this phase, which revolves round the mother as central object, the respective behaviour of the boy or girl still seems much the same.

We must not forget, however, that in the pregenital stages the dominant distinction lies between *activity* and *passivity*, for it is that which is mainly responsible for introducing and establishing the later distinction between *male* and *female*. As Freud wrote: "In maleness is concentrated subject, activity, and the possession of a penis; femaleness carries on the object, and passivity."[1]

Now activity, like passivity, as Freud has shown, begin to declare themselves when the child enters the sadistic-anal stage, towards the beginning of its second year. We then observe a concomitant development of the *active* muscular system with *passive anal* erotism of the mucosae. This is the time, in our opinion, when masculine and feminine or, rather, pre-masculine and pre-feminine, are prefigured *together* in the

[1] "The Infantile Genital Organization of the Libido" (1923): In *Coll. Papers*, Vol. II.

small creature, and this in proportion to the strength with which the aforementioned trends affect the erotization of its active muscular system as well as the passive, digestive, rectal, anal and cloacal mucous surfaces.

The tendency to aggression, seen sometimes in adult analyses, but principally in those of children—as also in many myths and primitive superstitions[1]—whose content is a projection, upon others, of the wish to injure and kill with one's excrement or urine, derives from the active sadistic muscular urge expressed in cloacal fashion and manifested by means of the only missiles (including spitting) which the child possesses and can use; namely, those of its body. Thus the cloaca, like the mouth, may be both active and passive, although passivity is generally its essential quality.

Now, at this stage, the libidinal emphasis, as the case may be, either reinforces the sadistic muscular activity, or else the passive erotogenic cloacal zone, but not always according to the *predominant* sex of the gonads. The boy, to become adequately virile later, must now present a greater libidinization of the active muscular system than of the passive cloacal zone, while the girl, to become truly womanly, must present a predominant erotization of that zone. It is thus that, at this stage, the greater or less predisposition towards a dominant unisexuality will be defined. Such, however, is not always the case, and the child's actual and future bisexuality thenceforth often expresses itself by an excessive erotization of the active sadistic muscular activity in the girl, as by a passive cloacal erotism in the boy. Any relative lack of these two erotisms, linked with sex, will similarly favour bisexuality.

This is not to say that the anal erotism of a boy, for instance, is so deplorable a bisexual phenomenon that its suppression, impossible though that were, would represent an ideal. Indeed no, for the adult man must be able to use this anal erotism, and to transform and integrate it as part of his character, his psycho-sexuality. I only refer here to an excessive degree

---

[1] See especially Melanie Klein: *The Psycho-Analysis of Children* (1932) and all Róheim's works on the aborigines of Central Australia.

of this erotism. The same also applies to excessive erotization of the active sadistic muscular system in the girl. It is a quantitative, an "economic" problem.

All we have just said, however, relates only to the first of the sadistic-anal phases: that in which muscular aggression is not yet inhibited, no more than is yet the primitive erotism of the anal zone. This is the period when the child would still like to abandon itself as freely to its excremental pleasures as to its muscular activity. But alas! training has already begun to check both these manifestations, though mainly the first.

Now the second anal stage is about to commence, in which the pleasure of freely abandoning itself to excretion will be converted into the duty, then pleasure, of retaining the faeces.

For a long time it surprised me not to find, at this point, any mention of the *positive* phallic phase in the table drawn by Abraham. This table, without transition, passes from the second sadistic-anal phase to that termed the *primitive genital* (phallic) *phase*, corresponding to object-love *with exclusion of the genitals*. Here is Abraham's table of the development of the libido (1924).[1]

STAGES OF LIBIDINAL ORGANIZATION	STAGES OF OBJECT-LOVE	
I. Earlier Oral Stage (sucking)	Auto-erotism (without object)	(Pre-ambivalent)
II. Later Oral Stage (cannibalistic)	Narcissism (total incorporation of object)	(Ambivalent)
III. Earlier Anal-sadistic Stage	Partial love with incorporation	
IV. Later Anal-sadistic Stage	Partial love	
V. Earlier Genital Stage (phallic)	Object-love with exclusion of genitals	
VI. Final Genital Stage	Object-love	(Post-ambivalent)

In the light of our present knowledge regarding the sexual development of the girl, but also of what we know of the boy's, it seems impossible to agree, so far as the earlier genital

[1] In *Selected Papers on Psycho-Analysis*.

phase is concerned, with this earlier phallic exclusion of the phallus; for it is the phallus, as the one primary genital organ, that is intended, as everything in Abraham's context shows.

True, just as he saw in the transition from the oral stage, to the anal stage which follows, a psycho-sexual repetition of what happens in certain embryos (Batrachia); namely, an actual changing of the primitive mouth[1] to function finally as a primitive anus, so Abraham imagines he recognizes, in the phallic stage, with exclusion of the phallus, an echo of the apparently initial sexual undifferentiation of the embryo. One might ask, however, whether one is justified in doing so, for it was, in fact, in a case of true hysteria, with kleptomania and *pseudologia*, that Abraham most clearly found "regression" to this stage, and we know that hysteria is a neurosis with a genital-phallic foundation, with repression, not regression, at its base. Thus we are justified in saying that the phallic stage with exclusion of the phallus must be, not the earlier phallic stage, but rather the final phallic stage resulting from repression of the earlier stage.

In the development of the human libido, there must have been an *affirmation* of the phallus before there could be a denial, whether hysterical or merely feminine, and this is just what we see it is in the *earlier phallic stage* of which Abraham's *earlier genital stage* is but a reaction-formation.[2]

[1] Which however, even in its first position, functions as an anus.

[2] At the meeting, in February, 1923, of the Berlin Psycho-Analytical Society, Abraham first expounded his theory of libidinal development and there drew a more elaborate table on the blackboard than that published in his book. Thanks to Dr. Odier, who was present, I have been able to consult a copy of this table. Now, opposite his earlier genital stage with exclusion of the genitals, Abraham had then written as corresponding to the Oedipal development at this stage: "Latency period with repression", which surely implies that this negative phallic stage could only be a reaction to an obviously implied earlier positive phallic stage. Besides, it was this positive phallic stage that Freud described in his *The Infantile Genital Organization of the Libido* which first appeared in the "Int. Zeitschrift für ärztliche Psychoanalyse" in 1923.

Since *A Short Study of the Development of the Libido* first appeared in 1924, it may seem strange that Abraham did not take this "phallic" paper of Freud's into account when drafting his

Now let us briefly review the customary development of masturbation in the child.

The masturbation of the nursling, as Freud has shown, is of very general occurrence. But at that age, masturbation will still, as it were, be embryonic and imperfectly focused on the erotogenic zones. True, the penis must already focus the boy's auto-erotism better than the small clitoris of the girl does hers, in whom it would be difficult to distinguish, at this time, between what is peri-cloacal masturbation and what phallic. Moreover, at this time, masturbation can doubtless do no more than provide a vague, diffuse fore-pleasure, for orgastic end-pleasure is only accessible to human organisms at stages of varying precocity though, for many, at roughly when puberty sets in.

Such masturbation is often spontaneously relinquished by the nursling, as though its muscular activity, awakening at the next stage, started off by drawing the child's active libidinal forces to itself.

The general activity now aroused soon flows, however, towards the phallus, the active erotogenic zone which, in its turn, seems destined to a later awakening. Ordinarily, beginning with the later sadistic-anal stage, that is, after earlier anal freedom is repressed, the child returns to true masturbation which, for the boy, ends in the active, positive, masculine Oedipus complex and, for the girl, in the same active Oedipus complex, (though femininely negative), both of which acknowledge the mother as object and doubtless, also, the same

---

table of the Development of the Libido for publication. Compare my division into two sections of the phallic stage with the ideas also expressed by Ernest Jones in his *The Phallic Phase*, delivered at the Wiesbaden Congress of 1932.

Jones, for his part, splits this stage into two parts: the protophallic and the deuterophallic, the former characterized by a unisexual conception of all beings, and the second by the concept of two different sexes. My ideas however diverge notably from Jones's as regards the primary nature of phallus-ness in the girl. The positive phallic stage does not seem to him to apply as a rule to the latter: he does not agree it represents a normal biological stage.

main executive organ, the penis, or its diminutive homologue, the clitoris.

This stage is only ended by the castration complex which, for the girl, as for the boy, as we shall hope to show later, inaugurates what Abraham has so justly termed the *phallic stage with exclusion of genitals (phallus)*, this, to our mind, being equivalent to the change brought about *in the phallic stage after the traumatic effects of the castration complex.*

It is not only in the hysteric, and pathologically, that we find *exclusion of the phallus*: it is what *should* happen normally, in the little girl, if she is later to adapt herself to her erotic function as woman. Abraham's exclusion of the genital is essentially, we would say, the first wave of the repression which *must* normally overtake the phallic masturbation of the little girl and her clitoris-excitability which, according to some, represents the executive organ of the girl's active transitory Oedipus complex, this being the highly attenuated and very truncated homologue of the boy's positive Oedipus complex, much as the female clitoris is of the male penis.

At this time also, an analogous wave seems generally to overtake the boy's phallic masturbation; his active Oedipus complex, as a result of the castration complex, declines, and with similar effect as in the girl, both as regards object, sexual aim and erotogenic zones. It is the castration complex which, in the girl and boy, terminates the primary Oedipus complex; that active Oedipus complex of which the mother, coveted with the active phallus, was object. It is this also, in both cases, which ushers in the second and passive Oedipus complex (chronologically speaking), in which the father, and his phallus, for the boy as for the girl, become objects, passively desired, in cloacal fashion.

Whereas, however, the girl's active Oedipus complex, (active strivings towards the mother) finally yields, in normal cases, to the passive Oedipus complex (lasting passivity to the father or his subsequent male surrogates), the boy's passive Oedipus complex, temporarily subject to the father, should only be a transitory phase from which he will victoriously emerge through narcissistic affirmation of his active masculinity turned back towards women, as substitutes for the given-up mother.[1]

It may perhaps be objected here that we have only dealt so far with exclusion of the phallus *in the subject* and not *in the object*, but Abraham himself, we feel, would have authorized it. Did he not write, in relation to this stage, which he himself postulated: "The rejection of the genital zone applies to the subject's own body as well as to that of his object."

It is now incumbent on us, given our own view, to speak about object-love with exclusion of the phallus in the object. To my mind, this stage of exclusion of the phallus, which is ushered in by the castration complex, will differ, in its primary orientation, according to the sex of the individual considered. In the girl, the cardinal features will be exclusion of the phallus on her own body, with compensatory narcissistic affirmation of the whole—in which, let me say, she shows a true perception of reality and, by its acceptance, takes a decisive step towards her future femininity.

In the boy, exclusion of the phallus is a feature which must pass over to the object: girl, woman or mother. It is not his own phallus, as subject, but the phallus of the love object, which he must learn to renounce if he is to become normally heterosexual. To be able to love woman masculinely, later, the boy must thenceforth, in effect, be able to love a whole being, with phallus excluded; the being, in short, that is woman. And success or failure in establishing these infantile

---

[1] *Active* Oedipus complex and *passive* Oedipus complex are terms which Freud himself proposed to designate the successive attitudes, with which we have dealt, of both girl and boy to the mother or father. I first became aware of this from Ruth Mack Brunswick's paper *Observations on pre-Oedipal Male Sexuality* read at the Wiesbaden Congress in 1932.

It will have been remarked that, whereas Freud in *The Passing of the Oedipus Complex* (1924) says that the castration complex, in the boy, makes an end of *both** Oedipus complexes, the active and passive, through narcissistic fears for the penis, and does not chronologically distinguish between the passing of either, I seem to lean towards splitting this passing into two stages. Nevertheless, the two currents, active and passive, are often so commingled, that it would be difficult to attach chronological periods to their decline.

* Author's italics.

positions which mirror each other, as it were, in each sex, will condition the psycho-sexual normality, or abnormality, of the future man or woman.

Whereas the boy, to become a man, must never, on any account, accept the loss of his penis, the girl, to become a woman, must normally accept the *loss of that penis*.

For the man whose psyche excludes the phallus from himself psychically castrates himself, whence will arise impotence in the varying degrees to which such exclusion occurred.

The woman, who, *per contra*, through jealousy of the male penis and revenge against its male possessor, psychically seeks to tear it from him, deprive him of it and thus, by a sort of talion, project her own castration on the male, is thereby preparing herself to reject a loving acceptation of the male penis, whence will arise divers forms of hysterical frigidity through the repression of acceptant vaginal response.

Both these forms of psycho-sexual inadequacy were, however, well observed by Abraham when he wrote: "This situation" (object-love with exclusion of genitals: phallus) "is to a great extent responsible for two very general and, from a practical point of view, important symptoms—impotence in men and frigidity in women."

In the light of what has been said, we believe we are justified in modifying Abraham's table.[1] He himself wrote that this "table is comparable with the timetable of an express train, in which only a few of the most important stations are enumerated", which thus leaves us space for others. He could thus only have approved of our inserting, as a forgotten important station, the first positive phallic stage, and our addition, to the two columns which relate to the libidinal organization and stages of object-love, of a third which marks the boy's and girl's active or passive attitudes to the object.

(c) *The Development of Passivity in the Girl and Boy*

Let us now follow, more closely, the fate of the libidinal cathexes of the passive cloaca, which parallels that of the libidinal cathexes of the active phallus. It seems that the

[1] See table p. 18.

future genital libido which begins to establish itself, though still diffuse, in both sexes throughout childhood, goes on oscillating between these neighbouring poles.

In the earlier anal stage, it was the cloaca that appeared as the erotogenic organ. Then, as throughout life, the cloaca is a passive organ as, largely, is the mouth before the teeth appear, in the primary stage. The cloaca, however, will never be dentated, except in the phantasies of impotent men who fear it, as such, in woman; or in certain primitive beliefs.[1] The cloaca, itself, all through life, will continue as the essential factor supporting passivity. Thus, any special accentuation of this passive primary anal erotism indicates a predisposition towards passive psycho-sexual attitudes, whatever the subject's sex.

We must not forget however that the girl, like the boy, originally knew only one love-object, the mother; this primary stage of passivity is constellated by the mother or woman by whom she is replaced (as with Kala, described by Ruth Mack Brunswick, where a feminine paranoia was shown directly to derive from a primary passive fixation on an elder sister as substitute for the mother)[2]. The cleansing ministrations of the mother, without any need for seduction, as such, will passively arouse the child's erotogenic cloacal zones. On the other hand, if the original tendency to welcome undifferentiated bodily caresses, diffuse and passive excitations of the skin and mucous membranes—a tendency opposed to the sadistic muscular activity which then awakens—proves more highly developed than this last, it must be considered a feminine trend, unfavourable to the boy's development, though favourable to the girl's; one additive to the effect of cloacal excitations in the prefeminine direction of passivity.

All this, however, soon leads to the later anal stage, characterized by the tendency of the cloaca to contract and shut. The child retains its faeces, in part because of early moral

[1] Among certain primitives, the mother-in-law's vagina is considered menacing because dentated, doubtless as a result of the repressed incest wishes transferred from the mother to the mother-in-law.

[2] "The Analysis of a Case of Paranoia" (1928).

prohibitions, "sphincter-morals", as Ferenczi calls them, which command it not to relax its sphincter muscles whenever or wherever it pleases, and, in part—which is perhaps what provides the foundation for sphincter-morals—by virtue of a kind of biological prohibition which coincides with increased control of these muscles. Abraham, pursuing his biological parallels, writes: "We recognized the fourth stage of the psycho-sexual development of the individual as that in which he has as his sexual aim the retention and control of his object. Its correlate, in biological ontogenesis, is to be found in the formation of the intestinal mechanisms for retaining what has been taken into the body. These consist in constrictions and enlargements, annular contractures, branching passages, divagations ending blindly, manifold convolutions, and finally the voluntary and involuntary sphincter muscles of the anus itself. At the time that this complicated arrangement for the retention of objects is being formed, there is as yet no sign of the appearance of the uro-genital apparatus."[1]

True, the uro-genital sinus begins to appear when the cloacal membrane has already vanished, but the intestine, nevertheless, is then far from complete, while the genital tubercle has only just started its evolution.

I am ready to believe that the later anal stage distantly reflects, as it were, this embryonic stage, but it is a parallel which may, perhaps, be carried a little further. At the point of the child's libidinal development with which we are dealing, the original freedom of the anal aperture has been controlled and, by virtue of the sphincter muscle, has learnt to close. But the erotism that clings to the anal zone does not at first lessen, for the sphincter muscles collaborate to serve it by helping to create hard, resistive sticks of faecal matter likely to excite the anal mucous surfaces: bodies which, to the female cloaca, will be the anal precursors of the vaginal penis. In my opinion, however, this stage of development is bivalent in relation to the cloacal erotism. First and foremost, it favours anal erotism but, with time, tends to eradicate this by the continuing trend towards anal closure.

[1] "A Short Study of the Development of the Libido" (1924).

	STAGES OF LIBIDINAL ORGANIZATION	ST OBJ
PRE-AMBIVALENT	1. Earlier Oral Stage (Sucking)	A (wit
AMBIVALENT	2. Late Oral Stage (Cannibalistic)	D (total incor
	3. Early Sadistic-anal stage (or Sadistic-cloacal)	Pa (with
	4. Late Sadistic-anal stage (or Sadistic-cloacal)	Pa (with
	5. Early Phallic Stage	Ob (with affir and partial CASTRA
	6. Late Phallic Stage	Ob (with excl partial re LATEN
POST-AMBIVALENT	7. Final Genital Stage	O

	ATTITUDES TOWARDS THE OBJECT	
	BOY	GIRL
sm ect) ... of object)	Pre-oedipal position Primary oral passivity and activity towards the mother.	
e tion) ... e on)	Primary cloacal and phallic passivity towards the mother. Diffuse muscular activity.	
of phallus of cloaca)	Primary phallic activity towards the mother. *Active Oedipus Complex*	
	Positive Oedipus complex of boy	Negative Oedipus complex of girl
OMPLEX	Secondary cloacal passivity towards the father *Passive Oedipus Complex*	
allus and of cloaca)	Negative Oedipus complex of boy	Positive Oedipus complex of girl
RIOD)	Ultimate genital activity towards the female (penoid)	Ultimate genital passivity towards the male (vaginal)

MALE

Early passive stage (cloacal) towards the mother.

Early active stage (phallic) towards the mother (active positive Oedipus complex).

CASTRATION COMPLEX

Late passive stage (phallic) with partial *exclusion* of the *phallus* and partial affirmation of the cloaca towards the father (*transitory* passive negative Oedipus complex).

TERMINATING, IN THE LATENCY PERIOD

In the late active stage (pubertal and penis-genital) towards *woman* with *affirmation of the phallus* and *erotogenic exclusion of the cloaca*.

FEMALE

Early passive stage (cloacal) towards the mother.

Early active stage (phallic) towards the mother (*transitory* active negative Oedipus complex).

CASTRATION COMPLEX

Late passive stage (cloacal with partial exclusion of the phallus) towards the father (*permanent* passive positive Oedipus complex).

TERMINATING, IN THE LATENCY PERIOD

In the third passive stage of woman (genital, vaginal, pubertal) with *permanent partial exclusion of the phallus* and *affirmation of the vagina*.

True, a vital condition is that the *digestive anus* must remain open, persist, but as this stage progresses, the *erotogenic anus* will tend to close. Whereupon, thanks to this mechanism, the anal libido of the young male, like the young female's, in girls as in boys, seems to be propelled, little by little, towards the then awakening phallus, in the same way that the genital tubercle first buds and then migrates forward and outward. It thus seems that the phallic phase, properly speaking, begins to appear during the late sadistic-anal stage, while the primary anal erotism is concomitantly being turned back on the phallus and the active muscular sadistic drives of the outlived early sadistic-anal stage are being so too.

This is the moment when the girl is her most masculine or rather, pre-masculine, as the boy was most feminine or rather, pre-feminine, in the early anal stage.

But now, the castration complex also intervenes, which complex is mainly cultural in the boy, and arises as the representative of patriarchal morality, whereas it is mainly biological in the girl, since it represents an anatomical reality which brooks no denial. Whereupon the situation then becomes reversed for the girl and the major part of her aggression will be turned against the mother, that mother who created her castrated; that is, without a phallus. The girl must, in effect, attribute her mutilation to the mother, for it is only secondarily, when she has accepted her own castration and eroticized it that, in voluptuous phantasies of sadistic coitus, she can masochistically imagine herself castrated by the father. It is a result of the primary effects of her disappointment, her castration, and of still deeper biological causes doubtless emanating from the gonads, that the girl finally passes over to predominant father-love and, to quote Helene Deutsch, to the masochistic wish to be subjected to the triad, *castration-violation-childbirth*.[1] Thus, the girl's wish for the phallus must be converted into the wish for the cloacal child, while, at the same time, the clitoris on her own body must undergo the kind of functional involution which culminates in that exclusion of the phallus to which we referred. Her cloacal erotism, however, must also be reactivated to prepare the adult erotization of the vagina, properly speaking, which, according to Freud, will only truly occur at puberty, after the menstrual blood has passed. If such are the facts, pursuing the biological parallel, we might recall that the embryonic vaginal plug begins by obliterating the vagina which, chronologically, only opens after the rectum and genital tubercle have been formed, and might thus consider these stages of development as prototypes of the post-anal, post-phallic

[1] "The Significance of Masochism in the Mental Life of Women" (1930).

advent of the vagina, that specifically female erotogenic organ, at puberty.

At any rate, the feminine organism achieves a remarkable feat on reaching puberty and full development of the sex glands, in its utilization of an originally male libidinal cathexis, namely the erotogenic and orgastic potentialities of the phallus (clitoris), for a purely passive feminine function, that of the vagina's receptive role. When and how this vaginal reversal of the phallic libido takes place is something we still do not know exactly. It was mainly in reference to this that Freud, in his *Female Sexuality*, wrote: "Subsequently, biological factors deflect them" (libidinal forces) "from their original aims and conduct even active and in every sense masculine strivings into feminine channels."

Here, too, we might ask ourselves, in a new biological parallel, whether the reflux of the phallic libido to the vagina, to the ovaries, would not be a regrouping comparable, though in the contrary direction, with the foetal descent of the testes towards the penis, as though the executive organs of sexuality, and the gonads proper to each sex, were mutually drawn together. In the male, the erotized penis seems to draw the gonads to itself: in the female, the gonads, which remain intraperitoneal, draw her erotogenic phallic sensitivity to themselves through her vaginalization.

(d) *Some Divergent Analytic Theories Discussed*

Of late, many women's voices have been raised to contest this secondary character of vaginal erotization which was assigned it by Freud. The works of Karen Horney, and of Melanie Klein, in particular, converge in that direction. Ernest Jones, moreover, in the light of Melanie Klein's observations of children, has constructed a whole new theory of the early development of female sexuality.

According to Karen Horney, the erotogenic awakening of the little girl's vagina occurs very early in life, as witness the instances of infantile or, at least, pre-coital vaginal masturbation that she was able, analytically, to deduce or observe, as well as memories, retained in the unconscious, of spontaneous vaginal sensations, often exceedingly early, and before any coitus took place. It would be mainly the effect of anxiety arising from the deep and dangerous wound to the body that coitus might cause, in punishment chiefly for the child's incestuous wishes, that certain girls would repress their native vaginal sensitivity and *secondarily* develop their male clitoridal sensitivity as a protection; almost, I would add, as one puts a lightning-conductor on a house to prevent it being struck.

Melanie Klein's theory, in many points, agrees with the foregoing, but draws far more widely on the vast field of the theory of instincts, in which so many regions still remain but barely explored.

For Melanie Klein, the Oedipus complex begins far earlier than the phallic stage; in fact, when the child is weaned. Then, according to her, its oral erotism will move from above to below, from the mouth to the cloaca and, in the girl, especially to the vagina. As a result of its deep disappointment in the mother who deprives it of milk and, as frequently happens, its perceptions of parental intercourse, or more rarely, its phylogenetic phantasies that take their place, the baby girl, furious with the mother, would then want to empty the latter of her body contents; namely bowels, foetus, and included father's penis, in order to devour them, more or less. It is through fear of the retaliation which the mother, like the witch in fairytales, may inflict for such aggressive phantasies, that the baby girl, between one and two, will develop her first *superego* and repress her primary aggression, in order to save the contents of her own body. This amounts to saying that the little girl will have a truly feminine *concave cloacal castration complex*, exact reflection of the *convex phallic castration complex* of the small boy. It is this cloacal castration complex which will put the brake on feminine aggression, and determine that vaginal anaesthesia so common among women who, in such cases, unconsciously continue to fear being wounded and robbed of their internal organs. As for *penis-envy*, Melanie Klein attributes this, in girls, in whom she fully recognizes its importance, to envy of the penis as *object*, and to the precociously oedipal wish to possess and incorporate the father's penis, which it has coveted from the mother, during its observations of parental coitus. The child's representation of the combined parents, to Melanie Klein, is the cardinal factor. Incorporation of the penis is originally desired in the only reality manner known to the child, i.e. *orally*, for the child imagines that, in coitus, the mother sucks and eats the father's penis, as it itself sucked and bit the mother's breast.

By a later displacement from above to below, now, however, on a reality basis, heralded by the passing from the oral to the sadistic-anal stage, the female child will begin to *covet* the father's penis, which the mother has taken over in abdominal fashion.

We thus see that Melanie Klein, like Karen Horney, more or less ends by denying the primary and basically bisexual nature of the *masculinity* complex in woman. The positive phallic stage disappears in these theories as an inevitable stage in feminine development, so that all we are left is an essentially psychogenic pathological reaction. It was to this that Freud objected in the authors who defend such ideas when, in connection with works published by Karen Horney and Ernest Jones, he wrote in *Female Sexuality*: "Certain as it is that the earliest libidinal tendencies are reinforced later by regression and reaction-formation and difficult as it is to estimate the relative strength of the various confluent libidinal components, I still think that we must not overlook the fact that those first impulses have an intensity of their own which is greater than anything that comes later and may indeed be said to be incommensurable with any other force. It is certainly true that there is an antithesis between the attachment to the father and the masculinity complex—this is the universal antithesis between activity and passivity, masculinity and femininity—but we have no right to assume that only the one is primary, while the other owes its strength merely to the process of defence. And if the defence against femininity is so vigorous, from what other source can it derive its strength than from that striving for masculinity which found its earliest expression in the child's penis-envy and might well take its name from this?"

The authors whom I have quoted might, from their angle, object that Freud has not sufficiently emphasized the *primary* nature of femininity in woman. The concept of a libidinal development of woman, in which the vagina, with no pre-history, would awake solely at puberty must, in effect, seem to them too stamped with the idea that the girl's masturbatory libidinal development began as purely male; they thus probably consider that it was because he was male that Freud so greatly emphasized the innate masculinity of woman, and above all, in his theory of instincts, her wish for masculinity.

Conversely, these women authors, protagonists of the equal importance of the vagina and penis, these feminine apologists of the vagina might be blamed with manifesting, in their theories, something of that same grievance which inspired the "suffragette" to tend to deny and obliterate just that desire for the penis which so truly exists deep in each woman. It is as though these women proclaimed: "Of what have these men to boast? Our woman's vagina is as good, and better, than their penis!"

Let us, however, abandon this contentious use of analysis in the eternal struggle between the sexes and, helped by biology, use our efforts to attempt a synthesis of these diverse viewpoints which all, it may be, hold part of the truth.

To me it seems that male analysts may have a tendency to emphasize masculinity, when they meet it again elsewhere, by projecting themselves externally on others. But women analysts, when dealing with the development of the little girl, may have the same retrospective trend to project their own mature femininity on others; the personality of their own adult vagina, so to speak.

One does not, however, see why one of these two viewpoints should so largely exclude the other or why, especially, in this "battle round the vagina", which is being fought out in psycho-analytic writing, the corollary to the significance of the vagina, from infancy on, should necessarily be a minimization of any biological phallus-ness in the little girl. Such indeed, would be the ideal of feminine development, but that ideal should not distort the picture of the facts as they are.

I am inclined to imagine, as my own analytic observations suggest, that when speaking of the early genital stage, with exclusion of genitals, Abraham was not altogether wrong and now I, myself, seem to be criticizing my earlier criticism of him. But, to confess him entirely right, we should have to forget that he himself qualifies this stage as corresponding "to the latency period with repression".[1]

From the moment the child enters the sadistic-anal stage—and we know how fluid the boundaries are that divide these developmental stages, how much they overlap each other—from that moment, libidinal development, in effect, comes under the supremacy of the cloaca.

I say of the cloaca and not anus for, though all that remains of the boy's deep cloacal aperture is the anus, if we consider that, in spite of urethral and genital remaining combined, the lengthening of the urethra to the tip of the penis withdraws it, as it were, from cloacal invagination, the little girl retains the depth and hollowness of the cloaca far better, since the anus and vaginal orifice constitute a hollow space only divided by the recto-vaginal septum.

Now, in the coenaesthetic condition of fairly undifferentiated infantile sensations, it appears that it is the totality of these openings which are frequently perceived or divined by the little girl, without any special preference as yet for the vagina or anus. Which is why, if we consider the libidinal development of both sexes, and not only the male's, it would doubtless be more correct to term the sadistic-anal stage the sadistic-cloacal.

In this stage, where the vagina is still only adumbrated as an adjunct to the anus, which in fact it is, it is the whole cloacal opening which dominates the libidinal organization. The *hole* seems to assert itself, so to speak, through all the libidinal organization, before the *protuberance*, and Freud long ago recognized the dominance of oral, as of anal erotism, as preceding that of phallic erotism. We may see here a psycho-biological confirmation of Marañon's specifically biological view, according to which, on the path of "progress", the male would be a later stage than the female. The hole, however, will stay female, and the protuberance establishes the male. Thus, the cloacal stage will remain the substratum of the *feminine*, and in the history of libidinal development, it is the feminine which exists before the masculine.

[1] See p. 19, Note 2.

But to return to Abraham. His early genital stage, phallic, with exclusion of genitals, might thus be conceived as simply with *exclusion of cloaca*, which would follow the erotogenic closure of the latter; this stage would then be that which would usher in the positive phallic stage (which he, however, omits to include in his table). That is to say, that according to the meaning we attach to "exclusion of genitals", whether feminine cloaca or masculine phallus, which Abraham postulates at this stage, the negative phallic stage it indicates would come either before, or after, Freud's positive phallic stage, according as it denies the feminine cloaca (male attitude), or the masculine phallus (female attitude).

But since Abraham could only have had in mind the denial of the phallus, my earlier reasoning must remain as it stands.

At any rate, in the light of what I have said, the positive phallic stage now appears as sandwiched, so to speak, between two main cloacal stages. The sadistic-cloacal stage thus precedes the establishment of phallic dominance, just as, in embryology, the intestinal convolutions, as Abraham noted, appear before the uro-genital apparatus.

However, a regression or return to cloacal organization follows the phallic organization after the trauma of the castration complex which, as we saw earlier, will at one time stamp the object, at another the subject, with the psychically perceived *exclusion of the phallus* which, then, will impart its adult psychic stamp on each sex in the degree to which it corresponds with the physiologically sexual reality of the subject or object.

In these oscillations between cloaca and phallus, and conversely, we may doubtless see a reflection of probable oscillations, in the embryonic stage, between female and male, as a result of their original bisexuality, even though the issue of the battle between the two sexes in each individual, as seems probable, is predetermined.

Thus, whereas the boy, leaving the sadistic-cloacal stage, should have entered the positive phallic stage once and for all, as it were, despite the powerful though temporary upheaval of the castration complex, the positive phallic stage of the girl, which to my mind is no mere reaction-formation, but a normal developmental stage, should, in ideal cases, be as temporary as that of the negative phallic stage of the boy ought to be, if the woman is eventually to prove biologically adapted to her feminine erotic function. The dominance of the cloaca should reappear to govern the infantile female organization; that cloaca which, in our civilizations, remains more or less dormant through the latency period and which passively awaits the man who will awaken it later in the elective form of the receptive vagina.

Yet, though the two feminine cloacal stages, pre-phallic and post-phallic, thus meet, as it were, over the pinnacle of the phallus, it may still be hard to imagine that no cloacal vaginal pre-history exists in the little girl.

Personally, I am inclined to think that, for most very small boys, the vagina, to use Freud's expression, remains "undiscovered". When Karen Horney, in her *The Dread of Woman* (1932) advances that the small boy, too, has a general idea of the vagina, I find it impossible to agree. There must be, in this theory, a "retrojection" derived from male analysts,[1] or at least, from women analysts. No, the small boy, following the universal anthropomorphic law of the human psyche, generally remains for a time "egomorphic" and continues to consider all human beings made in his own image; that is, possessed of the phallus and *without the vagina*.

We cannot adhere too strongly to this view of Freud's, justified as it is, save for the occasional exceptions, evidently due to special circumstances and unusual precocity, to be found in psycho-analytic literature.

Quite other must be the experience of the little girl. When the latter masturbates manually, as so frequently happens (other forms of infantile masturbation, as Freud told me, often being substitutes for the original manual masturbation), and plays with her little clitoris, it seems impossible that the small fingers do not, some day or other, perceive the adjacent opening.

I agree with Karen Horney when, seeing in certain typical

[1] Dr. Charles Odier told me he had analysed two men who seemed from a very early age to have known of the "hole in front" of the woman.

female dreams a probable echo of the discovery of this *orifice*, namely the vagina, she says: "For it occasionally happens that, when a general anxiety about the injurious consequences of masturbation makes its appearance, the patient has dreams with the following typical content: she is doing a piece of needlework and all at once a hole appears, of which she feels ashamed; or she is crossing a bridge which suddenly breaks off in the middle, above a river or a chasm; or she is walking along a slippery incline and all at once begins to slide and is in danger of falling over a precipice."[1]

I have dealt elsewhere[2] with the symbolism of bridges in general and truncated bridges in particular, in relation to phallic erotism, but in my opinion, the "phallic" interpretation does not exclude the cloacal, vaginal interpretation of the abysses they overhang.

The copy-books of a little girl I know are full of fantastic stories in which pits and precipices play a great part. Again, among the "vertigo" dreams which we so often observe, as often, indeed, as the real vertigo[3] of women, let me quote one:

"The dreamer is at the theatre, in the balcony. There is no parapet and she is sitting on the edge with her feet dangling over the stalls. She can only remain where she is by dint of great efforts to preserve her balance, yet these efforts against her giddiness spoil all her pleasure in the play she has come to see."

This recurrent dream, of a typically clitoridal woman, I may say, seems to confirm Karen Horney's view of the fears connected with the infantile "discovery" of the vagina. This woman, even as a child, had many opportunities to see the coitus of adults, and the "play" here, as in so many dreams, stands for it. As a result of the excitations this kind of play aroused in the young organism, the child, as so often happens, must have masturbated. But the small fingers then discovered the "pit" beside the clitoridal mount and thus giddiness of the

---

[1] "The Denial of the Vagina" (1933).
[2] *The Life and Works of Edgar Allan Poe* (1933). See my interpretation of the story: "Never Bet the Devil Your Head".
[3] Vertigo, as we know, is not exclusive to women and, when found in men, may be related to the femininity complex.

pit seized the child, to reappear later, in the adult woman, in symptoms of vaginal anaesthesia and her "falling dreams" at night. This recurrent dream therefore held the memory, retained in the depths of the unconscious, of the "terrifying" early discovery of the vaginal orifice, doubtless perceived, at that tender age (about two), as merely "cloacal".

Has not Freud himself, in so many passages of his works, referred to the castration "wound" that frightens both boys and girls? But a wound is a hole, and the vaginal orifice, as a hole perceived by the child's fingers, has its place even in the phallic theory of the infantile sexuality of little girls.

The so-frequent women's dreams in which an originally single house, room, closet or space is split into two are, according to Freud, typically anatomical dreams which topographically reproduce the way in which the cloaca is divided by the recto-vaginal septum into rectum and vagina. And is it only at puberty, after the first menstrual blood has passed the vagina, that these dreams appear? It would not surprise me to find that, sometimes, such dreams were present long before, dating from the second stage of infantile masturbation, that which the little girl gives up by degrees after the trauma of the castration complex and after the straying fingers have sensed the vaginal pit. Only psycho-analytic observation of children, however, can answer that question.

True, in this exploration of her genital organs, the little girl encounters an obstacle unknown to the boy: that of pain. The vagina is closed by a hymen which is more or less resistive in each woman. According to Karen Horney, three factors connected with self-preservation may contribute to create the infantile denial of the vagina; (1), the frightening dimensions of the adult penis compared with the smallness of the infant's vagina; (2), the occasional and frightening sight of menstrual blood; (3), slight but painful tears in the hymen as a result of manual exploration. Feminine masochism, of which we will speak in its place, must be capable of commingling voluptuous desire with these sensed or experienced pains. But the organism's self-preservation tends in the opposite direction and, apart from any element of moral repression, so does the basic bisexuality of the organism, the masculinity included in the woman.

Now, as we shall see later, since erotogenic masochism appears to be of feminine origin (Freud; Helene Deutsch), the more the little girl fears the "cloacal wound", the likelier will she be to possess an innate masculinity. The masculine, in effect, repels the passive and masochistic, for the masculine, active and sadistic presses forward, while the feminine works in the opposite way. The way girls react to the *cloacal castration complex* as to the *phallic castration complex*, before being psychically influenced by childhood traumas and events, is doubtless predetermined by the biologically innate degree of bisexuality they possess.

Every surgeon, every dentist knows how much "softer" men are than women. The fact that, in battle, they readily turn into heroes, when roused by an ideal or, more, by the premium offered their aggression, does not mean that, in the consulting room, under the drill, in hospital, or in cold blood, they support pain better than women. Women, however, will often suffer without flinching. These different reactions, at bottom, depend on the psycho-sexual constitution of the man or woman and it is this which, in girls destined to be clitoridals, must primarily condition the psycho-sexual response of their genital organs to the piercing, wounding penis. In this way, when in due course the "cloacal" vagina is "discovered", would arise what Karen Horney terms "the denial of the vagina", a denial which Ernest Jones compares to the pretended ignorance of certain primitives as to the consequences of coitus: in both cases, the "apparent" ignorance would merely be the repression of what, at one time, had been sensed.[1]

Here, a problem confronts us to which, as yet, I have found no answer. How far does the little girl when, as seems likely, she "discovers" the vagina during her infantile masturbation, sense that organ erotogenically? A precursive labile innervation must, in fact, anticipate the subsequent more or less successful feminization of this female receptive organ. In outline, it must exist at a very early stage. And these first and vague spontaneous or peripheral "sensations", when they exist, when exactly do they become converted into anxiety? What is the proportion, in each case, of primary *vagina-pleasure* and reactive *vagina-anxiety*

[1] "The Phallic Phase" (1933).

through vital fear of being wounded, through masculinity, or through moral fear of punishment for forbidden wishes?

And are there cases, given the elective erotization of the clitoris, so common in childhood, where the adjacent "hole" is only perceived as a "hole", a wound or scar; perceived dispassionately, as it were, without any recognized fear of vital danger, or sensuality either, but simply as a narcissistic wound to the female body castrated of its penis? Such a simple representation of the *vagina hole*, stripped of affect can, however, be but secondary, and derive from that well-known psychical mechanism which decathects an originally too highly charged representation when it sinks into the unconscious.

Thus, the vagina of many women, a simple, more or less insensitive hole, might be imagined as the residual of an outgrown stage, the cloacal, when the phallic stage has replaced it too completely. In such cases, the libidinal charge of the representation having sunk into the unconscious, the free floating affect would secondarily, more or less, be wholly transferred to the phallic clitoris, the primary mainstay of all masculinity.

On the other hand, where we meet with disturbed development in males, because of a disproportionate degree of innate femininity, the cloacal stage, which should have been outgrown, will continue more or less muted through the phallic stage, and the libidinal charge of the phallic representations, after the castration trauma, will abandon these more or less repressed phallic representations and erotogenically turn to recathect the cloaca.

Thus, what happens in girls who "deny the vagina" is, in a lesser degree, psycho-sexually similar to what embryologically, anatomically and physiologically constitutes the boy. In the male embryo, in fact, the cloaca closes and only the anus remains of the former deep invagination, the urethra being carried forward and outside the body with the lengthening of the genital bud. And this same psycho-sexual representation, this same innervation, as it were, is projected on the deep biopsychic make-up of the girl or clitoridal woman since for the latter, in woman, there is nothing below but an anus and a penis. Erotogenically, the vagina between them seems shut, even when, in fact, it allows itself to be penetrated. It is as though such women, in coitus, proclaim that, despite anatomy, they have no vagina.

Conversely, in males with too great an admixture of femininity, it is as though some part of the embryological development of the female were retained; the cloaca, in them, although it closes more completely, seems to persist, at least psycho-sexually, in wanting to stay open.

Having thus stressed the converse results of libidinal development, male development in the female, and female development in the male, the better to emphasize my ideas and the facts, let us now, to clarify our thoughts, draw up a table showing what would be the ideally normal development in both sexes, by strictly separating, contrary to what happens in nature, female from male.

MALE
(*Oral stages common to both sexes*)
Early passive stage (cloacal and phallic) towards object.
Early active stage (phallic) towards the mother (active positive Oedipus complex).

CASTRATION COMPLEX
Late passive stage (phallic) with partial *exclusion of phallus* and partial affirmation of cloaca towards the father (*transitory* passive negative Oedipus complex)
ending, after the latency period, in the late active stage (penis-genital, pubertal) towards *woman* with *affirmation of phallus and erotogenic exclusion of cloaca*.

FEMALE
(*Oral stages common to both sexes*)
Early passive stage (cloacal and phallic) towards object.
Early active stage (phallic) towards the mother (*transitory* active negative Oedipus complex.)

CASTRATION COMPLEX
Late passive stage (cloacal, with total or partial exclusion of phallus) towards the father (*permanent* passive positive Oedipus complex)
ending, after the latency period, in the third passive feminine stage (vaginal-genital, pubertal) with *permanent total or partial exclusion of phallus* and *affirmation of vagina*.

It is necessary to add here that the "little girl's" castration complex, according to psycho-analytic observations, must generally occur much earlier than the boy's, which should not greatly surprise us seeing that it is biologically determined and based on acknowledging reality. Also, it is in accord with the female rhythm of development which is completed earlier than the male's. Thus, the positive Oedipus complex in the girl, passively orientated towards the father, must chronologically establish itself at least as early as does the boy's positive Oedipus complex towards the mother, and still more so if earlier observations of coitus, for instance, have made the child realize the difference between the sexes.

(e) *The Passive Phallus*

It will doubtless have been remarked that, in the foregoing table, the early passive stage towards the object is termed both cloacal and phallic, although nothing in the text has yet authorized us to add the term phallic to that of cloacal. The reason is that, although I had reached this point of my paper, the table was only worked out after I had realized the great importance of what I shall call the *long, passive, prehistory of the phallus*.

My thoughts, in this respect, became confirmed as the result of an exchange of ideas with Dr. R. Loewenstein[1] in whose view my ideas (expounded later), relating to the passive, even masochistic stage of the little girl's clitoridal masturbation when in the passive Oedipus complex, confirmed suggestions of the existence of a *passive phallus* stage, which had arisen from his analyses of males with potency disturbances. In their turn, Loewenstein's views on the passive phallus stage in boys shed light, for me, on the corresponding phase in girls.

In fact, the phallus, whether penis or clitoris, following the widespread law to which all organic phenomena are subject,

[1] R. Loewenstein spoke on this subject at a meeting of the French Psycho-Analytic Society in June, 1934. He also read a paper on it at the XIIIth International Psycho-Analytic Congress, Lucerne, August, 1934: "Phallic Passivity in Men." *Int. J. Psycho-Anal.* **16**, 1935.

must begin with passivity before it can pass to activity. Passivity is first awakened in the pregenital phase, while the mother is supreme, as witness the tales, or phantasies, of seduction by the mother, which re-arise from the depths of the unconscious. And these are true in their way, since it was she, or her surrogates, who not only gave the child its first caresses, but also tended it and kept it clean.

At the beginning, what every small boy wants to get from his mother is that she titillate and touch that pleasurably sensitive organ and, only later, will he want to push and pierce actively with it. This first stage of development, or what should rather be called passive phallic awakening, which always doubtless precedes the active phallic flowering that ends in the Oedipus complex, would be that in which many semi-impotent males will linger or to which they will regress; such for instance, as those masturbators who find their phallic masturbation phantasies all-sufficient, or men who, though able to exercise object choice, demand only masturbation or fellatio from women and have no need for penetration. All degrees of retardation, in this attitude, however, may be met with, as well as every amalgam with the active phallic position which would challenge it, since certain men need but a few preliminaries by way of passive stimulation to be able to pass to active penetration. But here it would be best to define what we ourselves mean by the passive phallus. Some analysts, indeed, object that the phallus is always active when in erection, and however that may come about. By active phallus, therefore, we mean the phallus that is able to enter into erection and want to penetrate, whether spontaneously, through excitation of the central nervous system, or by sight or thought, for instance, of the love object. The passive phallus, however, needs localized peripheral excitations in order to function and then, in extreme cases of passivity, may even achieve orgasm without erection.

I once heard one of our best writers, coarsely, but lyrically too, praise "women who give men a good stand", in contrast to the far inferior fellatrix or masturbatrix who, however accomplished their art, can only artificially excite the male. No better masculine testimony could be given of the supremacy of the active over the passive phallus.

If, however, we now abandon male, and return to female sexuality, the long passive prehistory of the phallus must also have pursued its course in the little girl and, given the essential passivity of the female, with far more significance to her fate. The little girl, like the little boy, must have had the genital region cleansed, tended and involuntarily caressed by the mother: she it was who awoke the child's passive and phallic-cloacal sensuality.

Now it is only by slow and very various degrees, as the case may be, that the little girl comes later to covet her mother in clitoridal fashion with more or less active aims. Indeed, the child lacks the necessary truly penetrative organ for this, and it is understandable that Fenichel[1] for instance, rebelling against Jeanne Lampl-de Groot's ideas,[2] reacts so far as to deny all phallic strivings whatever in the little girl towards her mother, on whom, he says, she is never anything but pregenitally fixated, pre-oedipal being one with pregenital in his opinion.

The introduction, however, of the concept of a primarily passive phallus gives a different aspect to the libidinal development of woman, and better accounts for the facts.

The active phallic stage of the little girl, true homologue, in little, of the boy's, as Jeanne Lampl-de Groot so well appreciates, would thus, as it were, be sandwiched between two passive phallic stages, a primary phase originating while the babe is still a suckling and which continues as an undercurrent through the oral and anal pregenital stages, followed by a secondary phase succeeding the castration complex, that being the only phase with which we have so far dealt here. These two passive phallic stages, moreover, would be superimposed upon, and contemporary with, the two passive cloacal stages, which themselves as we said would enclose the active phallic stage, the second of which would equate to a normal, biological regression in woman. It is many years since Freud spoke of the two waves of repression which must overtake the active phallic sexuality of woman, one when the latency period begins, the other when puberty sets in.

[1] "The Pregenital Antecedents of the Oedipus Complex" (1930).
[2] "The Evolution of the Oedipus Complex in Women" (1927).

Now there is such simple, such striking proof of the prehistory of this passive phallus in woman that, probably just for that reason, it was not understood; namely, the predilection of so many women for clitoridal caresses. Every woman, thus stimulated, bears retarded, though living and irrefutable, witness to the long prehistory of the passive phallus which, in the ideally developed male, on the other hand, should have sunk into the unconscious without leaving any appreciable trace.

IV

DISTURBING FACTORS IN FEMININE DEVELOPMENT

(a) *Erotogenic Zones and Sexual Objects not necessarily Interdependent*

THE CONCEPT of the passive phallus will help us to understand certain phenomena which apparently contradict each other.

Although intensification of the erotogenic cloacal zone will generally predispose to feminoid attitudes in women as in male homosexuals, there is a whole category of males in whom poor erotization of the glans penis combines with an over-ready release of the orgasm when the zones which correspond to the introitus vaginae and its surrounding parts experience excitation, as in those cases of males with ejaculatio praecox unaccompanied by erection who did not become homosexuals but retained woman as the sexual object, which Abraham so fully explored.[1]

We must also mention here the many kinds of masochists and, in particular, the "flagellants" of different kinds. These men, as Freud has already shown in his paper *A Child is Being Beaten* (1919), have never emerged from the anal-erotic or, rather, the cloacal-erotic stage and, in them, the orgasm is released by thoughts or experiences connected with castigation, preferably on and around the buttocks. In the masturbatory phantasies of such men, however, this maltreatment must be inflicted by some domineering female so that, in fact, it is really an active mother that is envisaged in relation to an imagined passive subject.

Now in all such cases, with the survival of intense cloacal erotism, there is generally bound up a no-less persistent survival of the passive phallus. These men, according as to whether they are simply erotogenically passive or masochistic, readily phantasy their penis as caressed or beaten, and

[1] "Ejaculatio Praecox" (1917).

themselves thus passively excited; which passive phallic phantasy is always interwoven with the fact or phantasy of being cloacally or anally caressed or beaten by surrogates of the mother since, despite their passive, feminoid tendencies, they have not passed from the mother to the father, or replaced the female by the male as their love object.

As to the heterosexual clitoridal woman, she appears to covet the "convex" male with an organ adapted to desiring the "concave" woman; the phallus. But, given the atrophied size of the female phallus and the psychical phallic atrophy which corresponds to it, such women are obliged to content themselves, more or less, with the passive phallus and, generally, with caresses passively received from the male. Even homosexual women are reduced to these expedients, and it is only in phantasy that the hetero- or homosexual female can imagine herself endowed with the male phallus whose function is penetration and, in real and ambitious bestridings, or even by using artificial appendages, at times attempt to outdo the male.

In any case, clitoridal women who, whether manifestly homosexual or, having passed from the mother to the father, succeed in developing the object relation proper to the female, have always unconsciously remained mostly passively fixated, cloacally and phallically, on the mother they knew when a child. Manifest homosexuals, they re-enact to infinity the primary scene of the active-passive alternations of the mother's ministerings to the babe[1] and it is only the most active among them, superimposing identification with the father on the primary identification with the active mother, who will become that more specifically active type of homosexual female which wears a man's coat and tie.

(b) *Some Connections Between the Feminine Passive Oedipus Complex, the Maternal Instinct and Vaginal Function*

From what has been said it will be clear that, as was long thought, it is not an over-determined and persistent positive feminine Oedipus complex, or an over-tenacious fixation on the father, which most threatens the normal development of

[1] See Helene Deutsch: "On Female Sexuality" (1932).

the feminine libido. True, such a fixation may keep a woman from marriage, from men in general and, even in marriage and coitus, inhibit her vaginal function through fidelity to the omnipotent father. But an over-strong fixation on the mother, clitoridally coveted in infancy, is even more primarily pathogenic to the erotic feminine function.

Similarly pathogenic to the erotic feminine function would appear to be lack of identification with the mother, who remains over-determined as the love object in the unconscious and, deriving therefrom, the absence of a true maternal instinct, leading to a psychical rejection of motherhood, of children to come.

True, there are women, ever more numerous to-day, to whom love is all, who first and foremost love the man and that, vaginally, and whose main concern is not to have children at all. Yet acceptance of the child, comprised in that great feminine masochistic triad *castration-violation-childbirth* (Helene Deutsch), the substitution of the wish for the penis to the wish for the child, a wish appropriate to the girl's passive Oedipus complex, greatly favours the future vaginalization of the woman.

It would certainly not be facile, in such instances, to unravel cause from effect. Is it because the little girl is innately already highly feminine, highly cloacal, that she accepts the vagina, and the penis and child that will pass through, as also the dangers they imply; or is it because she has accepted these that she becomes highly cloacal, highly feminine? One must react on the other and femininity, like the primary masculinity, must have a snowball effect from the moment they are set into motion, as it were.

In any case, the wish for maternity—I do not say the more or less enforced acceptance of the child—is a factor so favourable to vaginalization that at times one is surprised to learn that highly domestic women are often the best adapted to their erotic function. Nothing wounds the narcissism of clitoridal women more, given their sense of resentment, than discovering this. Generally, however, they do not believe it.

Psychical inacceptance of the maternal function and defective maternal instinct, however, also seems no less frequently related to the normal failure in women to establish the erotic function.

(c) *Vital and Moral Dangers Inherent in the Feminine Sexual Functions*

Women are often afraid of motherhood and not only for economic reasons, which may also incite men to avoid procreation, for they dread the pain and danger that offsets the otherwise deep-rooted instinct to bear children.

This fear must have its roots very far back in the infancy of the girl. Some perception, or better, awareness of the biological facts, must therefore underlie this attitude which derives, primarily, from observation of the coitus of adults. When, as so often happenes, such coitus is observed by the child, its response will be very different, depending on the adult with whom it identifies most. This Karen Horney[1] has well shown.

In such cases, the boy, comparing his little penis with the orifice of his mother, sustains a narcissistic wound to his sense of adequacy and so pride; the girl, however, comparing her too small orifice with the father's large penis, justifiably fears some vital wound from an act which she otherwise desires, for anal or vaginal coitus with an adult male would result in severe bodily hurt.

True, the child, whether male or female, will always identify itself, though differently, with both the adults it observes in coitus.[2] This psychical and bisexual identification comes to

---

[1] In "The Denial of the Vagina" (1933.)
"When he" (the boy) "phantasies the fulfilment of genital impulses he is confronted with a fact very wounding to his self-esteem ('my penis is too small for my mother'); the little girl, on the other hand, is faced with destruction of part of her body. *Hence, carried back to its ultimate biological foundations, the man's dread of the woman is genital-narcissistic, while the woman's dread of the man is physical.*"*

* Author's italics.

[2] Freud maintains this view in all his writings. It surprises us therefore to find Karen Horney, discussing his views on the importance of the phallic position of the little girl, in "The Denial of the Vagina", saying: "whence comes the anxiety met with in the analyses of female patients —the dread of the gigantic penis which might pierce her . . . whence

pass just because of the child's primary and biological bisexuality. As a result, the boy cannot fail to fear, as well as desire, his passive penetration by the father's penis, nor the girl to feel some degree of phallic desire to penetrate, or rather push forward, actively, with her little clitoris.

All one can say is that, in instances that favour a psychical sexualization which corresponds to the gonadal sex, male attitudes should be dominant in the boy as female attitudes in the girl, and that from the very outset.

I cannot too much insist however that, in childhood, even girls do not truly vaginally apprehend the orifice which the penis is to penetrate; that is, with a clear representation of the recto-vaginal septum. Doubtless this orifice is then cloacally conceived, even if already discovered by the small fingers. True, the girl possesses an anatomical foundation for the concept of the "vagina-hole" which the boy lacks but, unlike ordinary holes, passages which already serve some purpose such as the mouth, ears, nostrils and anus, the vagina, through which nothing has so far passed, cannot doubtless be ideated so early as having an own and separable role. The horror, above all, of being castrated, of which the vulva would be the mark of the wound, must help to ward off from the girl any precise observation of this region.

Be that as it may, the possible penetration by the large adult penis of this nether orifice must be justifiably felt, though desired, as a danger by the small girl.

To this fear must be added the still more specifically feminine fear of motherhood.

The notion that babies grow in the body, in the mother's

---

comes that understanding of the female sexual role, evinced as the symbolism of sexual anxiety, in which those early excitations once more vibrate? And how can we account at all for the unbounded jealous fury with the mother, which commonly manifests itself in the analyses of some women when memories of the 'primal scene' are affectively revived? How does this come about if at that time the subject could only share in the excitations of the father?"

Freud considers fear of penetration by the father's large penis as present in the girl, but present in *anal* mode. Horney conceives it present solely in *vaginal* mode. I conceive it present in the less differentiated *cloacal* mode.

abdomen, arises very early in the child's life, whatever tales of storks or rose-bushes it may have heard or feigned to believe. To the child, however, the babe germinates, grows and is born in alimentary fashion, as Freud long ago pointed out,[1] and as is witnessed by many a myth and tale in which the queen conceives after eating this or that food and, especially, an apple. True, there may be some degree of displacement here, imposed by the censorship, but I am nevertheless inclined to think that the original symbolism which preceded such displacement and which is only secondarily displaced by the censorship, is a universal symbolism which underlies all these infantile sexual theories.

In any event, and even more than in the case of the penis, the phantasied cloacal baby, given its dimensions, must be conceived as dangerous to the child. How could such an object pass through the body without tearing it apart? Besides, in some sort, the little girl will have heard that childbirth hurts, and will have seen her sick mother, or other women, prostrate and in pain whenever a confinement occurred; the sick bed and the cradle are but a step from each other. What then shall we say of girls whose mothers died when they were born? For them, death becomes the ransom of maternity.

Girls, therefore, in their make-up, require a degree of erotogenic masochism which, however, is the masochism proper to the female needed to neutralize anxiety and enable her to accept the vital dangers inherent in the feminine function.[2]

Other dangers also threaten the small girl who aspires to identification, in the love-act, with the adult woman, the mother. To take the latter's place implies aggression against her, which aggression, in its turn, implies retaliation. Here we have the small girl's oedipal fear of her mother-rival, a fear, in essence, already moral.

It is appropriate here to recall Melanie Klein's ideas relative to the small girl's primary fear of her mother. Melanie Klein traces this anxiety as far back as late in the first year of life,

[1] "On the Sexual Theories of Children" (1908), *Coll. Papers.* Vol. II.
[2] See pp. 76 ff.

immediately after weaning and in hostile reaction to it when, according to her, the small girl's positive Oedipus complex is established, with its passive and vaginal orientation on the father. The small girl, witness of the primal scene, with the "combined parents" as the main actors, will be jealous, on the one hand, because the mother seems to "suckle" the father, and on the other because the father, with his penis, seems to "suckle" her in return, such being a suckling's concepts, the only kind of human interchange it can know. Thereafter, the small girl, beset by oral jealousy, will want to absorb, to suck, to devour the interior of the mother's body: intestines, faeces, foetus and incorporated father's penis while, as talion for these aggressive desires, she will develop fears that her own body will suffer similar treatment; this is that *internal castration complex* which, in the little girl, will give rise to the primary superego. Fairy tale ogresses, who so often eat children, would be the projections of this cannibalistic, because retaliatory, phantasy mother, who haunts the imagination of our small children. Such are the views of Melanie Klein.

My own opinion, however, is that though they contain some portion of truth, their author tends to *moralize* them too much. True, the child is highly aggressive but it is also, from a very early age, highly libidinal; its cannibalistic urges towards the mother, from the very start, express not only hatred and aggression, but also love. We "love" what we eat; we do not eat only to destroy but also to incorporate what we love; and lovers, for instance, "devour each other with kisses". The child's primary sadism towards its mother is wholly charged with infantile love; its instincts at this stage are still closely interwoven.

At the outset, two actors alone play out the sadistic drama of love plus aggression; namely, suckling and nurse. Only later do we find three; suckling, nurse and rival. If aggression then predominates towards one, love will be channelled towards the other. True, this may sometimes happen very early on, but the babe was, at first, only aware of its nurse, before it perceived the neighbouring rival.

Thus, to my mind, since we are dealing with the girl, it is only secondarily that hostility towards the mother, who in her turn has become a rival, superimposes itself on the primary sadistic loving aggression towards her. Thereupon, the talion of being devoured, for wishing to devour,[1] takes on a moral tinge and begins to erect the imposing structure of the superego.

Let us, however, return to the earliest stages of these retaliatory fears as seen by Melanie Klein, according to whom the clitoridalism of woman and the phallus position of the small girl can never be biologically primary, but only secondarily developed.

It is fear of the mother, from whom her jealous babe wishes to tear the body contents such as intestines, foetus, and incorporated paternal penis, which would contribute most to make the little girl renounce her primary cloacal desires and throw her back on the phallus position, which at least does not imperil the interior of her body.

Yet Melanie Klein[2] maintains that this reversal of libido from within to without, is proportionate to the infant's native sadism, and that, when strongly emphasized, it is a determinant factor. I believe this true, but consider it lacks precision, given her comparative indifference to the concept of bisexuality. If girls who, constitutionally, are powerfully sadistic, tend thus to take up the phallus position, it is because sadism, i.e. such dynamic and emphatic aggression, is an essentially male character and betrays a powerful, innate bisexuality. The centrifugal orientation of aggression, as of the libido, represents a male characteristic: the centripetal orientation of the libido, as of aggression, represents a feminine characteristic. Did the male or female genital organs precede this orientation, or did this orientation, this trend, create both the function and the organs? We should lose ourselves in speculative and philosophical problems were we to seek an *ad hoc* solution; it is far better to leave this problem open.

In any case, the aggression, the obdurate sadism which remains directed outwards, favours masculinity and the male

---

[1] See my *The Life and Works of Edgar Allan Poe* where, in my analysis of the tale of *Berenice*, I quote Freud's own ideas on the "vagina dentata" and the child's feared cannibalism by the mother.

[2] See *The Psycho-Analysis of Children* (1932).

functions, and prejudices, in similar degree, femininity and the female functions.

(d) *Infantile Masturbation, Seduction, and Constitutional Cathexes of Erotogenic Zones*

It has been said that excessive clitoridal masturbation, especially in infancy, when continued into the latency period, may contribute to subsequent libidinal fixation on the clitoris in women.

This, indeed, seems sure, but does not posit the problem correctly, for why, because of the traumatic effects of the castration complex, do some little girls abandon masturbation while others do not?

All children masturbate, in fact; at least all healthy children. Indeed, the phallic masturbation of the boy *must* manifest a certain resistance, must not suffer itself to be unduly intimidated by educative threats or the traumatic effects of the cultural castration complex. This phallic masturbation readily breaks through the latency period, and these preparative sexual exercises are most often favourable to future masculinity.

On the other hand, it would generally appear that, if the girl is to become a true woman, her phallic masturbation, normal up to the castration complex, *must* succumb even more to the biological castration complex than to educative prohibitions, and that the female vagina, erotized at puberty, must then be passively content to *await* the male penis that will awaken it.

For the role of everything female, from the ovum to the beloved, is a waiting one. The vagina must await the advent of the penis in the same passive, latent and dormant manner that the ovum awaits the spermatozoon. Indeed the eternally feminine myth of *The Sleeping Beauty* is the retelling of that first biological relation.

Thus one might claim that although the libido, in essence, seems masculine, the infantile latency period seems to be feminine in origin.

But there are little girls who are unable to *wait*, girls in whom the second passive, cloacal stage, following the castration complex, does not pursue an uneventful way to the ideal vaginal stage of puberty. We often find, during the latency period, active aggressive tomboyish recurrences of masculinity, when phallic masturbation reappears and breaks through in the latency period, possibly with passive phantasies pertaining to the new sex-object, i.e. the father, superimposed on primary and mixed active and passive unconscious phantasies connected with the mother.

May it perhaps be that, in such girls, the normal psychological development which would include anatomical development cannot take place, owing to a too powerful and innate bisexuality, a cardinal and preponderant trend of the nervous system towards masculinity? And what events, what infantile seductions, would have brought this about? What are the respective contributions in such cases, of the *wish for masculinity* or the *actual masculinity present*, of the *phantasied identification with the father* or *innate viriloid factors*? Both indeed may contribute their part, nor should we forget that seduction itself and, especially infantile observations of coitus, will affect each sex according to constitutional factors.

In any case, in clitoridal women, the evolutionary process which should have stabilized itself and stopped in the second cloacal phase with the *invagination of the phallic libido* at puberty, as well as with vaginal specificity of the cloacal libido, can be regarded as having, regrettably, evolved too *far* in an active masculine direction. They have not themselves, on their own bodies, accepted the *exclusion of the phallus*, despite the positive Oedipus complex, but have reacted too phallically, during the latency period, despite their attachment to the father, as though the clitoris were not an organ for ever condemned to be inadequate but, like the boy's, would continue to grow. Also, as counterpart to this, some innate psychophysiological awareness in them refuses, as it were, to acknowledge that immensely significant anatomical fact of the blossoming of femininity; namely, that the vagina enlarges at puberty.

Sometimes, however, in clitoridal women, no prepubertal masturbation seems to have occurred in the latency period. If, however, we analyse such women, we generally find that a neurotic symptom, most often obsessional, was then substituted for such masturbation; thus, indirectly, the infantile affirmation of the phallus was maintained.

Per contra, there are women who, during the latency period and beyond, have even masturbated clitoridally yet who, nevertheless, after their first contacts, speedily learn to react normally to the male. Such women are libidinally fortunate, since they possess both erotogenic zones, and thus can potentially achieve the orgasm by one or other, as the circumstances dictate.

(e) *Pre-pubertal Clitoridal Orgasm and Its Possible Relation to Fixation at the Phallic Stage*

Here, a problem of a general order arises, related to the above, to which our psycho-analytic investigations so far give no answer. To my mind, the relatively precocious period—infancy even—at which the orgasm, properly speaking, may have appeared in clitoridal women, must be a predisposing cause to fixating the libido on the clitoris. The time when the orgasm appears, in girl or boy, would seem to differ considerably in each case, and this cardinal libidinal event must help to fixate the libido to the stage and zone in which it occurred.

It seems probable that not only primary masturbation, that of the nursling, but also that of the first blossoming of infantile sexuality which corresponds to the early phallic stage, affirmation of the phallus and active Oedipus complex, may know nothing, as yet, of the orgasm, either as applies to the boy and, even more, to the girl.

Thus, the little girl who is destined to be truly feminine must generally have abandoned clitoridal masturbation before she succeeds in obtaining end-pleasure, orgasm, and so enters the latency period with only the memories of inadequate fore-pleasure. Thereupon, like the Sleeping Beauty, pierced in the hand—the hand of guilty masturbation—by the mother's phallic distaff, the preformed libidinal organization of the little girl will sink into slumber until such time as the husband's advent through the briars of the hymeneal forest awakes her from sleep. Such would be the ideal development of our girls.

Some little girls, however, as we have said, are unable to *wait*, and even more, are unable to accept the *exclusion of the phallus* from their own bodies. In such cases, phallic masturbation will outlive the discovery of the difference between the sexes and re-emerge and disrupt the latency period so that the child may learn to achieve full orgasm through *clitoris* masturbation even before menstruation appears.

What are the influences that help to produce such precocious erotic maturation? We may sometimes indict, and justly, direct seduction by another child, or even, adult. This is the exogenous factor which establishes the predisposition to eventual clitoridal fixation. But the growing girl will doubtless sometimes automatically preserve, or rediscover, phallic masturbation. Some degree of bisexuality should be enough, in which case the girl will behave more or less like the many boys in whom phallic masturbation reasserts itself in the latency period. This is the endogenous predisposing factor.

An exception, however, must be made for those women with dual erotogenic zones to whom I referred earlier; women who, despite the precocious advent of even clitoridal orgasm, become perfectly adapted to normal coitus after defloration.[1]

(f) *The Scylla and Charybdis of the Little Girl.*

A difficult biological problem confronts woman as regards her libidinal development. Infantile masturbation, in fact, far from

[1] Note added in 1948: Cf. the views expressed by Kinsey, Pomeroy and Martin in *Sexual Behavior in the Human Male* (Philadelphia and London, 1948, p. 180), in the following resumé of their behaviourist observations: "These data on the sexual activities of younger males provide an important substantiation of the Freudian view of sexuality as a component that is present in the human animal from earliest infancy, although it gives no support to the Freudian concept of a pre-genital stage of generalized erotic response that precedes more specific genital activity. . . ."

Whatever doubt may subsist as to the conclusions drawn by these authors relating to orgasm in the suckling, their observations anent the second period of infantile masturbation, that of the phallic stage, seem confirmed by the anamnesis of no few men and women. In some, the prepubertal appearance of the orgasm has never indeed been lost but has always been retained in consciousness.

being the exceptional vice still branded by so many educators, is a necessary stage in the libidinal development of every human being. It is to harmonious adult sexuality what play is to adult social activity; a preparation and training.

However inimical it may be, in other respects, to the strivings of civilization, achieved probably at the libido's expense and with its forces, and however justified the educator's attitude may be, to some extent, as a result, infantile masturbation, nevertheless, over and above all this, still retains the dignity of preparing the child for the most vital adult function, one which will surmount our mortality.

Now, the masturbation of the small boy is truly a preparing for the sexual activity of man. When the male phallus, however precociously, learns to experience the orgasm, it is but an early training for what *must* happen later, in more or less the same fashion. It has sometimes been justly said that the male, in the coital act, does something equivalent to masturbating in the woman. It will suffice him to learn psychically to prefer that "kind of masturbation" to the other.

The little girl, however, is caught between two perils. Her masturbation, in infancy, is often mainly phallic, the vagina being more or less dormant, and it is through the little clitoris, above all, that she *must* get to learn sexuality. With too little phallic activity in infancy, it is possible that sexuality will not have been well enough *learnt*, and the subsequent woman will remain in that condition of undifferentiated, diffuse and resigned sexual responsiveness that never quite reaches orgasm, which seems to be that of certain women. (It is true that this kind of woman, as Helene Deutsch so well saw, is gradually disappearing; on the other hand, in many, the part played by some degree of hysterical repression needs to be determined.) Nevertheless, with too much phallic masturbation in childhood (whether as a result of endogenous or exogenous factors, overemphasized bisexuality or clitoridal seduction) and, in particular, the precocious appearance of the clitoridal orgasm, the woman may remain fixated to that libidinal structure and never succeed in erotically accepting the passive attitude which nature demands of her in the male embrace.

A *dynamic stereotype*, as defined by Pavlov, would thus have been established, which the events of later life could only modify with extreme difficulty, a difficulty proportionately increased by any excess of bisexuality present in the underlying structure.

(g) *A Battle of Two Males*

In any case, proof that human bisexuality underlies the superstructures which it secondarily erects on this original foundation is provided by the anatomy itself of the external female genital organs, with their two erotogenic zones, each with its own degree of libidinal investment, a fact which no biologist or psycho-analyst would deny. Thus, a manifestation of the central nervous system, determined both by the degree of zygotic-endocrine masculinity present in the female organism and of the dynamic stereotype fortuitously acquired in infancy, will together establish the erotic behaviour of each woman.

Now, whatever the importance, in the psycho-sexual development of clitoridal women, of the long passive prehistory of the phallus, and the practice of passive caresses to which, given the atrophy of the female phallus, such women are reduced when with a male partner, it is none the less true that, in such women, the erectile clitoris, all said and done, tends to swell and push; in short, to behave like a little male phallus.

This form of behaviour may then activate the erotogenic zones of the clitoridal woman, as well as her whole psyche. Such women often present a generalized activity extending into everything connected with their lives. Not only are they often socially active, but they are even more so in the way they seek out their love-objects. They manifest a certain male activity in the way they choose and win them.

The tragedy of their erotic life will, however, be played out in the sex-act. If they decide in favour of heterosexuality, it will be dangerous for them, with their small phallus, the clitoris, to covet an object also endowed with the phallus and that, the large male phallus which such women especially admire. Since erotic reality insists that they be not the penetrator, but the penetrated, they will need to reconcile their unconscious desires, dictated by the pleasure-principle, with that inescapable reality.

To what strange shifts the clitoridal woman is at times put to reconcile the two phalli, her own and the loved male's, many dreams and phantasies of clitoridal women bear witness. For, with that scorn which the unconscious shows for reality, with that consummate distortion which the pleasure-principle manifests for reality, their overpowering desires often lead them to imagine that the anatomical functions, the changeless reality and very position of the sexual organs, have been converted into their opposites.

I once had the opportunity of recording what we might consider a typical dream of a clitoridal woman, in which she saw genital organs in the act of coitus. But, in place of the male penis, ejaculating, it was the woman who, with a small penis, concealed in the depths of her vagina, ejaculated into the male's urethra. Nothing could better express the wish to invert the respective positions and anatomical roles. This same woman, however, towards her tenth year, when a schoolmate revealed the mechanism of coitus, refused to believe it true and, in her superior wisdom, was sure that an opposite process took place; namely, that far from being penetrated by the male penis, the woman penetrated the male urethra with her clitoris in the sex act. Seduced soon after by a small boy, just as the latter's penis touched her clitoris, she experienced an immediate and intense orgasm and had thus been convinced that her little clitoris had truly entered the boy's urethra.

Certain clitoridal women, who are fiercely frigid in normal coitus, are not so, however, if they can invert the roles and take the superior position, so monopolising the sexual activity. For others, and those the majority, the penetration which so humiliates their masculine narcissism, that of the vagina by the male penis, despite the close contact of clitoris and penis which this implies, will suffice to inhibit all erotic feeling in the sex-act, when carried out in this position.

In any case, the coitus of such women with the male will always, more or less, resemble a battle. The coitus of a clitoridal woman with a male is, in effect, comparable with a battle between two males in which the weaker is defeated, penetrated and transfixed; one in which the victor, and he alone, wins the trophy of the orgasm, in the form of a return to the "womb".

It would appear that coitus in this form reflects, as it were, a vestigial remain of that primitive and biological struggle between male and female, postulated by Ferenczi;[1] the return to the yearned-for womb, which struggle ended in woman's defeat.

[1] *Thalassa, a Theory of Genitality* (1924).

PART II

THE EROTIC FUNCTION, A BIOPSYCHIC FUNCTION

I

PSYCHOLOGY, A BRANCH OF BIOLOGY

IN HIS *New Introductory Lectures on Psycho-Analysis* (1932), Freud very truly writes that, in effect, there are only two kinds of science: natural science and psychology. But in these immense categories we may attempt to regroup some portions and unite under the same heading that part of natural science, organic chemistry, for instance, that deals with life and which, combined with psychology, would constitute biology.

Psychology, in fact, is a branch of biology, a branch of vast importance to humanity. For which reason we cannot clearly separate the first part of this paper from the second.

We have continually mingled the light of psychology with the biological light by which we sought to illumine all we have so far said. Now the light of biology must mingle with the psychological lights with which we shall try to illumine other facets of our problems.

II

THE FEMALE AND HER LIBIDO

(a) *Poorer Libido of the Female and Basic Obstacles to Erotic Adaptation in Women*

FIRST, WE should recall that libido, like all energy, is *quantitative* in kind, and that all creatures are constitutionally charged with it in different degrees. This is what is meant when we say, for instance, without any clear idea what is meant, that a woman's disposition is more or less ardent.

True, it may be difficult to decide how much libido was originally present, given the inhibitions, the deflections, that culture, and even biology, impose on the individual libido in general, and on that of woman in particular, but some quantum certainly exists. No garment can be cut without stuff, however good or bad the tailor.

Now, whether or not it will please women to hear it, the feminine organism, quantitatively speaking, is in general more poorly endowed with libido than the male, a fact true of most animal species. Doubtless this is because more dynamic activity and sexual aggression are required in the male, if the race is to continue.

In the female, moreover, the libido seems often to have a longer distance to travel to achieve full adaptation to the erotic function for, like a deflected stream, it must, in some degree at least, flow through another channel, since it must change its erotogenic zone and pass, in the main, from the infantile clitoris—which, like the pronephros, should only be transitory —to the definitive adult organ, the vagina. We know that some power is generally lost when rivers change their courses. And the feminine libido, called upon to make this extra effort, is *ab initio* quantitatively less, therefore less dynamic, than the male. It need not therefore surprise us to find, given the longer road it must travel and the more numerous obstacles in its path—feminine anatomy and physiology on one hand,

and the stronger inhibitions which cultural morality imposes on female sexuality, on the other—that the originally weaker upsurge of feminine libido does not always suffice to surmount all obstacles in travelling its full path, and that its current should slow down, stop and stagnate, whether wholly or in part, at some point or other.

In any case, as a French biologist friend once pointed out, the divorce in woman, unlike man, between the erotic and reproductive functions, must work against the hereditary transmission of the progress acquired in woman's adaptation to her erotic function. And indeed, to go by the Mendelian theory, the adaptation of a creature to the erotic function proper to its sex, may be taken as a sex-linked character. In man, since male potency coincides with aptitude for reproduction, males of lesser potency will tend to perpetuate themselves less freely than the more potent, whereupon a natural selection towards adaptation to the male erotic function should follow and establish itself in future male generations. In woman, however, evolution follows a quite different pattern, for those defective in, or ill-adapted to the erotic function, reproduce as freely as those erotically adapted: woman has only to attract and accept the male, as indeed her feminine passivity inclines her. As a result, erotic selection functions badly and woman's hereditary adaptation to her erotic function has barely improved throughout the ages.

(b) *The Psycho-Physiological "Vitellinism" of Woman*

Woman offers us not a few enigmas and, in especial, this apparent contradiction; on the one hand, as we saw in all we have so far related, she generally seems less well endowed than man to achieve her erotic destiny, less charged with libido and more fettered in functional adaptation to it than he is; on the other, it is generally said, and apparently with reason, that woman is more instinctive and more deeply embedded in sexuality, often to the exclusion of all else.

True, woman has a far greater hunger than man to be loved, cherished, and petted, like some grown-up child. The male, bearer of the phallus, is far more self-sufficient; he has his social task which he loves and which occupies his mind and thus has more chance of satisfying and also of sublimating his sexual instinct. Woman, for her part, subsists and depends far more and much more exclusively on love; love of the male, love of husband and child.

Nevertheless, as regards the actual erotic function, this remains far more frequently defective in woman than in man. By which we mean that woman, in general, is both more hemmed in by instinct, her sexual instinct in its widest sense, than is man, though less well endowed than man to gratify that instinct erotically and explosively in orgasm, which perhaps amounts to saying, to achieve periodic discharge.

We cannot resolve this apparent contradiction without a general glance at the development of sexual differentiation in the evolutionary scale.[1] Underlying all, we find unicellular organisms, in which the simple conjugation of apparently, if not actually, undifferentiated cells, precedes multiplication. By degrees, with algae in especial, a division of labour is established, whereupon certain cells devote themselves to storing food for the provision of the future germ-cell, thus immobilizing themselves and adding to their weight. Others again specialize in the movement and activity needed to seek out the former and conjugate with them, in this way creating together, by virtue of the food reserves the former contain, the germ of the future organism. Here we have the first visible outline of differentiation between female and male. Higher in the evolutionary scale, the "vitellinism" of the female cell, if we may use such a term, reaches its maximum in the egg yolk of reptiles and, above all, of birds.

Despite the minuteness of the ovum in woman, we may consider that the female element, even in our own species, continues to be saturated with this vitellinism. But, with woman, it is as though the whole organism were charged with it. Actually, the mammal egg no longer needs a vitellus since it will have the placenta. Even more, when born, its young will find the breast. Later, the human mother will continue to prepare food for the family. Thus, in the nourishing aspect of woman, we meet again the vitellinism associated with

[1] See especially: Joseph Meisenheimer: *Geschlecht und Geschlechter*, (1921).

the bird's egg, but now extended to the total function of the female being.

Physically, too, the woman's body, more normally than the male's, appears as padded and permeated with adipose tissue imposed on a weaker muscular structure, one less adapted to motor activity, and one which provides a somatic testimony to her vitellinism. Often, indeed, the whole psyche of woman seems wholly saturated with this vitellinism, this relative dynamic inertia which is so essential a feature of everything female in nature.

This same inertia often attacks the libido of woman and hampers the dynamic expression necessary for orgastic fulfilment in the coital function.

(c) *Vitellinism and Human Motherhood*

Given the biological fact that the sexual life of woman is not limited solely to coitus, but covers every process of maternity, we might be tempted to conclude, from that alone, that the feminine libido must be less concentrated, less active, less explosive in the sexual act, which is the object and culmination of the male's whole sexuality. We have, however, shown elsewhere, that it is just this psychical acceptance of maternity which favours the vaginalization of woman and her erotic adaptation to the act which conditions that maternity. This new, apparent contradiction, will resolve itself if, as we should, we distinguish in the human maternal function the maternal activity proper from such residuals of passive female vitellinism as it may conceal.

Such residual vitellinism merely determines the inertia, the lesser degree of dynamism of the female libido. The vitellus, however, being replaced by the whole organism of the mammalian female, has therewith lost the greater part of its inertia. The nursing-mother, in effect, is a conscious vitellus which must know how to act, a vitellus endowed with a muscular system, a sort of vitellus which is no longer such in the true and original sense of negative vitelline inertia. Indeed, the active characteristics of human motherhood are emphasized both in the mother's active care of her child, and in her vaginal, orgastic acceptance of the act on which her maternity will be founded.

Actually, we frequently find full vaginal function and maternal instinct united in the same woman. It is as though one primary orientation of the libido conditioned both responses in their relation to the channel through which the penis and child are to pass; adaptive responses to specifically female transmitted functions.

(d) *The Triple Stratification of the Factors that Determine Feminine Frigidity*

These maximal vaginal and maternal adaptive responses, however, do not always occur and, as we know, there are innumerable women whom nature, it would seem, has more or less neglected to adapt to their sexual functions in general (even when it allows them the passively maternal sex act), and to their erotic function in particular.

If we investigate this defective function, the triple stratification of idiopathic female frigidity will appear.

Firstly, in so far as she is female, woman, as we have shown, has generally less libidinal energy, less libido than 'man: this is the specifically *female* condition of feminine frigidity.

Next, woman, in so far as she is a bisexual being, as we saw in the first part of this work, generally tolerates her masculinity complex better than the male does his femininity complex; but then, far from simply and purely correcting the primary biological inadequacy of the female function, this male contribution aggravates matters by making it harder for the libido to adapt to woman's passive, vaginal role. This is the specifically *male* condition of feminine frigidity.

Lastly, in our patriarchal civilizations, where a more or less double morality always holds sway, man imposes sexual inhibitions on woman while reserving a greater latitude for himself. As a result, women, from childhood on, undergo a much stronger repression of their sexuality than men, weaker though theirs already is and less clearly orientated. This is the specifically cultural, *moral* condition of feminine frigidity.

Thus, on the way leading to conquest of full erotic function, the woman encounters three great obstacles: her *femininity*, her *masculinity* and her *morality*.

III

ADULTS AND THE CHILD

(a) Contradictory Adult Attitudes to the Sexuality of the Child

MORALITY IN individuals begins by being imposed from without and thenceforth derives from the environmental influences to which the organism may be subjected.

But though this environment, in our civilizations, greatly inhibits the natural instincts, Nature, on the other hand, despite civilization, as it were, retains the right to awaken those same instincts through the environment in which the child grows and through the very medium of its education.

As a result, whether they suspect it or not, adults are both exciting and inhibiting agents in all that effects the psychosexuality of children.

There are many ways in which adults may excite the child's sexuality: let us recall them here. To begin with, even the nursling cannot escape the ministrations, connected with its toilet, to which we earlier referred, and which excite its erotogenic zones. But, if these ministrations are neglected, then it will be the secretions accumulating in the mucous folds which will assume that function, as though, whatever the event, Nature herself ensured that these zones awakened.

This is the first kind of seduction; involuntary seduction by the mother, which includes Dame Nature! To which, reverting to this same early stage, we may add the practices of uneducated and unscrupulous nurses who masturbate the child to keep it quiet, or to encourage it to sleep.

But adults seduce the child in yet another way; that of the activities they place before its eyes. In fact, adults hardly trouble to conceal their sexuality from the child. It often shares the same room, and is too innocent, in their eyes, to understand what takes place.

Now, in behaving thus, adults unconsciously fulfil a sort of mission prescribed by Nature and thus convey a mighty message to the little creature. For Nature has intended that the human child learn about sexuality, and that, from a very early age, with the result that the sex acts of adults, performed in its presence, indelibly impress its young mind. If it is perceived by that essential human function of sight, or merely as sound, the ineradicable traces of what was perceived at the time will for ever remain an unconscious memory, as is testified by many a psycho-analysis of patients of every age. We thus find conviction of the general fact that the child, often at an incredibly early age, a year and a half, for instance, is able, in its way, to respond to the sight or perception of adult coitus, as though to store up the impressions it will remodel psychically later. In effect, it already possesses all the mechanisms that will later compose its sexuality; the preformed instinct is already present, though dormant, and only asks to be wakened. Also, the sight or perception of the sex activity of adults reawakens and, in especial, reinforces the child's innate tendency towards masturbation, that cardinal manifestation of infantile sexuality.

* * *

Somewhat later, infantile sexuality may be stimulated by true seduction, carried out by other children. Sexual games between children, and between brothers and sisters, are not uncommon, and there is no need to go to savages for the visual proof! Also, from infancy on, the small human creature may, properly speaking, be sexually seduced by perverse adults, an occurrence less rare than is thought.

But even if we halt at the two first forms of seduction, those which most commonly occur and are rarely absent from the anamneses of our patients, namely unconsciously practised seductions by adults, such as cleansings, caresses, maternal pettings, or seduction through observation or perception of the coitus of adults, we find that the child, with its sexual development thus stimulated, as it were, by Nature's design, (such adults being but her delegated teachers), suddenly beholds a change in the attitude of those adults and thus of their mission. Then and there, they stop being *Nature's* proxies and become *Culture's*. For, confronted by the manifestations of infantile sexuality which these adults have themselves unwittingly awakened, and by the masturbation which is the only sexual activity within the child's scope, an activity in which it *lives* the instinctual phantasies which now begin to throng its imagination, they suddenly frown and threaten and scold. If the child goes on masturbating, they say, it will fall ill, infect itself, weaken its stomach or brain, even die! They may even, in fact, threaten the small boy with cultural castration—deprivation of his member. The girl, biologically castrated already, cannot be treated thus, but other threats are not spared her. In any case, the child who masturbates, whether boy or girl, is naughty, vicious, a pariah no one will love, a sinner whom God, if one there be, will condemn. And for the little girl, so naturally affectionate and eager to be loved, such threatened loss of love will often prove most effective.

But there are children whose masturbation is never discovered, and who are thus never directly rebuked. This is far from unimportant, for the discovery, or not, by its upbringers, of the child's masturbation, plays a great part in constituting an individual's future psycho-sexual reflexes and leaves an indelible stamp on the whole sexuality and even, character, of the later adult.

(b) *Sexual Ideation of the Child*

I confess to a sort of fear on entering the vast and shadowy realm which now confronts us. Here we risk going astray, and are faced by two dangers. If we are not to lose ourselves, we must either remain stockstill with shut eyes on the threshold (which is the attitude of all non-analysts), and so see nothing or, if ambitious to strike a direction and explore this dark continent, we do venture inside it, the arbitrary paths we trace may be too simple, too direct, and lead to ignoring vast though primordial regions.

Let us, however, dare the attempt. If we began by emphasizing, earlier, the manifest sexual activity of the child, which is masturbation, it was because masturbation is just that very activity and because that reality activity of infantile sexuality expresses the feelings, thoughts and volitions which are more or less shut in the helpless babe.

But the child's masturbation, with the fore-pleasure it includes and at whatever moment the orgasm may appear, this masturbation which is the manifestation, the expression of infantile sexuality, and so preformative of the modes of erotic satisfaction that will be proper to the adult, before becoming a cause, was itself an effect.

In speaking thus, I naturally refer to the later stage of infantile masturbation, that in which the emotions connected with the child's Oedipus complex are discharged, i.e. roughly between its third and sixth years.

At that stage, masturbation is wholly permeated with, and determined and directed by, the sexual phantasies proper, in each instance, to the child's oedipal attitudes. That is to say that sexual activity at this stage is governed not only by libidinal, atavistic and internal biological urges which foster its sexual dynamism but, also, by sexual ideas and representations drawn from the outer world.

This sexual ideation of the child is what we must now study, if we wish to find some path through the realm governed by the child's Oedipus complexes, from which its future sexuality develops.

First, however, let us try to define the term, *sexual ideation of the child*. By this I mean the combined representations, all charged with libidinal affect, lodged in the child's neuro-psychical apparatus. Some are but simple surface apparitions of the main unconscious complexes, and form part of what we call conscious thought, as when the small boy openly declares he wants to "marry mother". But the sexual ideation of the child is far bigger and deeper than that; it stretches in wide, thick layers into that unconscious which it is now our task to explore. There, for instance, dwell the demons and fairies that were the adults glimpsed, in particular, in the sacred and fearful performance of the sex-act. There rule the oedipal parents, like underground but all-powerful gods. Generally speaking, however, we have no very exact idea of the child's sexual ideation, for no clear demarcation exists, at that stage, between conscious and unconscious. It is only by degrees, as repression proceeds, that such boundaries are established.

In any case, though the child's earliest sexual ideation is dominated throughout by its infantile Oedipus complexes, and though this seems predetermined by constitutional libidinal drives, it is none the less determinant, in its turn, of the later adult fate of these same urges.

Now, since all human beings, in infancy, girls or boys, regularly pass through two successive Oedipus complexes, the active and passive, each, it is true, very differently stressed, according to sex and individual, it will be the greater or lesser strength of these Oedipus complexes, their persistence, and their partial vestiges present, more or less, in the individual's psycho-sexuality, which will condition the sexual attitude in general, and the erotic attitude in particular, of all men and women—all bisexual, in some degree—as so many major "reflexes", "conditioned", to use that word in its widest sense, in the dim past.

IV

ESSENTIAL FEMININE MASOCHISM

(a) *Respective Relations of Active or Passive Oedipus Complexes to Sadism and Masochism*

THUS, AT a given moment and probably successively, the two Oedipus complexes of the little girl replace each other after doubtless having, in most cases, for the unconscious knows nothing of contradictions, co-existed side by side. In the unconscious of many women, even that of the hetero-sexual, though especially that of the clitoridal woman, the little girl's active Oedipus complex, originally turned towards the mother, will for ever continue active, even though such women exclusively elect the male as their adult love object.

We know, however, that clitoridal masturbation often continues to be the activity which drains off not only the excitation bound up with the little girl's active Oedipus complex turned to the mother, but even that bound up with the passive Oedipus complex turned to the father.[1] This amounts to saying that when the little girl, having become aware of her castration—that is of the minuteness of her clitoris and, in my opinion, even of the hole of her vulva—indulges in phantasies with *passive* aims, such as phantasies of castration and ravishing by the father, she often lives them in terms of the pleasure dispensed by means of that very organ, the clitoris, and that, in general, until the advent of the latency period renders her masturbation dormant. The civilized child, despite her persistent love for the father, despite her never wholly cleared-up Oedipus complex, will then enter into that long waiting sleep, like that of the Sleeping Beauty's, which often characterizes the female's pre-pubertal sexuality.

In this sleep, as we said earlier, the feminine libido seems to

[1] See however, the works of Karen Horney and, in especial, of Melanie Klein, already quoted, for divergent views.

retire into itself before it is vaginally aroused by the male, when he appears. Such would be the ideal feminine sexual development. But when, as it were, the male clitoris "protests", when it does not permit itself to be eliminated or at least relegated to the background, when, at an early age, it achieves the orgasm and aggressively irrupts in the latency period, then disturbances may arise in the woman's adult sexuality.

How is it, then, that the infantile activity of this small phallic organ should be fated, in certain instances, if it continues, to be harmful to the adult erotic feminine function, and to resist and thwart that of the vagina while, in other cases, though doubtless present and continuing through childhood, it ends by fusing harmoniously with what has become a clitoridal-vaginal adult erotic feminine function, or even sometimes wholly succumbs in favour of the vagina, in cases of maximal adaptation to the function?

I believe that, where sado-masochism is concerned, the answer to these questions is to be sought largely in the different manner in which women react to infantile clitoridal masturbation itself, and so to the phantasies which accompany it.

* * *

The essential character of feminine masochism, as we have already recalled, was first brought to light by Freud[1]; later Helene Deutsch[2] thought it appeared to her as the primary condition needed to establish normal feminine erotic function. It seems to me, however, that we need a closer inquiry into the relation of this masochism to the clitoridal masturbation which helps to discharge the excitation proper to the little girl's passive Oedipus complex.

It is not possible to be masochistic without being passive, but the converse is not true. Nevertheless, though passivity and masochism are not identical, they are united by a deep

[1] "The Economic Problem in Masochism" (1924). *Coll. Papers*, Vol. II.
[2] "The Significance of Masochism in the Mental Life of Women" (1930).

bond, and numerous intermediate forms exist which lead from one to the other. Throughout the whole range of living creatures, animal or vegetal, passivity is characteristic of the female cell, the ovum, whose mission is to *await* the male cell, the active mobile spermatozoon, to come and *penetrate* it. Such penetration, however, implies infraction of its tissue, but infraction of a living creature's tissue may entail destruction: death as much as life. Thus the fecundation of the female cell is initiated by a kind of wound; in its way, the female cell is primordially "masochistic".

Now it would appear that these prototypal cellular reactions pass unchanged into the psychical apparatus of those who bear these same cells and, indeed, our psycho-sexual responses, whether male or female, seem thoroughly permeated with them. Originally, whether male or female, the nursling's attitude towards the active mother was mainly passive for, biologically helpless as it is, it must let itself be tended, cleansed, covered, rocked, petted and fed, even though the instinct to suck the proffered breast already implies an activity reflex, however basically receptive that may be. (Babies also differ in their capacity to learn to suck.) And though the deep current of infantile passivity, which is linked with the child's helplessness, does not wholly dry up, there begins to flow over it, as its strength grows, a counter-current of activity which reaches its maximal positive intensity in the active phallic stage of the boy or girl.

We should not, however, term this stage merely active. In these earliest years, in fact, the libidinal and aggressive urges are still closely intertwined and the child's whole activity is both libidinal and aggressive. It is this very combination which creates both the child's sadism and its phallic activity, which appear, as we already saw, when the child is well into the sadistic-anal muscular-erotism stage, following prolonged and passive earlier experiences of the phallus, which phallic activity is always, more or less, permeated with sadism. What the small boy apparently yearns to accomplish with his penis is an anal, cloacal intestinal penetration of the mother; a bloody disembowelling, even. The child of two, three, or four, despite, or rather, because of its infancy, is truly then a small, potential, Jack the Ripper. The little girl, though much more confusedly, also shows features of this same attitude, mingled with the strong oral and anal sadism common to all children.

Later, when the instincts begin to be disentangled and, taking shape, define the boy's Oedipus complex, a separation of the instincts will arise, and the major part of his aggression will be funneled towards the father, while the mother will retain his love, freed, more or less, from aggression. But we shall have more to say, later, of the complicated primary interminglings of the libidinal and aggressive drives and their oedipal unravelling, as well as of the eventual fate of the parricidal aggression which, after the passing of the Oedipus complex, by being turned back on the subject, becomes his moral conscience. Especially, we shall show how the boy's constitutionally stronger aggression succeeds in desexualizing itself better than the girl's, as also in releasing itself from libidinal fetters, thus partly determining the male's superiority in the struggle for existence and the stabler character of his superego.[1]

Aggression, in the oral stage, is manifested in cannibalistic fashion and, in the sadistic-anal stage which succeeds it, partly as a phantasied projection of the child's excremental products and partly, and more in accordance with reality, in muscular fashion. The voluntary muscular system will then, throughout life, remain the vehicle of aggression. The castration phantasies proper to the phallic stage imply an aggression reinforced by a second upsurge, a second libidinal charge, of erotism, and in this stage the truly erotogenic sadism breaks away from the general aggression, in the same way that the now ever more active phallus does from the rest of the body.

Depending on whether the libidinal or destructive urges are predominant in sadism, this erotogenic sadism will remain a subordinate factor of the sexual instinct or, as in extreme examples, will constitute that instinct itself (as for instance, with lust murderers such as Vacher or Kürten).

Ordinarily, however, when the active Oedipus complex appears in the little boy, a stage begins in which the drives

[1] See Freud: *Civilization and its Discontents* (1930).

begin to be sorted out, and the larger part of his aggression will then be turned on the father. This defusion of drives we might call the *Oedipal unravelling*. It is also valuable from the vital angle, for it enables the sexual object to be loved with the maximum freedom from aggression. From the social standpoint, however, it has its dangers, for no community tolerates parricide. Freud[1] has helped us to realize how, out of the inhibition of the two drives towards parricide and incest, morality and civilization were able to come into being in the dim past.

What now are the fates that respectively befall this libido and this aggression, both inhibited in our communities? The libido which, in childhood, would be biologically inadequate to conquer the mother, will later direct itself on other women, mother substitutes, and thus (leaving aside the indirect forms of satisfaction through sublimation), succeed in achieving reality satisfaction in direct erotic fashion. Man's aggression, however, inhibited in its parricidal trend, will retain a general homicidal inhibition except, of course, when mass-aggressions, national or social wars, or executions, are involved. It will then turn back, desexualized, on the subject, that is to say, maximally freed from its erotism, and thus constitute his moral conscience. In this we see another attempt at the defusion of drives normally experienced by the male child. Then, after the unravelling which takes place between oedipal objects of different sexes, the liquidation of the active Oedipus complex will bring about another attempt to unravel the drives, this time *moral*, by constituting the more or less impersonal superego. It is this last situation which Freud cites, in his *The Economic Problem of Masochism* (1924) as the typical example that proves this defusion of drives.

The fact that the girl has only the right to an active Oedipus complex as truncated as the little clitoris, her phallus, dooms her aggression to remain far more closely commingled with erotism than the boy's. Constitutionally, no doubt, female aggression, like her libido, is generally weaker than the male's; thus, through its risk of vital danger to himself, the latter is obliged to externalize his aggression more than she does hers.

[1] *Totem and Taboo* (1913).

But again, since the girl's active Oedipus complex, directed on the mother, does not develop, this defusion of drives cannot occur on the same scale as in the boy. The passive Oedipus complex, whose love object is the father and his big phallus, dominantly sets in in woman after her biological true castration complex is established, however early that may be. It is against the passive attitude and general masochism, which are not biologically imposed upon him, that the male *must* protest, whereas they *must* be accepted by the female. All forms of masochism are related and, in essence, are more or less female, from the wish to be eaten by the father in the cannibalistic oral phase, through that of being whipped or beaten by him in the sadistic-anal stage, and of being castrated in the phallic stage, to the wish, in the adult feminine stage, to be pierced and impregnated by the male as a substitute for the father.

Thus, on the one hand, aggression is much more constantly and intimately *bound* by the libido in woman than in man and, on the other, is far more preponderantly turned back upon the subject. Masochism in woman is far stronger than in man. The aggression against the mother, in the girl's passive Oedipus complex, can never result in a superego equal to that produced by the boy's active Oedipus complex turned on the father, since the characteristics of the two, often concomitant, Oedipus complexes, are so much more intricately commingled and confused in the girl than in the boy. And since woman, above all, remains always more or less dominated by her positive, passive, masochistic Oedipus complex, turned on the father, a position she never entirely erotogenically abandons, she remains, throughout life, more subject to her infantile libidinal urges than is man.

The fate of the active sadistic Oedipus complex turned on the mother is the same, at first, in girl and boy. Part of the aggression tends first to be canalized towards the rival father and proportionally reduces the sadistic aggression with which the love for the mother was originally charged. But this attempt to unravel the instincts remains merely adumbrated in the girl who, all too soon, discovers the difference between the sexes and then must submit to the castration complex, with all its disappointment as regards the too-small clitoris. This, the executive organ, properly speaking, of the infantile phallic sadism, soon therefore becomes depreciated and the envied penis, that big paternal penis with which the clitoris could never compare, must, in the little girl's eyes, take its place as the true representative of sadism. A sort of surrender of the clitoris to the greater and mightier power of the penis would occur, as it were. This is when the primary, passive masochistic drives dormant in the female are no doubt mobilized. The active clitoridal sadistic attitude, which must now be abandoned, is reversed, and the little girl desires the father's assaults and the blows of his big penis.

But how is she to enjoy these sensually, for the little girl is only aware of the clitoris as executive organ of her active Oedipus complex turned on the mother. True, the clitoris remains erotogenically cathected, but with the setting in of the passive Oedipus complex turned on the father, and its concomitant change of love object, it must also, as it were, alter its sensual direction. Of course, the concept of anal *penetration* by the male penis is not uncommon at this time, and indeed heralds that of vaginal penetration by the same penis. The little girl, however, has already known the primacy of the phallus, she already knows from experience that the focus of voluptuous pleasure lies rather in front than behind her. Thus, two linked phantasies must then take possession of her imagination: the father's assault on the anal zone by means of his penis, and the same attack on the clitoris.

Now the long passive prehistory of the phallus must greatly help to bring about this reversal which turns the clitoris, after its transient activity, which must vary greatly in different cases, into an organ that is once more passive. Here the regression, as regards the female, becomes part and parcel of her development. The passive clitoris of the woman directly derives from the originally passive infantile phallus.

Often, it may be, the active phase may have been so feebly defined that it must necessarily appear to have been entirely lacking. Perhaps even, in certain cases, the female phallus was never anything but passive, and never, indeed, adumbrated any activity.

(b) "A Child is Being Beaten" ... or a Woman

We return here to that famous feminine phantasy to which Freud devoted his paper *A Child is Being Beaten* (1919).[1] As will be remembered, Freud there considers, mainly from the analyses of women, the frequent infantile phantasy in which the small girl imagines she first sees another child, more or less vague, being beaten, which phantasy gratifies her jealousy of a rival sister or brother. Then, herself taking its place, she imagines she has been beaten by the father and, finally, that she has witnessed scenes where boys were whipped by a father figure, a schoolmaster perhaps, or some other person, which last phantasy, in childhood, was accompanied by masturbation. The same infantile phantasies were also presented by men analysed by Freud, with the difference that, in the third phase, it was the mother who beat these masochistic males. The second link of the chain, the central phantasy of the triptych, that of being beaten by the father, alike in form in both sexes, mostly however remained unconscious, due to a too powerful passive Oedipal guilt or fixation. Analysis alone, and that in indubitable fashion, enabled the phantasy to be reconstructed.

Now in reading this most thought-provoking paper on these typical flagellation phantasies, one has the impression that Freud has set even more problems than he solves. And, particularly, why is it nearly always boys who are beaten by father figures, in the girl's third phantasy—that accompanied by masturbation—and, practically never, girls? True, Freud justly saw this as an expression of the masculinity complex in women, but I believe we might venture even further. The equation faeces — money — child — penis is now a classical one to all psycho-analysts since his most fruitful *On the Transformation of Instincts with Special Reference to Anal Erotism* (1916).[2] Now, to me, it seems that, in regard to the phantasy "A Child is Being Beaten", the two last terms of this equation are to some extent equivalent. If the small girl substitutes boys for herself in her last phantasy of being beaten, it is indeed because

[1] *Coll. Papers*, Vol. II.
[2] Ibid.

she wishes to be a boy, but it is above all because she wishes her father to beat what is equivalent to the child in her unconscious, namely her small male phallus, the clitoris multiplied as a royal plural in the final beating phantasy. My own analyses of women permit me to assert it.[1]

The sadism, at this stage of libidinal development which follows the castration complex, has turned into its opposite, and the erotogenic infantile clitoris after having, for a time, it may be, functioned as an active sadistic organ, has once more become—or has remained—a masochistically cathected passive organ. I believe this masochistic-phallic evolutionary stage to be of normal occurrence in the libidinal development of the female. Every girl must have passed through it. Every small girl, passing through the passive Oedipus complex—which triumphantly asserts itself during the full phallic stage, and while the anal- or rather, sadistic-cloacal, erotism is still most active—must unconsciously have phantasied being beaten and on the clitoris, by *rods* or a rod, the executive organ, *in excelsis*, of the object sadism at this stage. For the phantasy *A Child is Being Beaten* is, in my opinion, the psychosexual connecting link by which the clitoridal libido of the girl when, for a time, it has been active and sadistic, by passive and masochistic regression evolves into full vaginality.

Beating, in fact, is an act preliminary to penetration, to effraction. One knocks at a door before entering. One shakes, if necessary, the lock or key. And it is the same primary organ, the clitoris, executive organ of the phallic-sadistic infantile sexual aggression turned on the mother which then becomes, through the subject's own sadism turning upon herself, the phantasied object of sadistic aggression by the father and his large penis. The clitoris, with its active external urge, may thus have become, or rather re-become, in the small girl's masturbation phantasies which the passive Oedipus complex has attached to the father, an organ of passive sensuality. And only later, if it ever is, will actual clitoridal masturbation

---

[1] Elsewhere Freud himself has related the beaten child to the clitoris in "Some Psychological Consequences of the Anatomical Distinction Between the Sexes" (1925). *Coll. Papers*, Vol. V.

be abandoned as a result of the narcissistic disappointment which, notwithstanding, pierces through. The penis is too big! The clitoris will thus finally *surrender* to it and the blows of the father's rod, of the male in general, will be kept for the vagina, which will then have become sensually receptive to the totality of the former; a vagina that is now the "hollow penis" referred to by certain analysts.

The sexual function proper to woman may then realize itself fully in this final acceptance, this accepted gliding of the penis within the destined sheath.

Vaginal sensitivity in coitus, for the adult female, in my opinion, is thus largely based on the existence, and the more or less unconscious acceptation, of the child's immense masochistic beating phantasies.

In coitus, the woman, in effect, is subjected to a sort of beating by the man's penis. She receives its blows and often, even, loves their violence.

Inquiry into the specific sensitivity of the vaginal membranes will confirm our views on this subject. We know that the vaginal mucosae are almost insensitive; they barely feel heat or cold or pain. Surgery operates inside the vagina almost without a local anaesthetic. Nevertheless, it is in the vagina itself and, more or less distant from the entrance according to the individual that, for the functionally adapted, evolved and adult woman, true erotic sensitivity dwells; it is from this point that, in coitus, the terminal orgasm starts.

An explanation offers itself for these apparently contradictory facts; the woman must not only, beginning in infancy, change her love object and her dominant erotogenic zone, but must also, in large degree, change her *kind* of sexual excitation. It is no longer through the sole medium of a superficial excitable mucous surface, responsive to rubbing, such as that of the glans penis or the clitoris which mild friction will arouse, that the typical and truly feminine orgasm will be released. Without denying the diffuse sensitivity of the vulvar mucosae which certainly play their part in procuring the feminine orgasm, and the frequent powerful erotization round the meatus or perineum, another kind of sensitivity must also contribute to it. This sensitivity must be a deep and truly vaginal sensitivity to the blows of the penis, and one in which the erectile tissue lining the vagina must play its part.[1]

Language itself, compact as it always is of unconscious "echoes", bears witness to this view. Is not the penis termed "rod", and is it not spoken of as "banging"? In any case, popular wisdom has it that women like "being beaten".

We know, besides, that women who show too great an aversion to men's brutal games may be suspected of masculine protest and excessive bisexuality. Such women may very well be clitoridal.

I also consider that such "masculine protest" (not in the Adlerian, but in the biologically bisexual sense), an attitude which is generally tinged with some sadism, only arises as a secondary reaction, and not mainly in reaction to a too powerful inherent feminine masochism so well described by Helene Deutsch in her *The Significance of Masochism in the Mental Life of Women* (1925). When a woman protests so energetically against her masochism, her passivity and her femininity, it is because the make-up against which she protests is already over-determined owing to a constitutionally preponderant bisexuality. But for that, she would perfectly, and without any great conflict, have accepted the feminine masochism essential to her sex.

All of which goes to confirm that, in woman, there must normally be less unravelling of drives than in man. Their aggression, already quantitatively less, is not nearly so much liberated from erotism as in man, and above all, it turns back on the subject early in life when, linked with erotism, it became masochism.

(c) *An Examination of Freud's "A Child is Being Beaten..."*

Here, an important parenthesis is necessary: that of examining Freud's paper in the light of our charts which showed the parallel development of the instincts in both sexes.

---

[1] Mme Dr. Afhild Tamm of Stockholm told me however (in Dec., 1932), that the erotic vaginal sensitivity of the female, in her opinion, must differ in kind from that of the glans penis or the clitoris.

(I) Freud begins by describing the phantasy of *A Child is Being Beaten* as it appeared to him from the analysis of many neurotics of both sexes, but mostly women. (This preponderance will not surprise us, masochism being, in fact, more feminine.) He also notes that the conscious masturbatory phantasy seems to appear before the child goes to school and not first in connection with witnessing punishment at school; that is, at latest, in the child's fifth or sixth year. This should not surprise us either, since this phantasy belongs essentially to the culmination of the passive Oedipus complex in both sexes, the maturation of which may generally be placed at about these ages; namely, immediately after the trauma which accompanies the realization of the difference between the sexes and ushers in the castration complex.

(II) In Freud's opinion, this phantasy expresses a perverse innate characteristic, a result of too precocious liberation and affirmation of the sado-masochistic components of the libido (with which we entirely agree though emphasizing that, in our opinion, such a characteristic would not merit calling perverse unless the beating phantasies were to pass, unchanged, into the subject's adult sexuality and there represent it more or less entirely; if, however, they are modified and integrated into the adult feminine sexuality in ways we shall later see, they there become a normal, indispensable factor in adult and adapted feminine function). Freud himself, I may say, informed me, in a written communication, that the four women to whom he referred in his paper were all virgin which, unfortunately, in those four cases, prevents us seeing the relation of such persistent beating phantasies to the erotic function, properly speaking. In this section of his paper, he also indicates that every infantile perversion, and thus the beating perversion in question, may suffer four fates: conservation, repression, reaction formation or sublimation. We shall return to this.

(III) Freud here reminds us that the lifting of the infantile amnesia is the aim of every psycho-analysis. Now, the conscious phantasies which the child remembers do not, in general, antedate its fifth or sixth years. They must therefore have a prehistory, situated during the upsurge of infantile sexuality which only blossoms at that age. Such, in fact, is the case. Freud also informs us that he will limit himself to the study of this phantasy in women. Analysis allows three phases of this phantasy to be reconstructed:

(1) *A child is being beaten:* i.e. generally a younger brother or sister; in short, a small rival for the parent's affection. It is the small girl's father who, in general, is charged with inflicting this punishment.

(2) *The father beats me.* This phase, contrary to the previous one, which the small girl vaguely remembers, generally remains quite unconscious, doubtless because too strongly charged with oedipal guilt (and perhaps, I would add, with narcissistic ego-defence against beating).

(3) *A father-substitute*, a schoolmaster or another, *beats children*, generally *boys*. This is the phantasy which adult memory retains. (It will not surprise us that those *beaten* are boys, representing, as they do, the phallic clitoris of the girl multiplied in the unconscious. It is in this phase that all the masochistic representations occur by a displacement in which the father as subject is replaced by some dominant male.)

(IV) Freud here considers the relation of the phantasy *A Child is Being Beaten* to the love the small girl desires from her father. The phantasy, he first declares, does not appear to be linked to her relation with the mother. (My own opinion is that the active phallic mother, at the very beginning and at the very end, in the first and third phases may, even as regards the girl, sometimes replace the father who, as we now know, regularly superimposes himself upon the mother in the course of the child's libidinal development.) Freud notes here that the first phase of this phantasy is generally linked to the jealousy felt for another child, a younger brother or sister. If "the father beats a child", the reason is that he does not love this other child, *he loves only me*. But the subject who, we must not forget, is still in the full anal or sadistic-cloacal stage, soon enters the phallic stage, whereupon the two phallic stages preceded, on the one hand, by the long passive prehistory of the phallus and, again, separated from each other by the feminine castration complex, mobilize all the forces of passivity that lie dormant in the girl. Such, in fact, it seems to me, must be the deepest source of that inversion which turns the sadistic phantasy of watching another child being beaten into that of being beaten, oneself, by the father. I think that the sense of guilt, of moral masochism, emphasized by Freud, certainly plays its part, but a part superimposed on the more primary part played by the erotogenic feminine masochism. Freud, indeed, admits this himself in this work when, after venturing to assert, an assertion retracted later, that a "sense of guilt is invariably the factor that transforms sadism into masochism", he adds, truly enough: "But this is certainly not the whole content of masochism". The sado-masochistic and sadistic-cloacal positions of the libido are regressively cathected. (In my opinion the phallic stages themselves are thoroughly permeated with it.)

Thus it is that the small girl may lovingly phantasy herself beaten by the father; that is, by his great rod. Thus, to be beaten by the father is not only "*the punishment for the forbidden genital relation, but also the regressive substitute for it,* and from this latter source it derives the libidinal excitation which is from this time forward attached to it, and which finds its outlet in onanistic acts. Here for the first time we have the essence of masochism."

Freud cites the case of a man in whom the passive erotogenic memory of *being beaten by his mother* had been fully retained, as opposed to the oblivion which generally overtakes the feminine phantasy of being beaten by the father, and asks why the tolerance by the ego in this instance? I would add that, in similar phantasies in men, one can always see a sort of counterpart to what occurs in clitoridal women; the man will have retained the heterosexual love object while still coveting it with the erotogenic zones and aims of the other sex.

Finally, Freud returns to the third phase of this phantasy—children beaten by a schoolmaster or other father figure—a phase upon which onanistic gratification is eventually consciously fixated and notes that, in the phantasies of both sexes, it is boys that are *almost invariably* beaten. Why? In the case of the boy, he says, it is understandable; he would simply be "projecting" himself on a number of boys. In the girl, however, there would be a revivification through regression to the masculinity complex, as a result of disappointed love for the father. The phallic girl would then externally project herself in the multiplied form of boys. (I think we should also add that it is not only the boy or girl, as total beings who, thus projected, are here beaten by the father, but an essential part of each which is common to both; namely the "phallus", whether, according to sex, it be clitoris or penis.)

(V) In this part of his paper, Freud states that, by the light of his analytic observations of the phantasy *A Child is Being Beaten*, he will try to elucidate, in some degree, the genesis of the perversions and the part the difference of sex plays in the dynamics of neurosis.

True, as we already thought, a perversion is always based on the constitutional reinforcement or premature maturation of a single libidinal component. Nevertheless, the study of the phantasy *A Child is Being Beaten* enables us to assert that the perverse component "is not an isolated fact in the child's sexual life, but falls into place among the typical, not to say normal, processes of development". It continues, says Freud, after the Oedipus complex has broken down, but continues oedipally tinged. (I would add that since the girl always remains in the passive Oedipus position directed on the father, it is not surprising that something of this phantasy which, in my opinion, is typical of this stage, should, even normally, remain an integral part of the adult sexuality of the truly feminine woman. Here, all is a question of degree and integration, with no clear break in continuity on a scale that reaches from the truly perverse beating masochism of woman to the integration of the masochistic drives which feed this infantile phantasy in the total, adult, feminine erotic function.)

Freud then explains some of the material he adduces on the

beating phantasy, in the light of its contribution towards elucidating the genesis of masochism. He also repeats the assertion which he later withdrew in *The Economic Problem of Masochism*, (1924) according to which masochism would never be the manifestation of a primary instinct but would always originate from sadism turned round and directed against the self. Impulses with a passive aim, he says, must be taken for granted as existing *ab initio*, especially among women, but passivity does not therefore constitute the whole of masochism; for passivity to be masochism, the characteristic of "pain" must also have been added. He considers that the transformation of sadism into masochism appears to be due to the influence of the sense of guilt which partly conditions repression. This repression, in the beating phantasy, would thus manifest itself in three ways: first by rendering the consequences of the phallic organization unconscious (I say phallic and not genital, since this term must be restricted to the pubertal organization and here we are dealing with the stage of *active* affirmation of the phallus, penis or clitoris already reached); it compels that organization itself to regress to the earlier sadistic-cloacal stage (in my opinion, the second normal phallic stage of this period, with negation of the phallus, plays a regular and dominant part in this regression, which itself regresses to the primary passive phallus, coeval with the earliest pregenital stages); thirdly, it transforms the sadism into masochism which, in a certain sense, is narcissistic. The sense of guilt, inherent not only in the incestuous object-choice, but in the aggression sadism implies, helps to bring about the reversal. (This is true of moral masochism, but in the genesis of the beating phantasy, erotogenic feminine masochism must be a dominant factor.) Freud, asking himself whence this sense of guilt might originate replies that, in his opinion, though still uncertain as to the structure of the ego, it should be assigned to that institution in the mind which sets itself over against the rest of the ego in the form of a *critical inner voice* (actually that super-ego which Freud only truly identified and named for the first time in *The Ego and the Id* [1923]). Freud then shows that the sense of guilt which Bleuler found so inexplicable in its cardinal relation to onanism in neurotics was, in fact, justly so related, since infantile onanism, as we so well see in the onanistic beating phantasy, is closely connected with the oedipal urges forbidden to the child.

Freud concludes this section of his paper by emphasizing that the second phase of this phantasy—that which has succumbed to repression and become masochistic and unconscious, and in which the girl has imagined herself beaten by the father—is by far the most significant to her libidinal development. He ends with a clinical picture of those moral masochists who attract all the blows of father-figures and of destiny, and touches on their perpetual sense of grievance. This is, however, outside the scope of the general problem of libidinal development which interests us here.

(VI) After recalling the three phases of the phantasy *A Child is Being Beaten*, as it occurs in the girl, Freud examines the same phantasy in the boy. One would have expected, he says, to find a complete analogy between the three phases of this phantasy in both girls and boys, except for a change in sex of beaters and beaten. Such, however, is not the case. In particular, the phantasy of being beaten by the mother, while remaining oneself a boy, which might be taken as the counterpart of that, in the girl, of being beaten by the father, far from remaining unconscious like the latter, is generally conscious in the boy and linked with his masturbatory activity.

True, the males analysed by Freud, in whom these phantasies were present, were mostly true perverts. These masochists who came to analysis might be divided into three categories: the first obtained sexual satisfaction exclusively from onanism accompanied by masochistic phantasies; the second were people who had succeeded in combining masochism with an object relationship by means of contrivances accompanying or preceding coitus; the third were those unfortunates who found their perverse activities disturbed by the appearance of obsessional representations which inhibited sexual activity and condemned them to impotence. Nor did the second category of perverts wholly experience full gratification, since the masochistic phantasies which preceded or accompanied the act would at times break down. Perverts content with their lot do not, indeed, resort to analysis.

Nevertheless, all these perverts who were analysed revealed one common feature. Their passivity, their masochism, coincided with a feminine attitude towards the beater object; they always imagined themselves in the woman's role when they were beaten. Their *masochism* thus seemed to be essentially feminine in nature. Some were fully aware of this; in others analysis enabled it to be easily revealed. Yet, though these perverts always thus attributed a feminine role to themselves in the onanistic flagellant phantasy, the flagellation was just as frequently administered by a woman.

Their infantile anamnesis, however, always yielded the same material; the conscious and masturbatory phantasy that *he, a boy, had been beaten by the mother* had always been preceded by another, unconscious phantasy that *he, a boy, had been beaten by the father*. Thus, the parallel relation between the beating phantasy of the boy or girl, with its reversal of sex as to subjects and objects, was replaced by an identical experience; the second phase of the beating phantasy, that is the unconscious phantasy of being beaten by the father, appeared as common to both sexes. (This need not surprise us, given the identical bi-oedipal development of the girl and boy, both of whom pass through an active and passive, though differently stressed, Oedipus complex, since the phantasy of having been beaten by the father is typical of the universal, passive, Oedipus complex.)

On the other hand, the first phase of the beating phantasy, in which a child of whom one is jealous is beaten by a vague indeterminate figure who, basically, will be the father, often seems lacking in the boy. Freud asks whether this gap may not be filled through more fortunate observations. (It is possible that the greater jealousy of girls, due to the castration complex, accounts for the more frequent emphasis on this phase in the anamneses of women. In any case, we may justifiably chart the following comparative table of development, in both sexes, of the phantasy *A Child is Being Beaten,* according to Freud.

GIRLS	BOYS
(1) A Child is beaten (a rival child): primary sadistic phantasy lost in the mists of memory.	(1) ....
(2) I am beaten by the father. (Unconscious masochistic phantasy.)	(2) I am beaten by the father. (Unconscious masochistic phantasy.)
(3) A father-figure beats a number of boys. (Masturbatory sadistic phantasy remaining conscious in the memory.)	(3) I am beaten by the mother. (Masturbatory masochistic phantasy remaining conscious and often transferred into sexual life with real women, mother-figures.)

(We see that the male, in the third phase of his beating phantasy, effects the counterpart of what is done by the heterosexual clitoridal female; he manifests a passive sexual aim opposed to his sex combined, nevertheless, with a heterosexual choice of love object. The clitoridal female has indeed transferred her libido from the mother to the father but, either in active or passive mode, she covets the heterosexual object with the male zone, the clitoris. The masochistic male flagellant has indeed succeeded in preserving his heterosexual object choice by relinquishing the father of his passive Oedipus complex to return to the mother, but he loves her, and the woman he will put in her place, in a passive feminine mode and with a passive phantasied use of his male phallus reduced to the same receptive role of receiving blows, which is the mode of the little girl's clitoris when the transient active Oedipus complex is reversed and becomes passive, accompanied by regressively phantasied, masochistic and onanistic clitoris activity.) Thus, as Freud notes, the content of the boy's masturbatory phantasy "has a feminine attitude without a homosexual object-choice". (We would add that what permits this compromise is the survival, in the boy's unconscious, of the primary passive attitude, both cloacal and phallic, to the mother—an attitude experienced by every child; passivity to the father is merely superimposed upon this and the original attitude, therefore, may always spring back into life. The predisposition towards this passive mode stems from the biological femininity linked with the masculinity of all males, which is why, where impotence derives from masochism, as Freud points out in *A Child is Being Beaten*, any prognosis must be very guarded, probably owing to the markedly bisexual make-up of the patient.)

Freud concludes his paper by discussing two theories in the light of this phantasy of *A Child is Being Beaten*, theories which claim to explain repression by the conflict of one sex with the other in the same individual. The first is inspired by purely biological, the second by sociological, considerations. The former suggests that, in every individual, the dominant sex tends to repress that part of the subordinate sex which strives to emerge: in men the feminine part, in women the masculine. (This was the theory of Wilhelm Fliess.) The second, that of Alfred Adler, a dissident disciple of Freud's, claims that the *masculine protest*, which turns against all that is feminine, and so inferior, determines the repression of these factors.

Study of the phantasy *A Child is Being Beaten*, however, reveals the inadequacy and falseness of both theories. To take the first, it will suffice to remark that what is repressed in the girl is just that second and most feminine phase of the phantasy "I am beaten by the father" and that what replaces it is a sadistic-masculine phantasy, for the biological theory to collapse. Also, why, were it correct, does the boy retain just the memory of a passive feminine attitude, even though to the mother?

Adler's sociological theory, tested against the masochistic phantasy, at first sight stands up rather better. It seems to apply fairly well to the girl, who thus would repress her passive-feminine attitude to the father in order, in the third phase of her phantasy, to replace it by the final sadistic phantasy. But why then does this phantasy become important as a symptom, if it is part of the normal process of health, of repression, according to Adler? As to the beaten boy, it can hardly be said to apply, for his passive feminine phantasies continue to be retained in consciousness. What, however, most conclusively refutes the theory of the *masculine protest* which, according to Adler, always instigates repression, is the mere observation of what generally happens during the boy's libidinal development. For the boy, during his active Oedipus complex, passes through a phase in which his active masculine incestuous desires to the mother mature and then are *repressed*. (As a result of the cultural castration complex, as Freud wrote later in *The Passing of the Oedipus Complex* [1924]). No one could claim that the repressing institution in this case was the *masculine protest*, since it is just the primary masculine drives that are repressed.

All in all, concludes Freud, study of the phantasy *A Child is Being Beaten*, and of the drives that give it strength, once more reveals that repression primarily derives from biological sources and tends to overtake what has been *left behind* in the advance to later phases of development. Among the most important drives, the sexual instincts offer especial resistance and by defeating repression act as the motive force in the formation of symptoms. And these symptoms, as study of the end results of the child-beating phantasy confirms, derive their main strength from repressed infantile sexuality, whose essential content, "the nuclear complex" of neuroses, is the Oedipus complex. (We should prefer to make it plural and say: the Oedipus *complexes*, active and passive, both general to the girl as to the boy.)[1]

(d) *The Different Vicissitudes of Infantile Phantasies and of Their Instinctual Impulses.*

In many analyses of men and women, however, we do not meet the masochistic phantasies with which we have dealt. If they were present once, what has become of them? Have they disappeared without trace? And why, then, are they so deeply buried that even with prolonged effort they cannot be disinterred?

Generally speaking, infantile phantasies, like the impulses which give them their drive, seem in fact to be subject to

[1] It is worth noting, in this context, that, among the Kirdis (tribes of the North Cameroons) beating rites are imposed on girls "who have seen blood": that is, their first menstruation. It is true that the blows are administered by old women (who also carry out the rite of excision). (From notes published by the Dakar-Djibuti expedition. See also *Minotaure* for 11th June, 1933.)

different vicissitudes. Infantile phantasies often succumb to repression, that is, are wholly forgotten. But what then becomes of the instinctual drives which brought them into being?

They, and their accompanying representations, may undergo repression, and together sink into the unconscious. There, they live on with more or less disturbance to the personality, according to the degree of repression. We then have the neurotic.

Again, the masochistic partial instinctual drive, with its representation, will remain conscious and prove obdurate to repression. Isolating itself thus, a primacy is established which is refused to the adult genital function. We then have the pervert.

A third category presents itself when the instinctual drive, detaching itself from the phantasy, sinks unaccompanied by it into the unconscious and thus becomes harmless, so finding paths of sublimation. Moral masochism, with its hunger for self-sacrifice, is already almost sublimation: those who devote themselves to humanity are, in general, such as have managed to sublimate their instinctual masochistic components.

Fourthly, those partial components of the libido which nourish the masochistic phantasies may convert themselves into their opposites and passivity deny itself by activity. This reversal may the more readily occur in that woman, to go back to women, is more bisexual and presents a more intense counterpart of masculine activity to her feminine passivity.

We thus see that the vicissitudes of which Freud wrote may be similar to those of the drives from which the phantasies derive their power; repression, conservation, sublimation and reaction-formation.

Nevertheless, in none of the instances cited of the fates that befall the instinctual drives which give rise to the erotogenic masochistic phantasies, have we seen any sign of their normal activity in the service of the feminine erotic function. If repressed, access to them has been lost, or if repression has proved imperfect, they will only reveal themselves as occasional neurotic manifestations. If sublimated, they will now serve other uses, purposes so approved by the ego, in such conformity with its ideals, that they will no longer reappear. If reaction-formations, they will run counter to their initial aim, and will radically oppose it. If retained as an isolated factor, they will disturb the adult function, the genital primacy, and will set a persistent perversion, such as beating, in its place.

What then is the fifth vicissitude, the normal fate of these drives, as of the phantasies on which, primarily, they were sustained, in the development and structure of the normal feminine erotic function?

In his *Three Essays on the Theory of Sexuality* (1905), Freud points out that, at puberty, all the partial components of the libido must combine, though without disappearing, in subordination to the primacy of the genital zone.

In what manner this combination takes place is not, however, very clear. It would seem, nevertheless, as Freud indicates in the same place, that these components have to play a special part in the indispensable fore-pleasure. It is here that the masochistic instinctual components, which instigate the perverse phantasies of childhood, must find their use by creating that receptive attitude in the woman towards the ever-renewed "wound" which coitus is to her.

As regards the masochistic phantasies, however, the instinctual impulse, at least in normal cases, must for the most part have been withdrawn and the masochistic phantasies, stripped of affect, have sunk into the unconscious, exactly as occurs in the case of sublimation. One part, nevertheless, of the representation may at times remain bound to the affect and save that part of the representation from sinking into the unconscious; it then tinges the sexuality of the adult woman with some "masochistic perversion", highly compatible with the woman's normal vaginal function in coitus.

In this latter case, memory of masochistic phantasies may, in part, be retained whereas, in the former, it may radically have disappeared and, in anamnesis, only be recalled with great difficulty or, indeed, not at all. In any case, the normal unanalysed woman little thinks she harbours such phantasies and does not even suspect the important part they play in the evolution of the feminine libido.

Such is the fifth vicissitude—the most ideal from the viewpoint of function—of the feminine masochistic drives. One might call it the *integration* of partial components in the terminal erotic function, under the primacy of the genital zone.

Here we should note that the masochistic impulses that relate to the little girl's clitoridal zone and which are linked with the above phantasies, seem to *disappear into the vagina or rather cloaca, en bloc*—doubtless while these phantasies are still attached to them—just when the little girl abandons her infantile clitoridal masturbation in narcissistic disappointment with her too small clitoris. The surrender of the small clitoris to the large phallus implies that the little girl cloacally yields to the latter; the reversal of the clitoridal sadism into first clitoridal, then cloacal masochism—corollaries of the passing from active to passive—must end by creating, in the unconscious infantile mind, erotogenic *hollow* phantasies which lead the way to that no longer *convex*, but *concave* representation of sexual pleasure to which we shall later return. This is the representation of sexual pleasure which will be that of the woman normally adapted to her erotic function.

* * *

In his paper *Female Sexuality* (1931), Freud enunciated the principle that all the impulses and emotions connected with the mother, which the little girl experiences during the phase dominated by the negative Oedipus complex, are eventually transferred *in toto*, and with equal intensity, to the father, when the girl passes to the positive Oedipus complex.

To this, we may add two further principles of such total displacement. On the one hand, the girl's masochistic phantasies, contemporaneous with the continued clitoridal masturbation but thenceforth directed on the father, represent a total inversion, though still effected by the same clitoris, of the sadistic phantasies which, in the girl as in the boy, were first directed on the mother; that is, phantasies of actively beating, penetrating, bursting the mother by means of the phallus, phantasied more or less clearly or vaguely, depending on individual and sex. Generally speaking, traces of these active sadistic phantasies are likely to be far more readily found and followed in the unconscious of the male, in whom the phallus, and its activity, remain directed upon women, than in woman, where not only are they generally much vaguer, but where at an early age masochistic phantasies come to replace and hide them. On the other hand, all the passive masochistic impulses which, during the passive Oedipus complex, accompany infantile clitoridal masturbation directed on the father, are transferred, *in toto*, and with equal intensity, to the neighbouring cloaca—although they have then become latent—when such masturbation is abandoned; that is assuming normal feminine development. Doubtless this is the time when electivity of the vagina begins to be established both in the organism and the unconscious, in preparation for puberty, which will enlarge the vagina and, with the passage of the menstrual flux, fully arouse it to await the male.

In short, then, the phallic clitoris which was first slowly and passively aroused to erotogeneticity during the child's toilet or by accidental caresses, becomes, for a time, the bearer of erotogenic and active sadistic drives during the passing active phallic phase. Then, by regression, it secondarily becomes that of the erotogenic passive and masochistic drives, whose function is finally to establish the girl's passive Oedipus complex, following on the castration complex, Lastly, by a final process of adaptation to the future erotic feminine function, these same passive drives must, as it were, glide into the adjacent hollow zones.

Three main principles thus govern the libidinal development of the woman: (1) the fate of the object relationships; (2) the fate of the instinctual urges and (3) the role played by the body zones.

(1) *The Fate of the Object Relationships.* The equation *mother = father* (Freud). The impulses and emotions relating to the mother, which often persist very late, towards the child's fifth and sixth years, and even—in my opinion, parallel with the choice of the male object—are transferred, *in toto*, from the mother to the father and that, whether the drives be passive or active; for the mother was originally passively experienced and it is this primary stratum of passivity to the mother on which the essentially preponderant feminine passivity to the male will be based. If, *per contra*, the active impulses remain dominant, despite the change in the love object and despite her gained heterosexuality, the male having become phallically, clitoridally

coveted, then the woman will not be well adapted to her feminine sexuality in general, and to her erotic function in particular, since her instinctual drives will run counter to her anatomy.

A first arrest in development may, thus, occur here.

(2) *The Fate of the Instinctual Urges.* The equation *sadism = masochism.* The active, masculine sadistic phantasies of beating, piercing, bursting, are regularly replaced by the masochistic feminine phantasies they reflect in opposite and passive terms, when the active Oedipus position is finally replaced by the passive position in the shift from the mother to the father. This reversal of the impulse is a necessary condition to the girl's later feminization. These urges, however, are doubtless experienced first through the clitoris, the usual executive organ, according to Freud, of infantile masturbation, which will continue for a time, even when constellated on the father, before it is given up through narcissistic disappointment. In this stage, it was the clitoris which the little girl, more or less consciously, imagined beaten or pierced or burst. If she remains at this stage of libidinal development and especially if the clitoris is fairly contiguous to the vagina, she may later acquire a satisfactory part-vaginal, part-clitoridal function, by accepting her passive masochistic impulses regarding the clitoris. This, however, is still not the ideal development of woman; i.e. supreme adaptation to her erotic function.

(3) *The Role played by the Body Zones.* The equation *clitoris = vagina.* The masochistic phantasies connected with the clitoris at the time clitoridal masturbation is abandoned through narcissistic disappointment are first *engulfed, in toto,* by the cloaca while, at the same time, or later, a biological electivity of the vagina takes place. This last step establishes the ideal feminine function, and the infantile phantasies which carry the feminine masochistic impulses may then disappear as having fulfilled their mission.

Thus, throughout this development, as we already saw, the phantasies detached from their free-floating impulses will, in the most normal cases, sink so completely into the feminine unconscious that they can often never again be found, even in protracted analyses.

* * *

Nevertheless, just because it is so essentially passive and masochistic, the girl's sexuality is threatened from three sides at the same time. In effect, repression of the masochistic impulses on which it is based may arise in three main directions.

First, from that of the masculinity innate in the woman; that masculinity which, so early in life, began to express itself, clitoridally, towards the mother. The more masculinity there is innate in a woman, and the more childhood events and her active Oedipus complex will have encouraged and reinforced that masculinity, through fixation or defiance, the stronger will be her *masculine protest* against masochistic phantasies. She will then refuse her feminine role as humiliating to her male narcissism and will adopt something of that defensive attitude towards it which the boy must normally develop in reaction to his passive Oedipus complex to the father and his dominating, threatening penis.

Secondly, this attitude will be the more readily established in proportion as the asexual *vital protest* of the biological ego, so to speak, works in the same direction. The ego always defends its integrity, more or less, and all living organisms invest their vital substance with defensive barriers. For each, despite osmosis, there is "an ideal, sacred limit where the body begins", and even cells partition themselves off with membranes.

Thus, every attempt at a violent penetration, at effraction, is felt as a danger threatening the life within; it is therefore more difficult for woman to accept her sexual mission, which implies penetration, effraction and, in any case, more danger than for man, who is so much luckier from this standpoint. True, other dangers threaten man, as more daring and aggressive, more exposed to the risks of war; nevertheless, the truth remains that the battlefield of life is strewn with women slain by their sexual and maternal function.[1]

---

[1] It is this vital protest that Karen Horney makes mainly responsible for *The Denial of the Vagina* (1933), which, according to her, is always secondary to the natural, primary erotization of the vagina,

Thirdly and lastly, the *moral repression* which generally overtakes the girl's sexuality more powerfully than the boy's (both because this repression is itself more powerful and because what it condemns is weaker, more passive and less resistive than in the boy, may also disturb the development of femininity. If the feminine erotic attitude towards the father, with all the masochistic passivity to him it implies, be too severely forbidden the girl, then all her erotism may come to grief. A total frigidity may arise if the phallic-clitoridal libidinal positions are not recathected. In such cases, a deprivative and punishing moral masochism will too wholly replace the erotogenic feminine masochism.

This is a problem of conflicting drives; of which will prevail, being stronger.

(e) *Affirmation of the Clitoris and Denial of the Vagina*

It is by no means easy to note, as it occurs, the mysterious passage of the feminine libido from its infantile clitoridal-cloacal positions to its adult and cardinal vaginal positions; a

---

in the small girl. The girl, by comparing her own small organ with the disproportionately large organ of the father, by observation of the woman's menstrual flow and also by the small hurts she may do the hymen in vaginal masturbation would feel terror of being wounded by penetration. I think that this fear of wounding is one of the factors in "the denial of the vagina" (or rather the cloaca in dealing with children) but it seems to me that Karen Horney, like many analysts, here takes the part for the whole. Her *vital protest*, in part, masks the significance of the distorting *moral protest* imposed on the child by its upbringers, and almost entirely ignores the importance of the *masculine protest* based on that biological bisexuality which is often so powerful in the small girl. For Karen Horney, penis envy in the girl would merely be a rather childish game expressing a vague bisexuality, of no biological intensity, in her opinion.

All this, however, does not mean that we should under-estimate the *vital protest*. The flight of the female from the male in so many animal species is doubtless itself based on a sort of endopsychic awareness of the vital perils of femaleness. And the coquetry which often enters into such flight might result from a compromise between the sexual instinct which urges the sexes to unite and the individual vital instinct which inspires flight.

process which continues for years in the depths of the biological psyche. Doubtless, we have here something akin to what takes place with the pronephros, mesonephros and final kidney: the replacement of temporary organs by a terminal one, but this time on a functional basis. Without psycho-analysis, we might say we understood nothing of these phenomena, that their very existence was unknown, as any work on gynaecology or psychiatry will prove.

Psycho-analysis, however, enables us to throw some light on these facts, difficult as they are to see, partly through the still too infrequent analyses of children and, again, through observation and interpretation of the erotic clinical picture in the adult woman.

I have not, so far, analysed a little girl, but have been able, directly, to observe different women in analysis or, again, through confidences which, even before I was a psycho-analyst, I seemed able, by a sort of predestination, to attract. I could thus convince myself, from the women themselves, of the practical and theoretical importance of sundry facts connected with the various attitudes of clitoridal women to the male.

Such women, in fact, have no single attitude to man: like everything which relates to that protean force, sexuality, their attitudes are of infinite variety.

Nevertheless, in the main, we can classify these clitoridal women into two groups: those primarily, in whom the clitoris is affirmed, and those who fundamentally deny the vagina.

True, both these attitudes are complementary and, in women who are not totally frigid through inhibitions of hysterical nature, *denial* of the vagina will imply *affirmation* of the clitoris; the converse also being true. None the less, the dominant emphasis of one or other of these complementary positions will stamp the sexuality of every clitoridal woman in different ways.

One observation will clearly illustrate the difference in these attitudes. We know that the clitoridal woman, in what is known as normal coitus, with the man above her, feels practically nothing, due to her vaginal anaesthesia. The clitoridal woman then readily complains, should she admit her frigidity, that the sensitive zone was *too high* and uncontacted, and will also suggest that if, by some means, this zone could be lowered in coitus, and thus contacted, she would perfectly participate in the man's pleasure. Here, in fact, she is not altogether wrong. For, if the man were solicitous to change his position for one which allowed manual stimulation of the clitoris during coitus, the clitoridal woman would generally, concomitantly, share her partner's pleasure. But if the man and woman succeed in adopting a position which ensures the actual contact of the clitoris and penis, as when the woman is in the superior position (kneeling upon the recumbent man or astraddle the man seated), the woman's voluptuous response is very different, depending on the clitoridal type to which she belongs.

Generally, however, despite the close contact between penis and clitoris in such positions, paradoxical though it seems, this form of coitus, even, will fail to satisfy the clitoridal woman, such is the strength of her protest against the male penis and its "sadistic" penetration of her body, and against the masochistic attitude in herself which it implies.

It was an analyst who, and with reason, formulated the concept of woman's "hollow penis". In her pleasure at incorporating the male penis, the vaginal woman, in her more or less unconscious phantasies, seems to represent her vagina as *hollow*; a mould, so to speak, of the coveted penis. Such women, one might justly say, have a *concave* mental representation of sexual pleasure which is totally opposed to the *convex* mental representation of sexual pleasure common to clitoridals and men.

We know, as psycho-analysts, how primordially mental representations may affect the biological functions, governed as they are by the nervous system. As a result, the rejection of the *concave* representation of sexual pleasure may become so strong, whatever the form of coitus, as to make the erotistic denial of the vagina, proper to such women, encroach on the sometimes extreme erotogenicity of the clitoris.

The "concave", in such women, is resisted to a degree where even a different kind of erotogenization, as regards the small clitoris, may ensue, depending on whether the inner posterior aspect or external anterior aspect is affected. This, in my opinion, explains the fact why stimulation of the external aspect of the clitoris in hyper-clitoridal women often seems far more pleasurable than that of the inner aspect: there is no "vertigo of the pit" adjacent to it. This elective erotogenization of different aspects of one erotogenic organ may also be found in some men, in whom it is just the anterior aspect of the glans that is often most erotogenic, as though male sexuality had to flee, as far as possible, from the cloacal danger.

Here we should recall the phenomenon of vaginismus which, as we know, consists of a spasmodic local condition that makes any penetration by the male impossible when coitus is threatened. Vaginismus may be temporary or chronic and either an episode, or an infirmity, in a woman's erotic life. We also know, in severe cases, that only psychogenic treatment will prevail against this extreme refusal of the feminine function. It may be considered as the extremest instance of the *denial of the vagina*.

Conversely, in truly feminine women, the erotogenization and psychogenic attraction of the cloaca and hole may prove so strong, that I can report a case where a woman, slowly devirginated by a solicitous lover, retained a gradually receding, distended hymen, for some weeks or months. To this woman, her hymen, and then its relics, became, as it were, her main erotogenic zone, such was the strength of the *concave* representation of sexual pleasure imprinted on her psyche. "What will happen when my hymen is completely torn" she even anxiously wondered for a time. However, this degree of "concave" erotogenicity, which had only been transferred to the transitory hymen, little by little and, without difficulty, also transferred itself to the already highly sensitized vulvo-vaginal walls or, rather, effected a normal return to the global concave representation of sexual pleasure from which the erotogenicity of these different internal zones was derived.

Here, one cannot prevent oneself thinking teleologically of the orgasm in Lamarck's sense, namely as an afflux of a sort of "vital fluid" governed by the nervous system, which would mould organ functions as the exigencies of the environment impose, which process, in some mysterious way, it appears that the organism, more or less, "understands".

* * *

What then is the significance of these facts as regards the *positions*, *aims* and *objects* of the libido?

As regards positions, in affirming the clitoris, that of the libido has obviously remained phallic and viriloid, even when the passive phallic attitude, naturally, in different degrees, will more or less have weakened this "virile" characteristic. We may see a concomitant to this in the *denial of the vagina*, where the libido, so to speak, has remained on another level, and does not come to recathect it, or may only have done so in part, for all degrees of vaginal anaesthesia may be met. How this has come about is what we must study in each instance, as also to define whether the dominant factor is affirmation of the clitoris or denial of the vagina.

As regards the libido's *aims*, these may be deduced from what was said in the previous chapter: in clitoridalism, the degree of active sadistic or passive masochistic impulses borne by the clitoris, varying in each case, will determine the degree to which the clitoridal is maladapted to her erotic function. As for the generally passive vagina, this also sometimes bears active sadistic impulses; phantasies of active castration of the male, tendencies to *retain*, to *tear off the penis*. There is, indeed, an "active cloaca", as there is a "passive phallus". Mostly, however, the vagina is invested with passive masochistic impulses, which alone are wholly favourable to the feminine erotic function.

The problem of *objects* as regards the respective erotogenicity of the clitoris or vagina is well worth study as being the most "psychological" of all, and to it we shall later return. The primary object of the passive, then active impulses of the clitoris, as we saw, is the mother. There seems to be an active Oedipus complex of the girl towards the mother, just as there is one of the boy, though far less accentuated. Secondarily, these impulses are displaced on the father and then undergo that transformation from sadism into masochism, which is the infantile clitoridal phase of the normal later development of feminine sexuality. It is, however, legitimate to think that when the clitoris, as it were, has refused to allow itself to be decathected, a deep and latent fixation on the mother has persisted in the feminine unconscious; that is, that underlying the positive Oedipus complex, the negative Oedipus complex has remained intensely alive. This doubtless comes about through a strong primary bisexuality, but the psychic attitude to which this gives rise will, in its turn, determine all future sexuality.

On the other hand, there can be no doubt as to the vagina's reality object; that can only be the penis and the male by whom it is borne. The vagina, or rather the cloaca which preceded it, is the executive organ (psychically, that is) of the girl's passive Oedipus complex when that is truly established. Earlier, however, the cloaca had also been the passive organ of the girl's fixation on the mother, at the same time as the passive clitoris-phallus awoke. Certain vaginal anaesthesias, and I have met some, may thus also be conditioned by a fixation, an anal or a cloacal fidelity to the mother, whose caresses, in that region, the girl child may have loved or desired too intensely.

It is the vagina however, which, in the relation of the female to the male, must electively detach itself from the cloaca to become the passive receptive organ. But, in the earliest period of sexual development, the vagina had not the support of erotic reality which infantile masturbation was for the clitoris, that executive organ of the active Oedipus complex and, then, for the passing over to the passive, masochistic Oedipus complex.

And indeed, in the little girl, it is just this masturbation which tends to be given up after the Oedipus complex is established. It is thus in the psyche that the future role of the vagina must be prepared, and the only real support it will find for this preparation, its only prototypes for what will later take place in coitus, must be taken from the bowel region; the passage of faeces through the rectum, or the enemas that children often endure so badly. Thus, given the great repression which, in our civilizations, overtakes everything anal, the erotic vaginal function, to which the anal component is far more necessary than to phallic erotism, will have an additional repression to avoid than the male phallic function, to establish itself later.

This, however, is not where the chief psychological obstacle to its establishment lies; it is the way the girl's passive Oedipus complex sets in, develops, culminates, continues or declines, that first and foremost determines the psychical destiny of the vaginal erotism of women. For though the cloacal and, even, phallic passivity was first awakened through the feeding, ministering, cleansing mother, a passivity soon succeeded by the wakening clitoridal activity also constellated on the mother, this activity, after its constellation on the father, comes to be given up. Whereupon the cloacal passivity is reawakened, augmented by all the organism's accrued powers, though now constellated on the father, the male, and will generally remain so throughout life.

This is so true that, as I was told by a woman who knew many homosexuals, when a girl happens, sensually, to be predominantly vaginal, despite the many adolescent seductions that may occasionally render her homosexual, she almost invariably ends by passing to the male, who is far more suited, with his penis, to satisfy the "concave" erotism with which she is endowed. Generally, it is only women whose erotism is purely or predominantly clitoridal that cling to homosexuality. But clitoridals, themselves, often go over wholly to the male and that, even from childhood, since their clitoridal erotogenicity allows them to pursue both active and passive aims.

(f) *Types of Women and Oedipus Complexes*

Let us now try to see what links exist between the different types of clitoridal and vaginal women and the Oedipus complexes through which they pass in childhood.

Before, however, we consider heterosexuals from this angle, we must look at various observations on homosexual women.

Homosexual women, as Helene Deutsch (1932)[1] has so well shown, very often go on playing at "mother and child",

[1] "On Female Sexuality."

to the exclusion of the disturbing father. Some tend to identify themselves with the active mother and are specially drawn to very young girls, their greatest pleasure being to "reveal" these latter to themselves. Others, again, go on being the child they once were, and are chiefly attracted to older, maternal, protective women, towards whom they remain, more or less, in a passive condition, or in one of infantile activity. Others, again, may demonstrate both attitudes together, or alternately. In all, however, the clitoris continues to be the executive organ of homosexual sensuous pleasure, as during the childhood of the little "phallic" girl. It is rare indeed for such homosexuals to try to "lengthen" the clitoris by artificial attachments. In general, the clitoris suffices them and the idea of the large, "disgusting", male penis generally inspires them with horror. Such homosexuals tend to exclude the male and his penis from the "Paradise Lost", but "Refound", where the mother once tended and petted her babe and, by her ministrations and caresses, aroused the yet passive clitoris of the girl. Thus, they do not tend to trick themselves out in masculine clothing and their appearance remains very feminine.[1]

The other type of homosexual woman, besides identifying herself with the primary active mother who cares for the child, has also identified herself, by superimposition, as it were, with the father who followed the mother in the succession of objects to be loved—or hated—by the child. Such women present far more active clitoridal phantasies than the former, and the ideal they have absorbed colours all their behaviour; these are the homosexual women who wear jackets and ties and who really strive to act the man in their relation to the loved women. Some, even, it is said, content themselves with caresses and giving pleasure, but refuse to accept caresses themselves, no doubt unable to admit such great passivity, as providing occasion to disclose the shameful absence of the penis.

To return, however, to the main object of our study, the

[1] Here we have one of the two types of homosexual women described by Marañon in his *The Evolution of Sex and Intersexual Conditions*. The other and more viriloid type of homosexual woman is dealt with in the next paragraph.

heterosexual female. If we consider the different types, we first find those who have achieved maximum adaptation to the erotic function. Such women remain insensitive to, or are irritated by, clitoridal caresses (which latter is a less degree of clitoridal involution). Only coitus will release orgastic pleasure and orgasm in these.

Next come those women with vaginal and clitoridal erotogenicity harmoniously attuned. Such women are capable of orgastic pleasure through clitoridal caresses, but generally prefer to keep them as a preliminary to coitus: a necessary preparative if some functional retardation be present. In any case, with such women, in coitus, both vagina *and* clitoris play their part in concert, subject however, it may be, to a certain proximity of the clitoris to the vagina.

Other women again, while possessing this composite function, may also achieve the orgasm through each of these *separate* zones: via the vagina *or* the clitoris. These are often women who feel the vagina and the clitoris to be mutually antagonistic: now one, now the other, plays its part. In such women, orgastic sensation in coitus is generally only vaginal.

Another category of women consists of those clitoridals with whom we have already dealt at length. In such women, the viriloid phallic function predominates at the expense of a more, or less, undeveloped or inhibited vaginalism.

Finally, there are those other women in whom a total inhibition of both erotogenic zones has occurred. These are the wholly frigid. Neither coitus, nor the most varied caresses of the male, will avail to give them pleasure.

* * *

We must now ask what vicissitudes will have overtaken the infantile Oedipus complexes of these different types of women?

With the first, those closest to ideal adaptation to the erotic function, the active Oedipus complex directed on the mother will, presumably, have been somewhat weak and, in any case, will have been successfully repressed, with all its representations, bag and baggage, so to speak; in this case the repression will be primarily biological. The woman has recognized, it would seem, that the love objects appropriate to her organism, which the external world can offer, are no longer the mother, no longer woman, and has abandoned both the feminine love object and the vainly active erotogenic zone, the clitoris, as wholly unfitted to be penetrated by the new object, which is the male with his penis. At the same time, the active aim of the impulses themselves, maximally rescued from repression, is abandoned and the sadistic impulses, converted into their masochistic opposite, have taken full possession of the penis-receptive vagina through which the child, in its turn, will pass. In these women, the representation of sexuality and orgastic pleasure has been fully established as no longer convex, but concave. In ideal cases, the woman triumphantly surmounts the primary fidelity to the mother, both as regards the erotogenic zone and impulse-aim as well as the love object; she will thus integrally, adaptively, have passed to the father and, thence, to the male who will take his place. We shall return to this *thence*, for it implies a new obstacle of oedipal fidelity, a second threshold of infidelity which female psycho-sexuality often finds hard to cross.

In the second type, where the two erotogenic zones have been retained harmoniously attuned, women, that is, in whom excitation of the clitoris, as Freud says, serves as "kindling" to excitation of the vagina, we may see a survival of that transient stage in which the clitoris, before the vagina, had become the operative, or rather "operated upon" organ of the masochistic impulses and phantasies which, in the girl, inaugurate the passage from mother to father, from the active, to the passive Oedipus complex. The passive oedipal object and aim, in this case, have been fully achieved; the active phantasies regarding the mother have been duly repressed and their afferent libidinal impulses duly saved and reversed to become their masochistic opposites. The clitoridal zone may thenceforth be harmlessly retained beside the vaginal zone, such traces of the former as remain assuming their subordinate part and place in the general adapted function.

In the third type we defined, where a sort of divorce occurs between vaginal and clitoridal erotogenicity, a conflict seems to appear. Here, the clitoris has remained bound to its active sadistic aims, and goes on wanting to push phallically forward;

thus, the mother, the primary unconscious object of these thrusts, must still be as tenaciously retained in the unconscious as she must originally have been strongly coveted in the same active mode. We must here ask how far a viriloid constitution more or less determines the intensity and persistence of these first attitudes. In any event, in such cases, the woman, though she has acquired an erotogenic and male-receptive vagina, adapted both to object, zone and aim, retains, as it were, in juxtaposition, an antagonistic phallic organization based on a very deep, very repressed "homosexuality". When this does not appear to disturb the receptive erotogenic function of the vagina, it is due to the indifference with which the unconscious regards contradictions; the passive Oedipus complex was able to establish itself in such women and remain dominant, side by side with residuals of the active Oedipus complex.

The extreme instance of inadaptation to function, to reality in general, and to erotic reality in particular, is provided by clitoridal women. Such women, in effect, have managed to pass from mother to father in infancy and so to change their love object; they continue, however, to covet that new object, with its active penetrating penis, with their own active zone, the clitoris, which has remained animated throughout by the active sadistic impulses it possessed when the active Oedipus complex was directed on the mother. We have here a striking instance of biological blindness and lack of direction. True, repression has overtaken the mother as the central object, but the mother, as the target, as it were, of the active impulses in the unconscious, must, nevertheless, have been retained; the father himself, furnished with the phallus which such women have been unable to abandon, either in themselves or in others, was merely vehemently substituted for the mother when the narcissistically wounding awareness of the mother's castration occurred. From the erotogenic viewpoint, the vagina in such women, as it were, has never "opened"; their erotogenic cloaca has reclosed, as must normally happen with the male.

The next category, that of the totally frigid, is most conclusive as regards psychogenic inhibitions. In these women, the erotic function appears abolished, whichever the zone that is excited: no kind of caress seems able to arouse them.

Here we see the utmost possible repression of the active, as of the passive Oedipus complex; the clitoris seems to have abandoned both its active aims and the mother, in the same way that the vagina, *in toto*, has renounced its passive aims and the father, or male. All this, however, is only in seeming, for a time often comes when, due to life itself, or to analysis, one zone or other will awake and that, at times, very violently. In such cases, it is generally the vaginal zone which takes the lead, since those with hysterically inhibited frigidity are often more womanly than the clitoridals who, as it were, have desperately clung to their male zone. In total frigidity, as with a Sleeping Beauty who has slept too long, the Prince's first kiss was not enough. She remains, however, ready for those kisses. In her, the passive aims are generally well established, though they have long remained latent in the unconscious. Even when the clitoris of such women is thus reanimated before or after the vagina, they will, when awakened, generally rank among those women in whom the two erotogenic feminine zones, harmoniously attuned, function under the common denominator of passivity.

In these last two types, the partially frigid, i.e. the clitoridals, and the totally frigid, with whom we have just dealt, we see a common vaginal anaesthesia. In the latter, however, the vaginal awakening generally occurs more readily than in the former, as we have already shown. Nevertheless, the example of these last suggests the question of the degree in which, in each of the former cases, this vaginal anaesthesia may be therapeutically removed. For if this excessive, exclusive and obdurate clitoridalism is, doubtless, determined by a constitutional bisexuality and must, when excessively pronounced, represent a sort of larval hermaphroditism in miniature, vaginal anaesthesia may always be suspected of including some large degree of hysterical inhibition and so of being psychically conditioned. Thus, the analyst's duty in such cases is to seek the probable psychic determination of the erotogenic "opening" as of the erotogenic "closing" of the feminine vagina.

Thus, when these inhibitions in the totally frigid are suddenly lifted, we are justified, as regards the partially frigid, in asking how far these inhibitions derive from developmental disturbances of biological origin or from some psychogenic cause. Faced by a clitoridal with vaginal anaesthesia, what does each contribute in each case? Only a prolonged analysis will permit us to decide.

In any case, a common principle seems to govern the psycho-sexuality of woman. *Inhibitions may be lifted, but what was acquired, in each case, tends to be retained.* I myself know very few cases where the vaginal function regressed to one that was clitoridal, except for some rare instances quoted by Helene Deutsch. A woman with vaginal erotism will generally retain it after the menopause, even despite a subsequent biological diminution in the erotic impulse. A woman of vaginal type in whom, say under the influence of analysis, clitoridal sensitivity is reawakened, will not, for that, lose her vaginal sensitivity. Similarly, a clitoridal might acquire vaginal function through some inhibition being lifted, but would not, for that, lose her clitoridal function. Nervous functions, once truly acquired, may indeed be masked by transitory inhibitions but, so long as the organism has not suffered irreparable damage, they remain irreversible.

V

THE MALE'S CONSTRUCTIVE ROLE IN FEMALE SEXUALITY

(a) *Real and Oedipal Erotic Initiation Compared*

EVERY SEXUAL occurrence to which an individual is subjected will leave its mark on his sexuality. And the more untouched and virgin the psyche so marked, the more determinant will be their stamp. That is why the first seductions to which girls are subjected deserve a separate chapter in this book.

Now, the seductions to which girls are subjected may be divided into two main kinds; those pertaining to the period before end-pleasure is possible, and which occur in the realm of still infantile, diffuse fore-pleasure, and those which succeed in releasing the orgasm in her for the first time.

The way in which a girl "learns" to know end-pleasure, via the vagina or the clitoris, cannot be unimportant, as we have shown. True, the pre-existent accentuation of one or other erotogenic zone, due partly to innate factors and again to childhood events, will trace their paths, in advance, for genital sensations. In its turn, however, the fact that the orgasm takes a certain nervous path will tend to establish that path and make it the elective erotic channel, by virtue of the compulsion to repetition that governs the instincts. Unlike the male who, wherever he goes, brings with and takes away his own forms of sexuality, with their dominant erotogenic zone the active, opposing penis, the more infantile, passive and malleable woman, in proportion as she is feminine, freely retains the stamp she is given. This was noted by Freud, when in *Three Essays on the Theory of Sexuality* (1905), he said that women, like children, are susceptible of acquiring all forms of perversion through seduction. And perhaps, through male influence, even normality?

I have met some instances of precocious seduction which

may prove of interest here as regards the form which the adult sexuality of such women may assume.

I begin with a case of incest. A girl, between ten and twelve, still unformed, was seduced by an eighteen-year-old brother whom, since babyhood, she had adored. Nothing but normal coitus took place, to which her reactions and the erotic pleasure she derived, soon became normal. Over a year later this incestuous relation was discovered by the parents, who sent the brother away. The girl claimed that she had never once felt "she was doing wrong" all the time this relation lasted. Nor could she have acquired this feeling in any strength later, despite the measures her family took and her father's solemn admonitions about its wickedness. This elder brother represented such an ideal in her eyes that his "permission of sex" must far have outweighed the others' disapproval, even her father's. Later, when the girl married, she manifested a normal clitoridal-vaginal erotic function as regards her husband, which allowed of regular satisfaction in coitus. The teachings of the initiator-brother had not been wasted.

All this happened in a very respectable, well-off family, and not amid working-class folk; in the "mansion" and not on the "ground floor". It will be remembered that Freud, in his *Introductory Lectures on Psycho-Analysis* (1916–17), pictures two girls in a relation of mutual seduction. One is the daughter of the owner of the mansion, the other the caretaker's daughter, living on the ground floor. Their misdeeds are discovered and the owner's daughter is subjected to an elaborate, strict and moral education which turns her into a virtuous and accomplished girl, while the caretaker's daughter is left to run about the streets, and promiscuously frequent her small playmates. This will continue until puberty. Soon after, the latter will marry, a workman probably, and become a healthy normal young woman, free from neurosis and sexually contented. The owner's daughter, on the other hand, far from continuing to feel the sexual games of her childhood as an initiation, has only retained the prohibitions that put an end to them, and which, so far as she is concerned, condemned sexuality *in toto*. As a result she becomes delicate, refined, able to sublimate, a musician or a painter it may be, but she also presents divers neurotic symptoms, and her "delicacy" repulses everything sexual as too "coarse". She may possibly refuse to marry and, if she does, to obey her parents or, perhaps, because some young man's "refined" appearance has pleased her, will prove incapable of responding to his "coarse" embraces; in short she will be a frigid, unsatisfied and neurotic wife, her husband's misfortune and her own, not to mention the resulting children's.

This is another way in which the discovery and punishment of an infantile seduction may end.

Wherein then lies the difference, as regards the development of sexuality, between the instance pictured by Freud and that which I myself have quoted though both, nevertheless, occurred in the "mansion"? Evidently, since this is an "economic" question, a quantitative relation, one might say that the parents were less brutally repressive in the case I quoted and, still more important, that this young wrongdoer must have had stronger, more resistant instincts. With Pavlov's experiments in mind, we might now attempt to establish the resultant of these two forces in the form of an algebraic equation.

Let us represent the brother's seduction—or the playmate's—and the ensuing repression in the three cases cited, by such equations: Then, if excitation through sexual seduction quantitatively equals x and inhibition through discovery and moral sanctions quantitatively equals y, the residual libido = z, thus:

$$x - y = z$$

If x is greater than y, the number denoted by the algebraical sign z will be plus and the subsequent reactions, the "reflexes" acquired through the excitations inculcated by seduction will, throughout life, in analogous situations, come under this plus sign. The response to analogous excitations will have remained positive.

If, on the other hand, y is greater than x, the number denoted by z will be minus; the inhibition will triumph, and subsequent sexual excitations will always release the inhibiting reflex; sexuality will remain impaired.

This was the case of the "owner's" daughter pictured by Freud: the former was the case of the "caretaker's" daughter and of the girl I cited.

In Freud's "owner's" daughter's case,
$$x < y \therefore z < 0$$
In that of Freud's "caretaker's" daughter and of the girl I cited:
$$x > y \therefore z > 0$$

True, we must not delude ourselves in regard to the seeming simplicity of this equation, for x and y are each the resultants of hundreds of factors which it is impossible to isolate, factors which vary throughout life, and to which others accrue, all of which may affect the result at any particular moment and even, at times, change the arithmetical sign temporarily or permanently. It is this possibility, in fact, that is the basis of psycho-analytic healing. In general, however, since the most constant factors, which constitute x or y, were incorporated into the psyche, the unconscious, the id and the superego very early in life, a given individual's erotistic responses, that is, of course, with a partner capable of evoking true excitation, will remain relatively constant, and retain a certain individual character more or less hard to modify.

Nevertheless, so long as we cannot measure psychical forces, our equation must regrettably remain imprecise. We see the sum total of z at work in everyone's existence; we know that instinct, libido, the psyche and life are governed by the same quantitative physical laws as those which rule the universe . . . but a psychometer, alas, has still to be invented.

We must therefore resign ourselves to its lack, though we should not, for that, abandon our scientific study of the psyche, as so many "scientists" are inclined to do.

To return to our earlier example, the girl seduced by her brother, a seduction undoubtedly beneficial as regards the erotic function. In that instance the resultant z was positively stressed, for the sense of guilt had not succeeded in stifling the instinctual function.

This plus, however, which therefore expresses the persistence of the positive response to excitations analogous to the first excitation x does not always fall so happily, since x, always positive, may have the plus sign attached where it should not, so to speak. I refer, once more, to the two erotogenic zones of woman.

I knew another woman of just as good class as the girl in my first instance. When about nine, she was also seduced by an adult male, in this case one of her parents' servants. This man would draw the child into dark corners or passages, and there masturbate her clitoridally without attempting possession. This continued for roughly a year, at which time the valet was discharged, though nothing was known of these relations.

Now, later in life, this woman was exclusively clitoridal. No coital position, not even contact with the clitoris, would procure the orgasm in coitus; only external caresses, while her clitoris remained untouched by the penis, would procure her satisfaction. And that in spite of the many times she changed her sexual partners.

For her, z had indeed become a positive factor but, since that plus was "badly placed", the early seduction, here, seems rather to have injured adaptation of the erotic function to the normal sex-act.

I know of other cases where the orgasm, *learnt* and experienced for the first time through the clitoris, seems to have permanently stamped the woman's sexuality.

Given these examples, we must ask one question: is it not really too ingenuous to attribute every subsequent orientation of the erotic feminine function to such-like seductions?

In effect, female erotism, like human psycho-sexuality in general, bases itself upon three main underlying strata: constitution, oedipal residuals, and prepubertal or adult formation. Who, therefore, can assert that the quantum of libido with which one or other of the erotogenic zones of the women we have cited was electively cathected, was not originally such that the orgasm, when it first appeared, *was forced*, willy-nilly, to discharge through one zone or the other? True, protracted fore-pleasure, which was all that the child at first knew, might still be borne, undifferentiated, by one zone or other, by the vulva or clitoris, even though the phallic clitoris may have dominated in its time. But end-pleasure, the violent discharge of an explosive accumulation of libido, could perhaps only occur where constitutional factors had already amassed the strongest charge of explosive. In that case, we should have a striking and conclusive example of "somatic compliance".

Thus, according to circumstances, and the girl's stronger or weaker constitutional bisexuality, we might conceive that the most powerful libidinal cathexis occurs, and that congenitally, as now borne by the clitoris or again by the bulbar-vaginal zone, which thus already prescribe the path by which the orgasm will discharge on its first appearance; that is, when the first *seduction* by another, or even by itself, takes place. Had this seduction been addressed to the other, more feebly cathected zone, it would have failed of effect, proved "unsuccessful"; that is, it would have yielded only the already familiar infantile fore-pleasure and not that preface to adult sexuality, end-pleasure.

Certain women, however, and again in advance, seem to have both zones, the clitoridal and bulbar-vaginal, each in its turn and from the first contacts, ready to yield end-pleasure. Thus, I knew a woman of fairly masculine make-up who, with her brother, as children, was taught to masturbate by a maid and retained the habit. She was then six but continued the practice, from time to time and always clitoridally, until she was thirty. Only then, for the first time, did she yield to a man. Whereupon, after coitus had occurred a few times and defloration been truly effected, she was then and there adapted to the bulbar-genital function and, with the utmost ease, with or without clitoridal preparation, enjoyed the fullest pleasure in normal coitus. She believes her pleasure comes mainly via the recto-vaginal septum, but is unable to localize the area clearly, as is often the case in women with internal orgastic sensitivity.

Such instances demonstrate the relative independence of the erotogenic zones, for we see that a long history of clitoridal masturbation did not injure vulvar-vaginal receptivity. The instance quoted is still more conclusive in that this woman's sexual impulse was fairly weak and that, between episodes which were always brief, she could live chastely for months without any apparent discomfort.

What complicates the interpretation of these facts is that the *predisposition*, not only to neurosis, but to modes of characterological and psycho-sexual response, and even to prepubertal, pubertal and adult seductions is, in each case, the resultant of two factors: those that are hereditary and constitutional and those represented by the preformative occurrences of infancy.

Such events, however, imply many kinds of trauma and every sort of oedipal disturbance, and to these we must again return in the light of what has been said.

Nevertheless, contrary to reality seductions, oedipal happenings generally occur solely in the child's mind; the parents, the father especially, who takes no part in his daughter's toilet, do not therefore *seduce* her in any true sense. Thus, when we consider the child's emotive disturbances and oedipal phantasies, and their nevertheless, vast repercussions, we find ourselves confronting the mystery, the darkness which, to the adult mind, enshrouds the immeasurable power of the imaginary.

Schopenhauer, in writing that the child lives in "representations", expressed a far deeper truth than appears at first sight.

True, the child does not live in the serene "representations" of which the philosopher thought here. On the contrary, it is a victim of that torturing "will" posited by the great pessimist, for most often the child is but an immense straining and impotent desire. Schopenhauer's formulation, however, becomes profoundly true, if we but alter it slightly: *the child lives in imagination.*

Now, imagination is governed by that *psychic reality* which moulds our beings to a degree at least equal to that exerted by the *physical reality* we do not always recognize, or even feel. And the facts, as every psycho-analysis reveals, suggest a general principle; namely, that infantile oedipal emotions affect the organism *as though they had occurred*. In them, the child takes his wishes for reality. As a result, its wish for incestuous union with one or other parent, and its wish for the death of one or the other, felt as a rival, evokes the same guilt-feelings it would have had, had it enacted these "crimes". Whence arises the inhibition that subsequently attaches itself to ideas of murder and of sexuality.

Another principle also appears; namely, that the manner in which the child phantasies sexuality, with active or passive possession of the mother or father, will condition the whole of its future psycho-sexual and even carnal-erotistic attitudes. Masochistic passivity in oedipal imaginings, in infantile phantasies, predisposes to feminoid attitudes whether in girl or boy. Phallic activity, if emphatic, whether in boy or girl, will also create an "engram" which will determine the form that the adult's erotic function will take.

At this time, however, the child by no means abandons the onanistic activities which lead the way to its later sexuality. True, masturbation does not, as yet, always yield end-pleasure, but the fore-pleasure sometimes suffices to lay down the paths and above all, to maintain, in a vague, undifferentiated and so to speak, asymptotic manner, its no less interminable oedipal phantasies.

True, the form of these oedipal phantasies is partly laid down by constitutional factors, but in their turn the phantasies determine the individuals' whole future sexuality.

Thus, whether the child will carry a wrecked or rescued sexuality into adult life will depend on whether the excitation of oedipal love, or moral oedipal inhibition arising from prohibitions of oedipal masturbation and the guilt resulting therefrom, was the predominant factor in these phantasies.

We thus come back, even without infantile seduction, to our equation:

$$x - y = z$$

in connection with the sum of the preformative oedipal excitations and inhibitions which, with constitutional factors, determine the individual's future psycho-sexuality.

Thus, just as infantile masturbation, as we said, is a preparation for adult sexuality, fulfilling, as regards the latter, an analogous role to the child's games when compared with adult social activities, so the child's Oedipus complex, or rather, complexes, may be conceived as a kind of psycho-sexual *play* preparative of the man's or woman's future psycho-sexuality.

In this way, the child *plays* at loving, loving sexually and totally; and, in so saying, I do not intend to minimize the Oedipus complexes! The nature of play, in fact, as Freud has shown, is not that it is not serious, but that it lacks support in reality, for no one could deny that at the time of the child's Oedipus complexes, the major part of reality support for its wishes is lacking, even though, contrary to what happens in games, the child, in its blind instinctive ardour, does not clearly perceive this most of the time. None the less, when the small boy phantasies himself marrying his mother, or the girl her father, something in them, despite these mighty phantasies, senses that it will never happen.

Thus, just as infantile masturbation which does not achieve orgasm is often automatically abandoned, especially by girls, and just as solitary infantile sexual investigation, because doomed to failure, is given up, so every infantile Oedipus complex, just because it is impossible that it can ever be gratified in reality, ends by fading, and that, independently even of those external inhibitory causes which, in all civilizations, have secondarily arisen to condemn it.

Humanity would need to regress to the cave-man, and beyond even, for the son, after the first infantile oedipal disappointment and the sexual play with other children, so common among primitives and among us, to dare, at puberty, to brave the authority of the old males, and return to battle with the aged father for the mother.

In any case, in our civilization, the frustration of the infantile Oedipus complex is generally final. At puberty, the son, as also the daughter, must turn towards strangers. Then, in the most favourable conditions, our children's Oedipus complexes will undergo the ideal fate of being successfully repressed; that is, the infantile oedipal *representations* will disappear into the unconscious, while the impulses and libidinal emotions afferent thereto will be detached and retained and, their evolution complete, at length enter the service of adult sexuality.

However, this absolute ideal of the total repression of the condemned representations, with retention and liberation of the impulses never, doubtless, altogether happens, due to the inertia which reigns in the realm of the instincts. In certain cases, one portion of the psycho-sexual impulses may follow the fate of the oedipal representations swallowed by the unconscious and, as it were, thus remain faithful to them, so depriving the adult psycho-sexuality of that much motive power. Here, repression will have been excessive and overshot its mark. In other cases, the fidelity of these impulses to representations will take a different path, that on the other side of the barricade, so to speak, and it will be the unrepressed impulses which draw to themselves those past oedipal representations which have re-emerged from the unconscious, doubtless with such displacements as to make them unrecognizable. In such cases repression will have been unsuccessful and have partly failed. Then, according as to whether oedipal excitations or inhibitions were dominant in the Oedipus complexes, the adult picture would be that of an individual who with unbridled, though unconscious fury, will seek parental imagos in his choice of love-objects, or of a man or woman who, unconsciously recognizing the oedipal object in every love object, will always recoil from the oedipal danger.

In the last two instances, a maladaptation to reality will have ensued, a sort of disturbance of the psychic vision, through projection of our inner phantoms on the outer world, which prevents our clearly discerning that other men and women who people the world are no longer, in fact, our parents. But only our last example will be truly disastrous to the erotic function, owing to the dominance of the inhibition.

(b) *Respective Roles of Father, Brother and Deflorator*

Detachment of the instinctual drives from the Oedipus complex, which can only occur through defeat of the stereotyped compulsion to repetition is sometimes approximately achieved by the male but apparently never, in equal degree, by the female who, from childhood, remains caught in her passive, never-resolved, Oedipus complex. As Freud once picturesquely said to me: "It is the father who always has first mortgage on a woman's heart: the husband never has anything but the second."

For, as we saw, if the clitoris originally wakes constellated on the mother, first passive, then active, the vagina, adjunct to the receptive cloaca, appears to "open" constellated on the father and on the passive Oedipus complex. Thus the father cannot but play a determinant part in this "opening" (a distant echo, it would seem, of the embryonic opening of the vagina through disappearance of the vaginal plug), by the quantity, as by the quality, of the love he bestows on his little daughter.

It will be objected, however, that the girl in the passive Oedipus complex, like the boy in the active Oedipus complex, which both, nevertheless, determine their sexuality, are doomed not only culturally, but biologically, to be frustrated in love.

How is it then that the inevitable frustration inherent in the Oedipus complexes will be inhibiting or pathogenic or create maladjustments in some cases and, in others, will not?

In the boy, his basic and quantitatively greater biological libidinal energy, borne by a highly differentiated organ, better adapted to its function than the girl's to hers, will enable him, oftener than her, to succeed in surmounting the inevitable oedipal frustration. As Freud has shown in *The Passing of the Oedipus Complex* (1924), for the man to be able to achieve normal adult sexuality, it is necessary that, as a small boy, he should, in part, have overcome the incest prohibition; that is, have succeeded in saving much of his oedipal instinctual drives from the threat of castration, nor had the upsurge of his sexuality broken by cultural castration threats. True, the drives must abandon the incestuous maternal object, but the libido, narcissistically saved by the love borne by the boy for his own penis, will then transfer itself, as wholly as possible, to other objects. I say "as possible", for Freud must be right in advancing that, in our communities, few men, doubtless, enjoy their total virility.[1] Part of it, more or less, must succumb in childhood to the inhibitive castration complex. In any case, the biological *libidinal urge*, generally stronger in the male than in the female, powerfully reinforces the normal development of sexuality in the male.

The position is quite different as regards woman. The *active libidinal* charge, borne by the clitoris, must be broken down for her to be able to acquire her true erotic function. It is therefore

[1] "Zur Einleitung der Onanie-Diskussion: Schlusswort" (1912).

this breaking down, caused partly by the biological castration complex, which inaugurates the girl's passive Oedipus complex, itself the psychical cause of truly feminine sexuality. From then on, the small girl's sexuality changes direction; it is as though she made a choice between her masculinity and her femininity; her instinctual aims from active, become passive, even though the *convex* clitoris sustains them a while longer, and the father, like a mighty god, presides over the whole process. Let us try and imagine what might then be happening in the child's soul. The mother, the original castrator, and herself castrated, is invested with feelings of hate and revenge and is more or less abandoned, while the father who bears the phallus is elected in her place. The larger part of the love directed on the mother has transferred itself to him and to what all her ripening organism and psyche dimly aspire; that is the psychical, physical desire to be the love object of this adored father. He is to love, want, monopolize, caress, enter and impregnate her so that, like the envied mother, she may have a child by him! The mechanism of these physiological acts is of course vague to the child still unaware of semen or vagina but, by her instinctual impulses, their male object and their passive drives, the little girl is already a complete, though miniature, woman.

As for the father, if he is normal, he loves his little girl and prefers her to his boy or boys. He pets her, takes her on his knee, caresses and spoils her and in this love she blossoms. Yet, deep down in herself, she senses approaching frustration and jealousy gnaws her, even if she does not possess a sister. "Why does father go out so often, without me, and with mother? Why does he shut himself in the bedroom at night, without me, to be alone with her? And why, when I am ill and Daddy and Mummy have my bed beside theirs, what are those moans, those sighs, I sometimes hear in the dark? Why does he sleep with her and not me?" And I do not refer here to working-class folk where the child must inevitably share the parents' bedroom.

Thus, infantile jealousy arises and the small girl's fate truly foreshadows the woman's, condemned as she is to share, be jealous, and suffer frustration. "Why, when I want to give Daddy a good hug, does he put me aside as though a nuisance?

Why, when I want to play with his pencils and paper, does he drive me out of his room? And what is that mysterious 'work' which takes him out so often?" Whereupon the small girl, again foreshadowing the woman, becomes jealous of man's work and occupations which too often, for her taste, distract him from his love for her.

And what the little girl longs to get from the father is not only psychical love! Has she not already discovered, whether at three, four or five, and even far earlier, the pleasure that comes, not only from all her cutaneous surface, but especially from the erotogenic genital zone? Thus, when she sits on her father's knee or when he lets her straddle his back, she strives to establish the closest contact between the beloved father and these sensitized zones and, by caressing the god she adores, to obtain the maximum pleasure accessible to her small body. Her father, however, if he realizes this or even, simply, tires of these games, will stop the pickaback ride, or dethrone her from his divine knees and put her down on the floor, vastly to her disappointment. And since every moral ban the parents impose, and even any fatigue on their part, is always interpreted by the child as lack of love, she thinks: "If father puts me down when I want it so much, it's because he doesn't love me enough to do it." Thus, to the psychical frustration, through jealousy of the woman her father sexually prefers, the mother, or her substitute, is added the no less serious reality-rejection of the helpless and frustrated child's physical solicitations. All this, day after day, will help to establish woman's primary frustration in love; that which the little girl experiences at five or six, with the first blossoming of her feminine psycho-sexuality. And this first bloom of her love will wilt and never again truly reflower if, as sometimes happens, the frost it encountered was severe or the blossom, especially, too frail.

In other cases, however, the gods, or rather god, proves kinder. For though, in our cultural communities, the father can never truly satisfy the physical, the sensual longings of his child, or be her real initiator into sexuality, it is all the more incumbent on him therefore to love her with that deep and lasting affection, that uninterrupted and constant tenderness into which sexual love, when inhibited in its aim, is converted, the love from which the enduring family will arise. This tenderness of the father's, so bestowed, is the clime in which feminine sexuality best develops.

When the little girl is thus offered tenderness and love, even aim-inhibited love, in exchange for what she desires, she far more readily adopts the psycho-sexual attitude that nature and men demand in woman, despite the narcissistic, even vital, risks this attitude implies. Though penetration of her body will be a wounding, what matter to one who is loved? The pain she fears will become a yearned-for pleasure and feminine masochism thus reaches its heights. Childbirth will imply the peril of death? Who bothers about that in love's realm? Woman, in exchange for love, is ready to accept every danger and give herself irrevocably to the beloved, so long as the man will keep her by him and not be first to deceive.

It is in this very fact that we sometimes find an oedipal obstacle to the eventual establishment of a normal psychosexuality which permits of marriage and children. Certain girls have irrevocably "surrendered" to the father. And because they were never physically possessed by this god who ruled over childhood's realm, they remain shut to all other men. It is as though, in such women, the receptor-vagina, psychically "open" for a while during the passive Oedipus complex, had psychically shut again through dint of vainly awaiting the male who was unable to come to it. Here we have an inhibition arising through useless waiting, through frustrated love.[1] In such women, who die with the hymen intact, it is as though fidelity had brought about a veritable closure of the vagina.

Possibly, in such women, the clitoridal zone had been retained, and found occasional activity in masturbation. The phantasies that would then accompany this act are of great interest psycho-analytically. They are rarely conscious, but when we do bring them to light, we often perceive that under those relating to the oedipal father, are others, deeper still,

---

[1] Compare Pavlov's dogs, which stopped reacting to the signal when it was repeatedly not followed by presentation of food. But in the dog, an animal less "cerebral" than man, the reflex reappears when, once the signal is resumed, food is offered again.

which have continued orientated on the mother, the mother of the active Oedipus complex to which the clitoris has thus remained faithful, in its way. It is as though such women had a specially "sticky" libido, a disease of chronic fidelity. In their unconscious, too faithful to the mother, they had kept their clitoris for her; too faithful to the father also, through love of him, they had closed the vagina to other men. For the fidelity of the clitoris is positive, that of the vagina negative; through fidelity, the clitoris *pursues* whereas the vagina *flees*. These instances, indeed, exemplify the principle which Freud enunciated: namely, that whatever relates to the mother in the girl's Oedipus complexes, fidelity included, is later transferred *en bloc* to the father.

Generally, however, the father's affection for his daughter is not so fateful as this for her psycho-sexuality; far otherwise indeed, for female sexuality, like our fine orchard fruit, needs sunshine in which to ripen. If, however, the father too much refuses his love, then rebellion will rise in his daughter's bosom. And though such rebellion may be nursed in the male heart without endangering masculinity, since it is active, sadistic and ego-syntonic, too much rebellion in the woman will only accentuate her masculinity complex and profoundly disturb her psycho-sexuality. Then, though such rebelling women may seek to flee the frustrating father by turning to successive males (prostitution complex), they will often stay faithful to him in spite of themselves. By rebelling, in fact, their clitoris will reactivate all its innate masculinity, and their vagina, despite the loss of the hymen, will remain erotically *"shut"*, as it once shut, in childhood, to the father, through frustration, disappointment and hate, after having offered itself fruitlessly to him.

Fortunate then are the women who have a brother upon whom to transfer the emotions aroused by their thwarted oedipal sexuality! For them, indeed, the brother may well have been the rescuer of their heterosexuality! The sexuality of the girl too deeply disappointed by the father, if she finds no other male to whom to cling may, in certain instances, forever turn from the male and wholly regress to the love object of the primary active Oedipus complex, the mother. Then, if the girl is markedly bisexual and the environment favourable, her only later outlet will be in homosexual mother-child play with other women.

We see from the foregoing that a "Scylla and Charybdis" threatens feminine sexuality which, at the oedipal crossroads, must avoid too much, or too little, love. In conclusion, however, and because women, unlike boys, remain throughout life enmeshed in their positive Oedipus complex, that of which the father, under later protective male transferences, will remain the object, we may assume that the father oftener risks far less in bestowing too much, rather than too little, love on his daughter. In any case, the male, engrossed in his work and other women, runs little risk of spoiling his daughter. What *spoils* girls far oftener is their rebellion against a father who has not loved them enough. For the father's love is all the more indispensable to his daughter in that, in our communities, he himself is prohibited from initiating her sexually; thus paternal love remains her sole compensation for the irrevocable fact that the father *must* repulse all that is sensual in his child's solicitations.

The father's tenderness is thus the "plea" by which he seeks forgiveness for being unable, himself, to initiate his daughter into true sexuality. And that "plea" must needs be eloquent for, as we have shown, the child, still unaware of abstract distinctions, always confuses *rejection on moral grounds*, with *rejection through lack of love*.

The child, in fact, finds hard to understand that one *must not* do what *one wants*, because of some abstract commandment: its superego has not yet become truly established. Had it the strength, it would certainly do what it wanted: it is only the grown-ups who prevent it. Why, since they have the power, should they not allow her all the petting she desires, if they truly love her? "Why doesn't my father", the little girl thinks, "fondle me as much as I'd like? It's because he doesn't love me enough!" This reproach to the father is the same as that of a passionate lover to his beloved who is too virtuous to elope: "You do not love me enough!" he will cry.

Yet both, the lover and the child are, in part, right. If the virtuous maid and the oedipal father each reject another's passion, it is because something is stronger in them than it.

The virtuous maid, however, like the oedipal father, may also be capable of loving intensely. But the counter-drive in them is even stronger, and morality can hold the natural instinct in leash. But to passionate natures nothing should exist that is stronger than passion, which is why the child experiences oedipal rejection on moral grounds as rejection through lack of love.

Only an ever-present affection, sublimated love, hovering over the carnally disappointed infant will eventually win the father pardon for his rejection, and give the girl that lasting premium of paternal affection in exchange for which she will accept *moral* oedipal renunciation.

But if the mission which fate prescribes for the father is that of initiating his little daughter into the turmoils of love—if not into heterosexual object-pleasure—and equally, into the age-old morality built up by humanity, the brother, on the other hand, when the little girl is so fortunate as to have one, must play a quite different part.

If they are young enough, morality, as between brother and sister, will not have established itself yet: to them morality, imposed from without by their upbringers, will as yet be only more or less introjected. And nature, in them, despite its atavistic hereditary readiness to run in moral grooves, will, with its primitive instincts, demand its rights.

For which reason, despite the vigilance of parents and servants, and despite adult prohibitions, children not only masturbate, but seek out others to share their pleasures; in short, to live their object-sexuality, inhibited as that is towards the parents.

Then, if the brother is nearest in age to his sister, is it strange that the sexual play of children should so often be *incestuous*?

In my opinion, educators do not fully realize the frequency of such childish relations, blinded as they are by their own infantile amnesia. We, however, often find them in our analyses of children and adults.

It has been said that "infantile seduction" is the cause of many evils. Whether the seduction was by a child or, more rarely, by an adult, it does, in fact, leave deep marks on the psycho-sexuality and indeed, whole nature, of the child.

Nevertheless, it seems that "seduction", even when of very early occurrence, is a two-edged weapon; one that Freud well understood and expressed in his "ground-floor and mansion" story. What dooms seduction to pathogenicity is far more the moral repression which it more or less inevitably involves in our civilized communities, than the seduction itself, which is part of the preparative training in sexuality.

It is not only as regards a pathogenic morality that seduction may drag other evils in its wake, since it may also injure the individual's psycho-sexuality and whole character. For, if woman's biological mission is passivity, the male must preserve his activity. For which reason, whereas juvenile seducers, if boys, often show no ill after-effects, since seduction, as an activity, is properly male, *seduction* of the boy will be harmful, whether by an adult or other child, and even by an elder sister, since an element of passivity will, doubtless, be incorporated in his sexuality and nature. Seduction of the little girl, however, is less pathogenic, if not to her morality, at least to her future sexuality; that is, if the moral condemnation of her upbringers has not been too severe.

Let me now cite some instances of seduction by brothers with favourable effects on the psycho-sexual adaptation, the erotic function of the woman.

Apart from the case of prepubertal incest I cited earlier, here are two other cases of early passive seduction which ended well.

I knew a small couple in which the brother was barely a year older than his sister. When they were children, despite all supervision, they played the following game. Both slept in the same room. Immediately their nurse had left them, the brother got up and softly approached his sister's bed. Then, he would begin to tease her, saying: "I dare you to touch it" (meaning his penis). She did not, in fact, dare, or almost.... He, however, went on: "I dare!" and would touch her genitals. These children were then about five and six.

Now, as things were, this little girl had had to put up with a serious oedipal frustration in that her father greatly preferred the boy. And this had made her conceive an immense oedipal aggression, a hatred of the "father" in all shapes and forms. Her amorous solicitations had then turned back towards the mother, but she, like a normal woman, preferred her small boy, whence arose further frustration.

The brother, however, appearing as the seducer, here seems to have been fated to become the preserver of his little sister's normality. Actually, this game of theirs was never discovered. Their exploits were told me by the grown-up woman. She also gave me much other valuable information for, in fact, this woman became perfectly normal as regards her erotic function. Her awakening by the male came after a long latency period and, rare though that is, the function proved normal from the very first contact.

In this case, the brother had rendered his sister a signal service in teaching her not to continue hankering after her impossible oedipal love; he had taught her to resort, when need arose, to the salutary, indispensable, infidelity.

In another case, where I am less acquainted with the part the brother played, though it may be inferred from the woman's later reactions, the girl was so strongly fixated on a father, who himself adored her, that it was long doubted whether she would marry. Though her father urged her to do so, she went on refusing. Then, near thirty, an attractive young man offered his hand and was accepted. But during the engagement she suddenly changed her mind. The young man, passionately in love, did not, however, give her up. And indeed, her conflict needed time in which to work itself out.

This young woman had a brother, a few years younger than herself. I think it was due to him that the lover finally won her. We do not know what happened, in childhood, between the girl and her brother nor, doubtless, does either of them now. Was the seduction actual or emotive only? Or perhaps, in some degree, both? In any case, if this girl who was so powerfully fixated on the father had had no brother, it is highly probable that, despite her father's desire, she would never have married, nor been as completely happy as she physically and psychically was in her marriage.

Thus, early attachment to a brother and, even, actual seduction by him, may have fortunate results.

Conversely, even when the little girl is seduced by an elder brother, in conformity, as it were, with the passivity of her sex, the consequence may prove very harmful. I shall quote only one case, but one I know very well. Her analysis revealed that this woman, in childhood, had in fact been seduced by an elder brother, a seduction in the form of caresses, unaccompanied by actual coitus. They were discovered and the brother punished. For the sister this resulted in a complete retreat from sexuality. At forty, despite many lovers and a sex-life which began at twenty-three, this woman had never been able to experience end-pleasure with a male, whether through coitus or caresses. Only vulvar-clitoridal masturbation would at times procure it for her. All this time, however, the brother held first place in her unconscious imagination. I emphasize *unconscious*, for no memory of all these infantile events existed and analysis alone enabled them to be reconstructed, which it did with great precision. Indeed, such was the dominance of this brother, that every lover she chose corresponded to his type, while the obligation she had felt, as a child, to succour him from the father, had become transferred into a most obdurate repetition-compulsion in her life. This woman was perpetually *compelled* to demand money for her indigent lovers, from those who were rich and who, as it happened, would often refuse it. (This case, in my opinion, throws an interesting light on the psychology of girls who bestow on their "fancy man" what they extract from their rich "protectors"; we have here a predilection for the brother "who can love", as against the oedipal father whose rejection is never forgiven.) Her analysis, by lifting the moral prohibitions of her childhood, by substituting the analyst, as one "Beyond Good and Evil", for the severe, prohibitive mother of her childhood, permitted the return of the erotic function, under the preferred transference from the "brother", that lover with whom she had so long been anaesthetic. This, after various rather haphazard adventures which the analyst, in this case of hypersensitivity to morality, was careful not to condemn. The erotic function thereupon reappeared, vaginal and fully normal, after its long repression. This woman, doubtless innately very feminine, had reacted to her seduction, as to its repression, with feminine passive plasticity and, with the same plasticity, was able to recover her erotic function, though forty years had passed. Here we see the cure of a case of hysterical inhibition in a woman born, to her misfortune, in the "mansion".

These cases will suffice to show that, though the father, following our civilized code, must not erotically initiate his daughter, the brother, though by parental injunctions he *must not* do so either, nevertheless frequently *does* and often with beneficial results, thus applying a corrective to his sister's oedipal frustration, as well as teaching her to change her object and return to lovers of her own age, which is biologically desirable, since every succeeding generation must make its life together.

In the same way, the sister, as substitute for that unsatisfactory initiator into sexuality, the oedipal mother, may play an analogous part for her little brother.

Even more important, however, is the part the brother may play towards establishing a normal function in his sister. For, from a very early age he becomes the male for whose sake she will be ready to accept all the disadvantages and risks of femininity.

Thus, generally speaking, the male plays his part in several guises in the psycho-sexual formation of woman, and more particularly, in her erotic formation. At first he appears as the father, or his surrogate, for many a girl, in the passive Oedipus complex, will have seen that part played by several actors. Then, wearing the brother's features, or his substitute's, cousin or friend, the little girl's more equal partner will appear, often her sole true initiator into infantile object-sexuality. Finally, after the Sleeping Beauty slumber of the latency period will come the deflorator, lover or spouse, whose mission is to initiate the woman into true adult feminine sexuality.

Thus, whereas the father, as regards true sexual initiation, *must not*, and the brother *may* but *should not*, the deflorator, himself, *must*.

When the male approaches the young female, he is confronted by a sort of Sleeping Beauty (I omit girls deflowered early in life by a brother or young playmate), whose vagina is still sealed by the hymen, and whose psyche is already traversed by congenitally laid down paths which are more or less sexual, as well as more or less bisexual, a psychical make-up which early events, and the active and passive Oedipus complexes will have corrected or emphasized. First the mother, then the father and brothers or their surrogates, will each in turn have left their mark on the statue and thus, of the clay furnished by Nature, composed a more or less finished statue. Nevertheless, the last touch to the statue will be given by her first lover, the deflorator, whether husband or not.

The importance of this last factor has always been sensed by popular wisdom, which has even attributed more to it than its due, in its ignorance, before psycho-analysis, of the preformative role of infantile sexuality.

When the young woman faces her deflorator, the latter's task is not always facile. Pain cannot always be spared the woman and, if not too intense may, in any case, favour that erotogenic masochistic attitude which should be that of woman in the sex act. For which reason we may wonder how far artificial defloration by surgeons favours the subsequent acquisition of a normal function. This, however, is possibly but a return to a customary primitive practice, as Freud noted,[1] according to which defloration of the girl was, or is, confided to ritual figures, who thus relieve the husband from any enduring resentment the pain would cause and, in addition, as parental forms, in part satisfy the girl's oedipal wishes, after their long childhood frustration. In one way or other, once the hymen is torn, the way is open to the initiator, and it is then that the male's adaptative role begins.

If the woman, because of an innate over-strong bisexuality, accentuated by the vicissitudes of her Oedipus complexes (clitoridal fixation on the mother, rebellion against the father and denial of the vagina), is too wholly clitoridal, the tenderest efforts of her mate will fail against that wall; there will be no adaptation to coitus, and the woman will only respond to external caresses.

[1] "Contributions to the Psychology of Love: The Taboo of Virginity" (1918). *Coll. Papers*, Vol. IV.

If vaginal potentiality, however, is present, whether wholly so or combined with residuals of clitoridal erotogenicity, then the role of the deflorator, who adds the last touch to this feminine statue, may prove decisive.

In any case, the male should always remember that, in the love act, he is the sole lord of time. True, there are men who can more or less "wait" before or during the act, but there are others who do not even try. Woman, however, not only because she generally needs more time, physically, than the male, but also because she takes the time she is given, whether in the love act, or in loving, as a sign, a proof she is loved, is often highly sensitised to its lack. One might indeed say, to vary a well-known tag, that *Time is Love* to women.

However, women with a combined clitoridal-vaginal function have one advantage over those that are solely vaginal, these last being all but reduced to simple coitus, which internal digital caresses do little to replace. Thus, if their function has remained somewhat slow, there are fewer partners who will be apt to satisfy them. The clitoridal-vaginals, on the other hand, admit preliminaries (sole sustenance of so many clitoridals) before the coital act which, while postponing end-pleasure till the normal act, submits male patience to a less harsh ordeal during coitus.

All of which amounts to saying that, in love, the male must be endowed with patience: *erotized patience*, in fact.

The behaviour of the deflorator, the first real initiator, is thus often of decisive importance. He may correct or exacerbate deficiencies that date from childhood. If he defaults in his mission, his punishment will often be that the woman, hungering for love and its pleasures, will turn for initiation to another and, if he also defaults, to still others.

But here we come back to frigidity, a condition with a long prehistory and one which the adult initiator may, but sometimes proves unable, to relieve.

VI

AN OUTLINE OF THE DEVELOPMENT OF FEMALE SEXUALITY

FEMALE SEXUALITY may be conceived to develop as follows. Initially, Nature does not create the girl wholly feminine, but only more or less so, plus an added masculine factor. These constituent factors will soon find organic expression in the earliest forms assumed by the child's infantile, cloacal masturbation which, originally undifferentiated as to a specific zone, later become more or less fixated on the clitoris alone or on the contiguous entrance to the vulva. In each case, a degree of innate erotization of either of the erectile zones comprised in the external female genitals, the clitoris, or the bulbar-vaginal zone, will respectively predispose the child to one or other form of masturbation. Thus, depending on the child, masturbation will predominantly be either *convex* or *concave*, though not to the entire exclusion of the less dominant form.

Whereas the clitoris tends to push and pierce, the vagina demands penetration. All this, at first, is diffuse, indefinite and vague since neither organ is conscious, at first, of what should be pierced or should pierce. Nevertheless, the biological trend exists: a *somatic compliance* which already advances to meet the object.

The little girl, in the primary cloacal stages, where the mother alone rules over her needs and cleansings, doubtless has vague and passive desires for cloacal caresses from the mother's hands, since everything that protrudes on the mother's body may, in the diffuseness of its desires, take the place of the originally sucked nipple.

Anally, the small boy also passes through an analogous passive stage which, in the homosexual male, will serve as a base for that feminoid component which allows a response to pederasty.

The clitoris, first awakened as it is by the mother's cleansings, has a long prehistory. But when, as always happens, phallic activity comes to replace the primary cloacal and phallic passivity, the tendency to *penetrate* becomes superimposed on that of *being penetrated*, and the girl then lives through the sado-phallic stage, more or less emphasized in each instance, which will be brought to an end by the properly feminine reversal of sadism into masochism, originally always phallic, but eventually returning the libido to the concave, vaginal, erectile-tissue zones. I believe that it is during this passive oedipal phase that the direction taken by a woman's erotism will be determined: the menstrual flow, passing later through the vagina, will only confirm an erotogenic mode already present.

Whereas, in the boy, the phallic stage must persist and, in line with the male organ, become the genital stage, it seems that in woman, taking an ideal instance, the clitoris, that small female phallus, must experience the fate of those temporary organs which, like the thymus, having played their part for a time, will succumb to involution, due to the development of another organ which fulfils an analogous function, on which the adult function will devolve.

Since the clitoris and vagina, however, were together from the start, I do not think that the little girl, when masturbating, can completely ignore the vagina. Such ignorance is reserved to the boy. Her little fingers, to my mind, could not avoid gliding into the small pit beside the clitoris, with more or less pleasure or fear, depending on whether the vagina is already more or less erotized, as well as on how far she is innately feminine, or on the strength of her masculine vital protest against that *wound,* that *hole.*

Nor should we forget that, in all we have pointed out, this biological, this infantile prologue to adult sexuality may operate, more or less lengthily, solely in the form of forepleasure. This is why these erotogenic zones may readily replace one another, the libido being far more labile at this time, and so abler to take one or other channel.

Since both the clitoridal and bulbar-vaginal zones are *primary*, they may, secondarily, become emphasized through assuming the excitation or inhibiting stamp which external events impose upon them. It is thus that grown-ups, the mother, father, even brothers and sisters, and all who stand for them to the child, it is thus that all these greater and lesser gods may help to trace its path for the woman's future sexuality.

This they may do in two manners; firstly in reality and sensual fashion, by seduction, which no child wholly escapes since, to be washed, fed, fondled, it must at least be touched by the mother. But again, the pattern is stamped in imaginative fashion, not only by the sensations, but also by the feelings aroused in the child by the emotional reactions of those around it. And these emotions, together with the representations they create, these preformative "engrams", contribute towards making the woman accept or reject her femininity, with all the phantasies which that implies of giving oneself and of accepting or rejecting penetration.

Then one day, sooner or later, as may happen, the girl will experience orgasm, either as a result of seduction, or alone.

When she achieves this alone, it is evident that the pre-existent orientation of her sexuality, including phantasies, the more or less pronounced erotogenicity of one or other zone, must elicit contact, caresses, here or there. But when the orgasm is taught the woman, as often happens, by means of seduction, then the manner of the seduction may, in its turn, affect what was already present. True, in very pronounced instances of vaginality or clitoridalism, the seduction, if addressed to the less sensitive zone will simply have no effect. *Per contra*, it will be maximally effective if addressed to the sensitized zone. Where, however, a combined clitoridal-vaginal function is involved, clitoridal seduction could no doubt hinder or merely retard the subsequent establishment of vaginal function which, but for that, would soon have come to pass. Conversely, vaginal seduction will help to push the clitoris into the background.

It is on these diverse superimposed courses that the edifice of female sexuality rises. Constitutional factors are its foundation, and life builds thereon. Finally, we see the feminine psycho-sexual structure in its main varieties, varieties more multiform even than those to which male sexuality is susceptible, centred as it is on the phallus, that highly differentiated organ developed to serve the male erotic function.

PART III

EVOLUTIONARY PERSPECTIVES

I

ALLO- AND AUTOPLASTIC ADAPTATION

(a) *Normality and Health*

WE SHOULD never confuse normality with health. Female, as indeed all human psycho-sexuality, contains much possibility of suffering but also of satisfaction too, and general psychical health may be compatible with striking deviations from the ideal instinctual norm.

In his paper, *Female Sexuality* (1931), Freud established an important distinction between three main types of women: those we have called *the acceptive, the renunciatory*, and *the claimant*.

With the acceptives, there is a maximal incidence between psychical health and normality; these are the vaginal women, whether loved ones or mothers; those who have adopted their femininity best.

With the renouncers, we may sometimes see the renunciation of the sexual object co-exist with health, as in certain virgins in whom the highly sublimated libido seems saturated with intense social activity. In other cases, however, this renunciation is poorly tolerated, a neurosis appears, and analysis alone will enable the woman to reconcile herself to her renunciation by adopting a till then absent social activity or, what is instinctually simpler, by reconciling herself to the real sexual life which she had denied herself so far.

With the claimers, we have already dealt at more length than the others. Here, we shall first consider them in their sub-groups and, first and foremost, the *homosexuals*, in whom the masculine protest is maximally displayed.

Where the ego of the homosexual female fully accepts its psycho-sexual make-up and its own mode of erotic satisfaction, health may then be compatible with this "anomaly". If suffering, however, attends such a compulsive homosexual object choice, then psycho-analytic treatment is indicated.

Such of the claimers as are clitoridals, with a pronounced masculinity complex that nevertheless displays heterosexual object choice may, as we saw, support their frigidity, their infirmity, rather, in coitus, in different ways, Either they adjust, or pride themselves on it, or it gives them pain. Thus, some greater or less degree of impaired psychical health, as may be, is their lot.

All living organisms, however, strive to adapt to their environment either allo-plastically, by seeking to modify or even select it in terms of themselves, or again auto-plastically by seeking to modify themselves in terms of their environment. The psycho-analyst daily observes the nervous, psychical forces employed to shape the bodily and functional. And heterosexual, clitoridal women, so instructive if considered as regards bisexuality and maladaptation of the important erotic function to the conditions imposed by environment, here represented by the male partners, are an especially instructive subject of observation in respect to an organism's now allo-, now auto-plastic efforts to adapt to environment.

(b) *Alloplastic Adaptation: the Male as Mirror*

Primarily, what so often enables such women to endure their fate, hard as that basically is, is passivity; the characteristic masochism of the feminine sex which we meet even in this kind of woman. In addition, there is a factor of a similar bisexual order, to which it is worth drawing attention, a factor related to certain qualities of the love-objects that may offer themselves to such women.

In accordance with the picture of libidinal development which we have outlined, many men, on their side, will retain a number of feminoid characters. Such men, partly fixated at the cloacal-phallic stage, present a partial *exclusion of the phallus* as regards their own bodies, and even at times some overstressing of the peri-cloacal zone. While they will have retained woman as object, they sometimes, at least, present slight potency disturbances. But the male who has not psychically, and determinedly, clung to possession of his own phallus, never suppresses as radically as highly virile men do all idea of woman's phallus. In the unconscious of such men, the phallic woman, common to the infantile phantasy of all boys, goes on surviving with special intensity.

Now the female clitoris is, in fact, a small penis, a miniature phallus. And such males, pronouncedly masculine as they may otherwise have become as regards their intellectual, social and even psycho-sexual activities remain, more or less, unconscious worshippers of the female phallus. Thus it will be the clitoris they love in woman, though this will become more or less unattractive to the more wholly masculine and integrated male. To the former, coitus may even become less important than the preliminaries involving the female clitoris before or during the sex-act.

Clitoridal women, thus, nevertheless, succeed in gratifying their essentially phallic erotogenicity by their sure instinct in discovering and attaching such men, men whom civilization tends to multiply, given the obstacles which it presents to normal sexual development and which encourage arrests in development as much as regression.

In this way of compensating their feminine sexual maladaptation with another and male kind of sexual maladaptation, which mirrors their own, we see a fairly successful attempt on their part at *alloplastic* adaptation.

It would be unfair, however, to suggest that only this sort of "male as mirror" will bother about satisfying clitoridal women.

In the West, the male, by the mere fact of his excessive cerebralization, is well aware that many women prefer activities which involve the clitoris, to simple penetration. Thus, even though his own degree of feminoid sexuality may not be especially high, and even though he be very masculine, the "civilized" male, when he loves, often comes to adapt himself to the woman's desires. Actually, once the "civilized" male loves, he is far less purely egotistical than he is sometimes accused of being; his need to share his pleasure and his loving identification with the woman result in a consideration for her wishes. In this way, therefore, clitoridals may find a compensation for their functional disability. It will not happen, however, with the firstcomer, but only with a male who loves them enough to care.

Nevertheless, clitoridals exist who do suffer because of their maladaptation, including perhaps even those who claim it as a mark of superiority. Whatever the satisfaction those women may feel who, as Abraham so well saw, belong to the type which reacts with "revenge" to the castration complex, whatever pleasure they may feel in *cheating* the male with their frigidity, in proving his uselessness to him, his *impotence*, as it were, when with them, it is none the less true that they are cheated themselves, and even more than the male. Besides these, however, we find women who, despite their masculinity, are nevertheless feminine enough to want to be different; women too masculine to be satisfied with normal coitus, but too feminine not to suffer thereby; for one may be partly male and yet very feminine. For such women, their tragedy is especially poignant when the object, the male on whom they happen to fixate, is too fiercely male to adapt to their clitoridal wishes, which may the more freely happen in proportion to the degree in which femininity preponderates over the masculinity in them. Some modification, some autoplastic adaptation is then necessary.

(c) *Psycho-Analysis and Autoplastic Adaptation of the Central Nervous System*

Only *post hoc* reconstruction of the developmental stages unresolved in childhood, and thus distorted at puberty, can truly modify and produce true autoplastic adaptation.

Life alone but rarely achieves this, as regards truly clitoridal women. In such cases, contrary to the frigidity that arises from neurotic repression of full cloacal and vaginal development, from which the woman's sexuality may suddenly emerge perfect, frigidity resulting from excessive phallic accentuation, with concomitant erotogenic cloacal effacement, shows far more difficulty in being modified by life. But even when such frigidity is hysterical in essence, it often remains fiercely obdurate to the usual suggestive psycho-therapies.[1]

[1] Dr. Paul Sollier, a year before his death, told me that in all his long psycho-therapeutical career, he had never seen a clitoridal woman change into one that was vaginal.

Only psycho-analysis is capable of influencing it, a by no means easy task when the fixation and clitoridal habits are old-established.

Here, the difficulty is to know just when analysis has given everything it can. Libidinal fixation on the female clitoris, like all psycho-sexual phenomena is, in fact, conditioned both by the innate bisexuality, and the childhood and even adult events which may have thwarted or encouraged it. But this disturbance in libidinal development will be corrected if the analysis, in its course from current to past events, succeeds in eradicating the exclusive clitoridal fixation and causing vaginal sensitivity to appear. In that case we might say that the analysis (which would surely have affected the total personality and its symptoms) was successful. When, however, despite the progress of our theoretical discoveries and, especially, despite deep analysis of the first phallic fixations on the mother, no modification of the erotogenic zones occurs, or not enough to permit a fully normal satisfaction in coitus, what is the attitude the analyst should adopt?

At what moment can we tell ourselves that the impassable biological borderline has been reached, as in certain kinds of homosexuality, and have we not always the right to believe that some bit of psychical ground remains to be conquered?

The therapeutic surprises we often encounter in the last stages of analysis should encourage us to prolonged and persevering efforts in treating such cases. We know that analyses of the perversions are generally protracted, and no analyst will miss the analogy between feminine frigidity, due to a tenacious clitoridal fixation, and a "perversion". Contrary to frigidity through total genital neurotic repression, does not libido share with the perversion the possibility of seeking discharge through a lateral route, and is not this route, collateral, alas, in woman, the main route of discharge of the male libido of the all-powerful phallus?

Thus, we should only reluctantly resign ourselves to admitting, when we meet but partial success in the therapeutic treatment of these frigidities, that we have already encountered the impassable bounds of the organic.

(d) *A Peripheral Attempt at Autoplastic Adaptation: The Halban-Narjani Operation*

When I first began to be interested in psycho-analysis, the problem of female sexuality, aroused by the many confidences entrusted me by women, began to occupy my mind. I was struck by the great number of clitoridal women and wondered what could cause so frequent an anomaly. It then occurred to me to inquire whether something in the genital anatomy of these women might contribute to their defective erotic reactions and, with the collaboration of various doctors, both in Paris and Vienna, who were kind enough to help my research, I was able anatomically to observe, and question, a fair number of women during their gynaecological consultations.

What these observations seemed to reveal was that, whereas the size of the clitoris hardly mattered, the distance from the clitoris to the urinary meatus might be important. This distance varies considerably in different women, ranging between 1 and 4 cm., and those in whom the distance was greatest tended to be purely clitoridal. The results of these observations were published in the issue of *Bruxelles-Medical* for April, 1924[1] under the pseudonym of A. E. Narjani. They appeared prematurely, as it proved, for I subsequently observed that frigidity through clitoridal fixation also occurred in women in whom the space was small, whereas wider spaces were often compatible with entirely normal vaginal sensitivity. In particular, as regards erotic enjoyment, I attributed too cardinal a part to the proximity of the clitoris to the vaginal zone; the vaginal utilization of the clitoris, as it were.

Nevertheless, these observations did establish that largish gaps between the meatus and clitoris were not in general favourable to normal transference of clitoris response to the vagina, as though the gap were too wide to leap. A wide gap therefore fairly often appeared as a real stigma of bisexuality.

[1] "Considérations sur les causes anatomiques de la frigidité chez la femme." I have not reproduced this article here since it was pre-analytic and erroneous.

It then occurred to me that where, in certain women, this gap was excessive, and the clitoridal fixation obdurate, a clitoridal-vaginal reconciliation might be effected by surgical means, which would then benefit the normal erotic function. Professor Halban, of Vienna, as much biologist as surgeon, became interested in the problem and worked out a simple operative technique. In this, the suspensory ligament of the clitoris was severed and the clitoris secured to the underlying structures, thus fixing it in a lower position, with eventual reduction of the labia minora.[1]

The results of five such operations are highly interesting from the psycho-sexual point of view. Two cases, unfortunately, could not be followed up, while the third proved unsuccessful. The woman, thirty-five and a divorcee, had lived for some years in concubinage with a lover, and was enraged at having allowed the operation, which evidently had neither damaged her nor proved very successful. She had only been fully satisfied twice in normal coitus and then only while the cut, which became infected, remained unhealed, thus temporarily mobilizing the essential feminine masochism. Once the cut healed, she had to revert to the sole form of coitus which had so far satisfied her: the kneeling posture on the man lying flat.

A short analysis demonstrated that this woman, who belonged to the category of ultra-claimers, had hoped that by this operation the surgeon-father would give her the wished-for penis. This woman's masculinity complex was exceptionally strong.

The two remaining cases showed generally favourable, though not decisive, results: vaginal erotization and potential excitation in normal coitus, neither of which were present before. Nevertheless, capacity for orgasm in the normal coital act did not immediately establish itself regularly, but with long intervals between its occurrence. The clitoris continued as the dominant erotogenic zone.

In these women (one twenty-five and newly married, the other forty, and married twice, first at twenty and then at

[1] See Halban: *Gynäkologische Operationslehre* (1932).

thirty-five), a markedly feminine attitude was present, side by side with the masculinity complex, in contrast to the case already cited, which doubtless was what allowed such a duplication of what normally happens so much more perfectly in normal development; *the use of a male energy in female fashion*; i.e. the vaginal utilization of the clitoris in such cases.

We therefore find that this sort of operation should only be tried in carefully selected, psycho-analytically explored cases, since its degree of success is prescribed by the strength of the "dynamic stereotype" imposed by the autonomous nervous system electively erotizing the clitoris and the practices which involve it alone, while correlatively excluding the vagina. The results of an operation, therefore, remain more than doubtful.

Thus, when it gains its ends without such surgical intervention, psycho-analysis, because more purely psycho-physiological, will be a surer and more elegant solution of such disturbances of instinct until we possess those yet undiscovered, if not undiscoverable, hormones which will enable us to masculinize the male and feminize the female, with their erotogenic zones and psyches, when the need should arise.

II

FEMALE MUTILATION AMONG PRIMITIVE PEOPLES AND THEIR PSYCHICAL PARALLELS IN CIVILIZATION

IT is interesting to note that in antiquity, as to-day, whole races have practised, and still practise, surgical operations on the external female genitals, which practices, unlike the Halban-Narjani operation, are generally not pro- but anti-clitoridal.

True, these practices were never so widespread as that of male circumcision. Still, we do know that, in ancient Egypt, as nowadays among the Egyptians, the Abyssinians, many Eastern races, and even in West Africa, clitoridectomy is practised on the young girls and that the Somalis' cruel rite of infibulation, preceded by ablation of the labia minora and clitoris, results moreover in sealing the vagina which can only be opened again by the husband's flint or knife or penis.

Whereas, however, since Freud, we more or less understand the significance of male circumcision, which may be seen as a milder form of cultural castration, a sort of reduction of the punishment for incestuous desires, a ransom, in fact, accompanied by many rites, which is generally paid at puberty, and which allows the young males to enter the world of adults and their sex-life, we are less certain about the significance of the mutilation of young girls.

The excision of the clitoris, which many tribes practise, seemed to Freud a way of seeking to further *feminize* the female by removing this cardinal vestige of her masculinity. Such operations, as he once said to me, must be intended to complete the *biological castration* of the female which Nature, in the eyes of these tribes, has not sufficiently effected.[1]

---

[1] Compare these practices on the female with that of ablation of the male nipple in certain tribes. On this, Prof. Cerulli wrote to me as follows: "The tribes which practise ablation of the male nipple are the Djanjero who inhabit the high valley of the Omo

Freud also said that the same tendency towards further feminization of woman, but displaced on the foot—a frequent phallic symbol, especially with fetishists—might be found in the Chinese practice of crushing and shrivelling the girls' feet, often the very girls who, from early childhood, had had the vagina opened by the mother's quasi-ritualistic cleansings, with the result that in certain regions there were no longer any "virgins".[1]

However, given the over-determination of these practices, we may ask ourselves how far other trends than the wish to maximally feminize women may have dictated such rituals.

In his *Neger Eros*, Felix Bryk takes almost the same view as Freud.

On the other hand, when certain peoples are asked why they practise clitoridectomy, the reply most generally given is that it is customary. Yet we are sometimes told that it is intended either to remove something "ugly" or to curb the licentiousness of the girls. Here, clitoridectomy would appear as a sort of "cultural" castration inflicted for their own benefit, as the girls' owners, by the fathers, the husbands of the tribe.

Possibly all these motives are simultaneously at work. But another problem than that of the motive for clitoridectomy arises, for, though we should like to know *why* primitives practise excision, we should no less like to know its physiological, functional result, as well as its psycho-sexual effects.

Is its motivation mainly biological; was Freud right? Is the male, in excising that phallic vestige, the clitoris, principally

[1] Ploss and Bartels. *Das Weib* (1884).

Bottego, details in regard to whom I gave in my *Etiopia Occidentale*, Vol. II, p. 13–23 (and chart, *le Populazione ed il Languagio dell' Etiopia*, attached to Vol. I). The Djanjero whom I questioned on the subject of their custom of cutting the breasts, told me: 'We do this because we do not wish to resemble women in any way.' The French traveller, Borelli, who explored Southern Ethiopia, noted on 2nd January, 1888, in his diary: 'My Zingero has returned with a compatriot who, like him, has his breasts cut. Both assured me yet again that it is a general practice inspired by scorn for women: A man should not resemble them in anything, they both say.' This is almost word for word the reply they gave me forty years later."

concerned to achieve the utmost "feminization" of the woman and, by thus burning her boats, to force her libido to take the vaginal path, now the only one left to it? We should then need to know whether such operations were generally crowned with success. Are African women more frequently, and better, "vaginalized" than their European sisters, or even than the still more primitive Australian aborigine, for instance, who retains the clitoris? One sees how vast a field must be covered before we can give a reply. But none of the necessary information is so far available; no ethnologist, to my knowledge, has sought it out.

It will be said that numberless whites have had sexual relations with excised women. I myself, indeed, have met many. Their evidence as regards such women's erotic response, however, is contradictory: according to some, they are completely frigid, while others endow them with internalized response. The truth is that such testimony lacks any objective worth, for the male is not a trustworthy observer as regards his partners' erotism, doubtless because, at such times, he lacks the detachment necessary for scientific observation and, also, because woman, always and everywhere, is the great Dissembler, the supreme Liar, and one far from disinterested, given the fact that where sexual pleasure is not shared, the male demands its simulacrum.

Now, self-evident though it seems, it is worth emphasizing that any "behaviourist" study of the female orgasm must always give uncertain results, unlike the case of the male orgasm. No man can really pretend to ejaculate; he cannot simulate erection and at most we would need his testimony to appraise the quality of his pleasure. With woman, however, even though we are able to note clitoridal erection, we can never very positively infer a clitoridal orgasm from her behaviour. As to orgasms of vaginal origin, it is even less possible to vouch for them from the purely "behaviourist" viewpoint, for any contractions that accompany it may also have been present before. The same confusion may arise for the two kinds of orgasm, as regards the secretions discharged by the glands of Bartholin, which may precede it. It is for that reason that, to understand the female orgasm and woman's general erotic reactions, we are forced, far more than with man, to take the unavoidable detour of psychology; women must be persuaded to talk and to talk truly. This requirement will apply to every woman, to the white woman of our civilization as much as to the excised black. But though the white has at last surrendered some of her secrets through psycho-analysis, the black, so far, has not.

The latter, no doubt, will talk only to women, intimidated as she is by the male, whose slave she has more or less been throughout the ages. How much more then will she fear a stranger of the white race? Much preliminary work would be needed to gain her confidence, and establish that prime condition of a "positive transference". It is a task for which knowledge of the native tongue would be indispensable. Also, we should need to be able to judge, from external gynaecological examination, whether the excision be total or partial, and to compare functional response with anatomical changes. For this purpose, two women researchers would doubtless be best, given the difficulty of the task and its anthropological, linguistic, gynaecological and psycho-analytic requirements.

Meanwhile, we may perhaps conjecture what results such an inquiry would give, though bearing in mind that this is all hypothetical. Apart from instances where the glans clitoris is not completely excised, instances in which it might retain some degree of specific response, I think it likely that the functional, physiological and biological results of the excision cannot always be the same. For, according as to whether the primitive female innately, and through her earliest experiences (these less determinant, says Freud, in the less repressed primitives than among us) is more or less bisexual, these results must differ.

In the vaginals, excision would not be likely to change much and they would retain orgastic capacity. In clitoridals, depending on the strength of the clitoridal libidinal cathexis, the result should be either complete suppression of external orgastic capacity, with no libidinal vaginal gain, or no change at all.

In support of the latter possibility, let me recall the oft cited instance of the clitoridectomy practised in Europe to remedy excessive infantile or pubertal masturbation. We know that, for fifty years, European surgeons did not hesitate to resort to it at times. Yet the children and adolescents who underwent this operation, continued to masturbate as much after it as before. We might, of course, ask whether it ended in orgasm, remembering cases where nymphomania or masturbation continues for hours, just because it does not end in orgasm. I consider myself justified, however, in thinking that, with such confirmed masturbators, no change in orgastic capacity occurs, as a result of my observations in the following instance, the only case of excision I have so far been able to observe.

In 1929, at the neuro-psychiatric clinic of Leipzig, and thanks to the kindness of Drs. Weigel and Hupfer, I was able to observe a thirty-six year old woman who was afflicted with compulsive masturbation, repeated up to fifteen times a day. She was married and had herself asked to be cured. The nerves of the genital region had therefore been severed, the labia minora and clitoris abraded, and both Fallopian tubes and ovaries removed, which operations dated from at least two years before. She still, however, continued to masturbate just as frequently and compulsively on the scar of the glans clitoris, which she showed me, this being originally placed very high. She masturbated exactly where she had always done, with no diminution of "clitoridal" sensitivity and no gain of vaginal sensitivity which latter, in her marital relations, was almost completely lacking. Only twice, she said, had she experienced some slight pleasure in normal coitus and that only when slightly tipsy.

True, this case, with its striking testimony to the dominance of the "dynamic stereotyping" of the autonomous nervous system (this woman went on feeling her clitoris as cripples do their amputated leg or arm), constitutes an exception, due to the intensity and tenacious fixation of the libido. We may wonder whether, in constitutionally mixed clitoridal-vaginal cases, excision of the clitoris, depending on the degree of defiance or docility in the woman, contributes, or does not, to election of the vagina as the dominant erotogenic zone.

Let us now, however, consider the other aspect of this problem; not the physiological and functional success of excision, but its cultural results.

It seems to me very likely that in the more or less unconscious motives for excision, there is a factor tending to repress the feminine sexuality present. All over the world, something in the male wants the erotic partner to be as feminine as possible (whence the tendency to "feminize" the female by removing her small phallus). At the same time, however, something in the man wants his partner to be "chaste" and not to be driven to seek other embraces, whence arises the tendency to reduce female desire by excising the clitoris. And since this latter coincides with that which inspires the older women, who are jealous of the young, it is not strange that, in primitive races, the males find zealous females to practise the mutilations they prescribe.

Here a parallel seems to arise between our hypotheses anent the different ways in which primitive girls may react to clitoridectomy and the feminine types established by Freud according to the various ways our own little girls react to the castration complex.

To our group of the psychically *acceptive*, there would correspond those primitive girls who, as it were, have accepted reality excision; those in whom, whether innately or as part of their development, psycho-sexual involution of the clitoris and erotistic cathexis of the vagina had already occurred, those with a psycho-sexual acceptance of the female's *biological castration*, which excision, as it were, confirms. This would present us with very feminine women, either lovers or vaginal mothers; women content with their feminine lot whether, as with us, they retained a useless clitoris or, as in Africa, had lost what, to them, was a superfluous organ.

To the *renouncer* type of woman among us would correspond those primitive clitoridals who, after the removal of the tiny phallus, which thus completed Nature's cruel work in prejudicing them as compared with man, would renounce all erotic end-pleasure, despite the solicitations of the male which primitive women can less evade than obdurate virgins in our own society. Such women will have found ways of renouncing their erotism though forced, or constrained, to dispense pleasure to the male. Their nearest counterpart would be those total and persistently frigid women among us who, while not renouncing the male, at least renounce the clitoris without, however, gaining vaginal sensitivity.

The last category, that of the *claimers*, possessed of a strong masculinity complex, marked bisexuality and a stubborn clitoris, would be represented by those of the type of the "Leipzig woman" who, despite excision, would retain their erotogenic sensitivity phallically placed on the scar, their clitoridal libido, as it were, refusing to abdicate its phallic position and take the internal vaginal route. Thus despite, and even in defiance of, the ablation of the glans clitoris, an attitude analogous to that of the women who remain stubbornly clitoridal in our own civilization would be established.

If such be the case, the diverse fashions in which women react to the castration complex, reactions parallel in primitive women and our own, will be seen faithfully to reflect the dual nature of the feminine castration complex.

In the male, the castration complex is mainly cultural: it should not be biological for it does not imply actual exclusion of the phallus, against which the normal male must strongly protest. Thus, as regards ritual mutilations, the male has generally confined himself to mutilation of the prepuce or other modes which ensure continuation of the erotistic phallic function; this is the case even with the subincision of the aborigines of Central Australia.

In woman, however, the ritual mutilation is generally directed at the erotogenic organ itself since human excision of the female phallus but follows Nature which created it in stunted form. Nevertheless, a cultural significance must have been superimposed on this biological meaning of ritual mutilation, and the intention must be repression of sexual licence in women, as well as their additional feminization, which amounts to saying that the deepest, unconscious motives for excision reflect the dual nature of the feminine castration complex which, it must not be forgotten, though cultural, is also in reality biological.

In any case, an important principle seems to emerge from the comparative study of civilizations which, like ours, have abandoned ritual mutilation and those where it still obtains.

It would appear that humans, living in communities, cannot dispense with sexual repression of some kind and that, if it has not succeeded in coming from within, it must go on coming from without. Many problems still remain to be solved from the comparative study of primitive societies with our own; those, in particular, connected with the latency period. Is this totally absent in many tribes, as for instance, the Trobrianders of Malinowski? Such examples might give us a closer insight into instinctual human development than those taken from nearer home.

It would seem, however, that the sexual freedom of children, certainly greater among primitives than with us, is overtaken at puberty, and sometimes before—unlike what happens among the Trobrianders— by the traumatic effects of ritual mutilation, whether circumcision, excision, or substitute forms like the knocked-out tooth of some Australian tribes. Only then does the boy become adult and enter the men's group; and only when the woman is branded with the feminine sign of the tribe is she considered worthy of marriage.

In proportion, however, as cultures progress, such ritual mutilations are thrust ever further backwards into the individual's ontogenetic history: Abyssinians and Jews are circumcised a few days after birth, and the excision of Abyssinian girls takes place equally early. It is as though the mark of a real intimidation gradually faded into a mere symbol, before totally disappearing, as with us.

In our society, apart from the ritual Jewish circumcision or occasional circumcision for medical reasons, males and females grow up anatomically intact. This integrity vanishes, however, if we pass to the psychical domain, for it is here that our civilizations practise their "mutilations". The sexual instinct, together indeed with the aggressive instinct, suffers very early mutilation through our educative prohibitions regarding masturbation, in particular, prohibitions of which the primitive child knows nothing. As a result, highly civilized and intellectualized though our rising generations may sometimes be, we also find them desexualized in equal degree, which thus gives rise to diverse neuroses which march parallel with sexual disturbances of functional origin, such as the many degrees of male impotence and the different kinds of feminine frigidity.

Thus, from the primitive to ourselves or, rather, from our

ancestors to ourselves (for contemporary primitives, with as long, though a different, chain of development, are but our cousins), we see the evolutionary path along which morality has travelled for, originating first in the external repression imposed by the fierce hands of the father and the strong, it has gradually become, by internalization, our moral conscience. It is no longer externally clamorous and brutal but is just as fierce and inescapable, for we carry it everywhere with us.

III

NATURE AND CULTURE

OBSERVATION OF the excised females of primitive tribes should provide many an interesting answer for if, among them, as I imagine, we were to find *acceptives*, *renouncers* and *claimers*, their relative proportions would surely be significant.

Also given the fact that, apart from excision, primitive girls are generally allowed far more sexual liberty than ours, if the proportions are analogous to those encountered in our society, functional sexual disturbances in women would then need to be first referred to natural causes since, teleologically, Nature appears to have bothered far less with the female's erotic function than the male's, to whom fertilization is entrusted. One may indeed wonder, to take the creature closest to hand and, for instance, observe the bitch when coupling, whether Nature was much concerned to secure erotic satisfaction for the female.

Is, then, the proportion of *acceptives*, though excised, greater among primitives than with us: are their women more often vaginal, more easily satisfied than ours, following the belief which credits the negress, the primitive woman, with being more sensual than the white? In that case we should have valuable evidence in the charge we might justly bring against our culture.

Male potency disturbances, however, according to most ethnologists and explorers, seem less frequent among primitives than with us. If disturbances of the feminine erotic function are also less frequent, then the total frigidities, and the frigidities most markedly bisexual in appearance, as well as the reinforcement of the feminine masculinity complex which engenders them, will appear as principally conditioned by a regression deriving from our cultural moral prohibitions which overtakes feminine sexuality during the course of its development. In that case, primitive woman would owe her greater normality less to the fact that more freedom is allowed infantile masturbation than to the fact that, far earlier than with us, where girls are better protected, she becomes a prey to "seduction", i.e. to the normal, vaginal enterprise of the boys and men.

The importance of all this will be realized if we consider what problems the study of feminine sexuality in general, and woman's erotic response in particular, which expresses it in different cultures, will permit us to answer; nothing less, in fact, than the respective values of biological or cultural factors in conditioning human sexuality and that, not only in its degree of intensity, but also in its more or less bisexual orientation.

We may in fact ask ourselves in what direction our species is moving: towards a greater or less degree of sexual differentiation? The theory propounded by Marañon, for instance, in his *The Evolution of Sex and Intersexual Conditions* rests on the progressive differentiation of the sexes from hermaphroditism to gonochorism, as one ascends the biological scale, according to which the male tends to become more and more male as the female more and more female. From the purely biological point of view it may doubtless be so, but man's purely biological evolution has been strangely hampered by his civilizing processes.

Nor are we the only species whose sexual development is disturbed by social progress, for many hymenoptera, whether termites, bees or ants, have only raised their communities on the sexual repression of their soldiers, or male or female workers. With them, the social burden of the community is mainly borne by an all-but asexual type of female, since sexual specialization is reserved to the queen and males, which latter are mostly superfluous.

True, humanity itself could never resort to such means to solve the antagonism between work and sex, given the relative infecundity of woman. Nevertheless, as we have seen, some resemblance to what we find in the hive or anthill is suggested by the atrophied sex life of the many *renouncers*, women who hold themselves aloof from all true object-sexuality, while remaining otherwise socially useful.

As for the others, males and females who have not renounced

sexuality, we may ask what direction their libido will take as civilization progresses; whether towards a greater or lesser sexual differentiation?

According to what Dr. Rudolph Loewenstein, who is also interested in these problems, told me, to go by psycho-analytic observation, sexual differentiation in the West appears, in general, to be decreasing, the woman becoming less frankly female and the male less frankly male. In support of this, he cites, in fact, the cultural frequency of potency disturbances in the male and of clitoridal fixation in the female.

As regards primitive societies, the counterpart of these facts still remains to be established but, given the picture we see of our own civilization, I incline to think that it will rather favour a regressive undifferentiation than a continuing sexual differentiation.

Most striking of all is the progressive masculinization of woman, women often aspiring to, and succeeding in, becoming the male's equal in many tasks. Is a sexual masculinization the corollary of that social masculinization to which, in fact, the so-frequent clitoridal fixation of the white woman would be the physiological witness?

This opinion, contrary to Marañon's predictions, nevertheless conforms to other of his views for, does he not, throughout his book on intersexual conditions, write that virility is *progressive* and femininity *regressive*? The progressive social masculinization of woman would thus, biologically, find a favouring factor.

Also, since women remain the boys' educators and, as Abraham has so well shown, a mother's over-strong, active castration complex disturbs her son's psycho-sexual development, it should not surprise us to find such boys often inhibited in their masculinity, thus causing them to regress to a certain femininity which then links up with their own masculinity.

Nevertheless, and thanks indeed to psycho-analysis, the first science to venture to study human psycho-sexuality, to comprehend and accept it, we may hope that this tendency in civilization to regress to the primary bisexuality of the individual may find a corrective.

Not only the psycho-analysis of adults but, above all, that

of children, should be able to direct sexuality proper into normal channels. Indeed, the nervous system largely controls the adaptation of organisms, in a given environment, to their function.

But though woman will oftener, and better, succeed in adapting her organism to its erotic function, and in achieving full satisfaction in her relations with the male, whether as wife or even as mother, it need not therefore imply the renunciation of all social and intellectual activity.

Though Marañon has so truly written "woman encounters either the obstacle of maternity, which blocks her intellectual progress, or the obstacle of sterility, which is a bar to the transmission of any progress", humanity, fortunately, does not always have to accept such extremes. The main thing here, not always easy, one must admit, is, as Freud once said to me, "for woman to know where to apply her masculinity appropriately".

II

PASSIVITY, MASOCHISM AND FEMININITY

PASSIVITY, MASOCHISM AND FEMININITY[1]

I. *The Pain Inherent in the Female Reproductive Functions*

THE MOST superficial observer cannot help noting that in the sphere of reproduction the lot of men and of women, in respect of pain suffered, is an unequal one. The man's share in the reproductive functions is confined to a single act —that of coitus—which he necessarily experiences as pleasurable, since, for him, the function of reproduction coincides with the erotic function. The woman, on the other hand, periodically undergoes the suffering of menstruation, the severity of which varies with the individual; for her, sexual intercourse itself is initiated by a process which involves in some degree the shedding of her blood, namely, the act of defloration; finally, gestation is accompanied by discomfort and parturition by pain, while even lactation is frequently subject to painful disturbances.

Already in the Bible[2] woman is marked out for the pain of childbearing, the punishment for original sin. Michelet[3] describes her as *"l'éternelle blessée"* ("the everlastingly wounded one"). And, in psycho-analytical literature, Freud,[4] discussing the problem of masochism, that bewildering product of human psychosexuality, characterizes it, in its erotogenic form, as "feminine", while Helene Deutsch[5] regards it as a constant factor in female development and as an indispensable constituent in woman's acceptance of the whole of her sexuality, intermingled, as it is, with so much pain.

---

[1] Based on a paper read before the Thirteenth International Psycho-Analytical Congress, Lucerne, August, 1934; originally entitled "Du masochisme féminin essentiel". Published in *Int. J. Psycho-Anal.* **16**, 1935.
[2] Genesis iii. 16.
[3] *L'Amour* (1858).
[4] "The Economic Problem in Masochism" (1924).
[5] "The Significance of Masochism in the Mental Life of Women" (1930).

II. Erotic Pleasure in Women

There is, however, another fact no less striking even to a superficial observer. In sexual relations women are often capable of a high degree of erotic pleasure; they crave for caresses, it may be of the whole body or of some particular zone, and in these caresses the element of suffering, of masochism, is entirely and essentially absent. Moreover, in actual copulation the woman can experience pleasurable orgasm analogous to that of the man.

Of course, in this connection we must bear in mind that biological fact which, for that matter, many biologists seem not to know, although Freud has accurately appraised its importance; namely, that in women, as contrasted with men, there are two adjacent erotogenic zones—the clitoris and the vagina—which reflect and confirm the bisexuality inherent in every woman. In some instances there is an open antagonism between the two zones, with the result that the woman's genital erotism becomes centred exclusively either in the vagina or in the clitoris, with, in the latter case, vaginal anaesthesia. In other instances, and I think these are the more common, the two zones settle into harmonious collaboration, enabling her to perform her erotic function in the normal act of copulation.

Nevertheless, woman's share in sexual pleasure seems to be derived from whatever virility the female organism contains. The Spanish biologist, Marañon, was in the right when he compared woman to a male organism arrested in its development, half-way between the child and the man—arrested, that is to say, precisely by the inhibitory influence exercised by the apparatus of maternity, which is subjoined to and exists in a kind of symbiosis side by side with the rest of her delicate organism.

The residue of virility in the woman's organism is utilized by Nature in order to eroticize her: otherwise the functioning of the maternal apparatus would wholly submerge her in the painful tasks of reproduction and motherhood.

On the one hand, then, in the reproductive functions proper—menstruation, defloration, pregnancy and parturition

—woman is biologically doomed to suffer. Nature seems to have no hesitation in administering to her strong doses of pain, and she can do nothing but submit passively to the regimen prescribed. On the other hand, as regards sexual attraction, which is necessary for the act of impregnation, and as regards the erotic pleasure experienced during the act itself, the woman may be on equal footing with the man. It must be added, however, that the feminine erotic function is often imperfectly and tardily established and that, owing to the woman's passive role in copulation, it always depends— and this is a point which we must not forget—upon the potency of her partner and especially upon the time which he allows for her gratification, which is usually achieved more slowly than his own.

III. *The Infantile Sadistic Conception of Coitus*

Let us now go back to the childhood situation.

Psycho-analytical observations have proved beyond any doubt that when, as often happens, a child observes the coitus of adults, he invariably perceives the sexual act as an act of sadistic aggression perpetrated by the male upon the female —an act primarily of an oral character, as little children so conceive it, because the only relations between one human being and another of which they have at first any knowledge are of an oral nature. But, seeing how early the cannibalistic phase occurs, it seems certain that this *oral* relation is itself conceived of as aggressive. Nevertheless, it so frequently happens that the child is in the anal-sadistic phase when he makes these observations that his predominating impression is that of an attack made by the male upon the female, in which she is wounded and her body penetrated. Having regard to the primitive fusion of instincts we may perhaps say that the earlier these observations occur the more marked is the sadistic tinge which they assume in the child's mind. In his perception of the acts of adults the degree of his own aggressiveness, which varies with the individual child, must also play a decisive part, being projected on to what he sees.

In the mind of a child who has witnessed the sexual act the impressions received form, as it were, a stereotyped picture which persists in the infantile unconscious. As he develops and his ego becomes more firmly established, this picture is modified and worked over, and doubtless there are added to it all the sado-masochistic phantasies[1] which analysis has brought to light in children of both sexes.

The very early observations of coitus, made when the child was still in the midst of the sadistic-cloacal and sadistic-phallic phases (which, indeed, often overlap), were effected in the first instance with partial object-cathexes relating to the *organs* which children covet to gratify their libidinal and sadistic impulses. Little by little, however, the whole being of the man and of the woman becomes more clearly defined as male or female, and the difference between the sexes is at last recognized.

Thereafter, the destiny and influence of the infantile sadistic phantasies will differ with the sex of the child. The sadistic conception of coitus in boys, the actual possessors of the penetrating penis, will evade the centripetal cloacal danger and tend to take a form which is centrifugal and vital and which involves no immediate danger to their own organism. Of course it will subsequently come into collision with the *moral* barriers erected by civilization against human aggressiveness, with the castration complex especially; but the oedipal defusion of instincts through which the boy's aggression is diverted to his father, while the greater part of his love goes to his mother, is of considerable assistance to him in distinguishing sadism from activity and subsequently orientating his penis—active but no longer sadistic—in the direction of women.

In girls, the sadistic conception of coitus, when strongly emphasized, is much more likely to disturb ideal erotic development. The time comes when the little girl compares her own genitals with the large penis of the adult male, and inevitably she draws the conclusion that she has been castrated. The consequence is that not only is her narcissism mortified by her

[1] Cf. especially Melanie Klein, *The Psycho-Analysis of Children*, (1932).

castration but also, in her sexual relations with men, the possessors of the penis which henceforth her eroticism covets, she is haunted by the dread that her body will undergo some fearful penetration.

Now every living organism dreads invasion from without, and this is a dread bound up with life itself and governed by the biological law of self-preservation.

Moreover, not only do little girls hear talk or whispers about the sufferings of childbirth and catch sight, somehow or other, of menstrual blood: they also bear imprinted on their minds from earliest childhood the terrifying vision of a sexual attack by a man upon a woman, which they believe to be the cause of the bleeding. It follows therefore that, in spite of the instinct which urges them forward, they draw back from the feminine erotic function itself, although of all the reproductive functions of woman this is the only one which should really be free from suffering and purely pleasurable.[1]

IV. *The Necessary Fundamental Distinction between Masochism and Passivity*

As the little girl grows up, her reactions to the primal scene become more pronounced in one direction or another, according to the individual case, the determining factors being, on the one hand, her childhood experiences and, on the other, her constitutional disposition.

---

[1] In my opinion this primitive drawing back is a motion of the *vital ego* and not primarily, as Melanie Klein holds, that of a precocious *moral super-ego*. In this connection my view agrees more nearly with that of Karen Horney, though I differ from her on another point, namely, the constitutional phallic element—what I should term the bisexuality—in the nature of women. Cf. Melanie Klein, *The Psycho-Analysis of Children*, quoted earlier in this paper, and Karen Horney, "The Flight from Womanhood" (1926), and "The Denial of the Vagina" (1933). The outbreak of rage to be observed in so many children, when an attempt is made to give them an enema, is, I believe, to be explained as the defence set up by this same instinct of self-preservation against penetration of their bodies. This seems to me much more probable than that it is the expression of a kind of orgasm, as Freud holds (no doubt with some justice in certain cases), following Ruth Mack Brunswick. (Freud, "Female Sexuality" (1931).)

In the first place, there is bound to be a distinct difference between the reactions of a little girl who has actually witnessed the coitus of adults and those of a little girl who has fallen back upon phylogenetic phantasies, based on her inevitable observations of the copulation of animals. It seems that the severity of the traumatic shock is in proportion to the earliness of the period in which the child observes human coitus and to the actuality of what she observes.

Above all, however, the violence of the little girl's recoil from the sexual aggression of the male will depend on the degree of her constitutional bisexuality and the extent of the biological bases of her masculinity complex. Where both these factors are marked, she will react in very much the same way as a little boy, whose reaction, since he also is bisexual, will be likewise of the cloacal type, though very soon his vital phallic rejection of the passive, cloacal attitude will turn his libido into the convex, centrifugal track of masculinity.

For there are only two main modes of reaction to the sadistic conception of coitus harboured by the little girl's unconscious mind throughout childhood and right up to adult life. Either she must accept it and, in this case, in order to bind masochistically her passive aggression there must be an admixture of eros equivalent to the danger which, she feels, threatens her very existence. Or else, as the years pass and her knowledge of reality increases, she must recognize that the penetrating penis is neither a whip nor an awl nor a knife nor a cartridge (as in her sadistic, infantile phantasies) and must dissociate passive coitus from the other feminine reproductive functions (menstruation, pregnancy, parturition); she must accept it as the only act which is really purely pleasurable, in sharp contrast to the dark background of feminine suffering, an act in which libido—that biological force of masculine extraction—is deflected to feminine aims, always passive but here not normally masochistic.

It is true that in woman's acceptance of her role there may be a slight tincture—a homoeopathic dose, so to speak—of masochism, and this, combining with her passivity in coitus, impels her to welcome and to value some measure of brutality on the man's part. Martine declared that she wished "to be beaten". But a real distinction between masochism and passivity must be established in the feminine psyche if her passive erotic function is to be normally accepted upon a firm basis. Actually, normal vaginal coitus does not hurt a woman: quite the contrary.

If, however, in childhood, when she is brought up against the sadistic conception of coitus, she has, if I may so put it, voted for the first solution, namely, a masochism which includes within its scope passivity in copulation, it by no means follows that she will accept the masochistic erotization of the vagina in coitus. Often the dose of masochism is in that case too strong for the vital ego, and it is a fact that even those women in whom the masochistic perversion is very pronounced often shun penetration and content themselves with being beaten on the buttocks, regarding this as a more harmless mode of aggression since only the outer surface of the body is concerned.

The vital, biological ego protests against and takes flight from masochism in general and may establish very powerful hypercathexes of the libido's defensive positions.

V. The Cloaca and the Phallus in Women

At this point we must remind ourselves that in females there are two erotogenic zones and that woman is bisexual in a far higher degree than man.

Earlier in this paper I quoted the views of the Spanish biologist, Marañon, who holds that a woman is a man whose development has been arrested, a sort of adolescent to whose organism is subjoined, in a kind of symbiosis, the apparatus of maternity, which is responsible for the check in development.

In woman the external sexual organs, or, more correctly, the erotogenic organs, appear to reflect her twofold nature. A woman, in fact, possesses a cloaca, divided by the recto-vaginal septum into the anus and the specifically feminine vagina, the gateway to the additional structure of the maternal apparatus, and a phallus, atrophied in comparison with the male penis—the little clitoris.

How do these two zones react, on the one hand to the little

girl's constitution and, on the other, to the experiences which exercise a formative influence upon her psycho-sexuality?

There are various stages and phases[1] in libidinal development. The oral phase is succeeded by the sadistic-anal phase which, in view of the anatomical fact of the existence of the vagina in little girls, I should prefer to call the sadistic-cloacal phase.

There is, therefore, a cavity (as yet, no doubt, imperfectly differentiated in the child's mind) which in the little girl's sadistic conception of coitus is penetrated in a manner highly dangerous. (The little boy, for his part, arguing from his own physical structure, often recognizes the existence of the anus only.) Consequently, when coitus is observed at this early age, the result is the mobilization, firstly, of the erotic wish for the penis, coveted by the oral and cloacal libidinal components, and, secondly, of the dread of penetration which wounds and is to be feared.

Before long, however, the phallic phase, which is a regular stage in the biological development of both sexes, is reached by little girls, as by little boys, being accompanied in the former by clitoridal masturbation. Doubtless, at this period, masturbation is not confined exclusively to the clitoris but is extended in a greater or lesser degree to the vulva and the entrance to the adjacent vagina. How far this is so depends on the individual and on the amount of her constitutional femininity (her pre-feminine, erotogenic cloacality).

At this point, however, through a confusion of passivity with masochism, the little girl may take fright and reject her passive role. The dread of male aggression may be too strong, the admixture of masochism already present too great, or too potent a dose of it may be required to bind and accept the dread. When this is the case, her ego draws back and her eroticism will cling, so to speak, to the clitoris. The process is something like that of fixing a lightning-conductor to a house in order to prevent its being struck: the electricity (in this case, the child's eroticism) is diverted into a channel in which it does not endanger life.

[1] Freud, *Three Essays on the Theory of Sexuality* (1905); Abraham, "A Short Study of the Development of the Libido" (1924).

Thus a sort of *convex erotic engram,* upon which her erotic function as a woman will be modelled, is set up in opposition to the *concave erotic engram* which is properly that of the female in coitus.

Now the convex orientation of libido is the very direction taken by the eroticism of the male, as he develops anatomically, and, further, the erotogenic, centrifugal orientation of the penis. Consequently, such an orientation of libido in a woman is highly suggestive of a considerable degree of constitutional masculinity. Here, passivity being more or less inextricably confused with erotogenic masochism, its *vital* (self-preservative) rejection and its *masculine* rejection coincide. *Moral* repression, on the other hand, which has its source in educational influences and is maintained by the super-ego, tends to attack feminine sexuality as a whole, without discrimination of its specifically vaginal or clitoridal character, and, when carried to its extreme, tends to result in total frigidity.

Nevertheless the phallus itself, an organ essentially male even when it goes by the name of the clitoris, can be used for ends which are, at bottom, feminine.

It is true that the clitoris, the rudimentary phallus, is never destined to achieve, even in its owner's imagination, the degree of activity to which the penis can lay claim, for in this respect the male organ is far better endowed by Nature. The clitoris, like the little boy's penis, is first aroused when the mother is attending to the child's toilet, the experience being a passive one. Normally the clitoris, after passing through an active phase, should have a stronger tendency than the penis to revert to passivity: the little girl's biological castration complex paves the way for her regression. Next, when her positive Oedipus complex is established, with its orientation to the father, the clitoris readily becomes the instrument of those libidinal desires whose aim is passive. And this prepares the way for the clitoridal-vaginal erotic function by means of which, in so many women, the two zones fulfil harmoniously their passive role in coitus and which is opposed to the functional maladjustment of women of the clitoridal type, in whom the phallus is too highly charged with active impulses.

From the biological standpoint, nevertheless, the ideal

adaptation of woman to her erotic function involves the functional suppression of the active, and even of the passive, clitoris in favour of the vagina, whose role is that of purely passive reception. But in order that the vital ego may accept this erotic passivity, which is specifically and essentially feminine, a woman, when she reaches full maturity, must as far as possible have rid herself of the infantile fear which has its origin in the sadistic conception of coitus and from the defensive reactions against the possibility of masochism which are to be traced to the same source.

III

SOME PALAEOBIOLOGICAL AND BIOPSYCHICAL REFLECTIONS

SOME PALAEOBIOLOGICAL AND BIOPSYCHICAL REFLECTIONS[1]

I. *The Castration Complex and the Perforation Complex*

PSYCHO-ANALYSIS HAS long recognized the importance of the phallic castration complex in men, and also in women, in whom it generates penis-envy. The phantasies of being ripped open which have been so effectively demonstrated by Melanie Klein seem to me to form a counterpart, in every respect as significant, in the psycho-sexual make-up of women.

But, as I have indicated in a previous communication,[2] I differ from Melanie Klein on a point of fundamental importance in holding that the source of the little girl's anxiety connected with her fear of being penetrated, perforated or ripped open is something anterior to and independent of a super-ego in any shape or form.

II. *The Primitive Fear of Irruption into the Protoplasm*

I believe that the biological reaction of fear manifested by an organism in the face of what may be described in very general terms as penetration or irruption into its own substance, is something extremely primitive.

Let us try to imagine for a moment a mass of primal protoplasm. Surrounded and threatened from every quarter by hostile forces this primitive organism must defend itself against these dangers if it is to survive at all. But what forms do these threats and dangers take? There is the danger of desiccation; or the danger of solid objects of greater strength penetrating into the substance and even destroying it. We may suppose that the tiny protoplasmic mass will, in virtue of life's

---

[1] Read before the Fourteenth International Psycho-Analytical Congress, Marienbad, 1936. Published in *Int. J. Psycho-Anal.* **19**, 1938.

[2] "Passivity, Masochism and Femininity" (1935).

mysterious powers of adaptation to environment, have had to learn to react with some signal to the external dangers which threaten it. It will surround itself with a protective membrane against desiccation; it will draw back or take to flight from solid objects which threaten to penetrate it.

This defence, this garrisoning of the "sacred frontiers of the body", persists throughout the increasing complexity of organic life. Every living organism from the lowliest microbe to the mammals recoils before anything which threatens to force its way inside its body.

III. Penetration and Nutrition

Nevertheless living organisms cannot survive without penetration by the outside world: exchanges must occur in connection with the acts of respiration and nutrition, accompanied by the constant anabolism and katabolism which are of the very essence of life. And so the organism will also have had to learn to absorb what is beneficial to it while avoiding penetration by injurious substances. It has to look for the necessities of existence in the world surrounding it, to possess itself of foreign substances which it can assimilate, and indeed more often than not this means that it must kill in order to live itself. The digestive juices enable it to "bind" or assimilate by osmosis the foreign bodies penetrating it and to make them part of itself.

Moreover a sure sign that the nutritional impulse has been satisfied is a feeling of pleasure; oral-erotism, in virtue of which living creatures derive enjoyment from oral ingestion, is its ally. The elimination of substance can itself be a source of vital pleasure, and anal and urethral erotism give appropriate expression to the satisfaction of an organism whose digestive system is functioning as it should.

IV. The Antagonism between the Individual and the Species

From the very beginning of living substance, however, it was impossible for the protoplasm to remain, as such, in security unless it refrained from perpetuating itself. For the individual is ephemeral and the absolute narcissism of the earliest cells would have brought the beginnings of life to an early close. The cells, the earliest individual entities, must multiply if the dynamism of life is not to fail. At this point the fissiparity of cells originated, and the productive union of two cells prior to fission.

I have no desire to endow the cells at this early stage with a psychology. But, if it is granted that man must psychologize his thoughts before he can make his meaning understood, I shall consider myself justified in maintaining that these primitive acts leading to reproduction must already have been felt biologically as in some sense a wound to the cell's primitive narcissism. The antagonism between the integrity of the individual and the perpetuation of the species was already operative at the early palaeobiological stages we are trying to visualize.

V. Penetration and Disintegration: Perforation Complex and Castration Complex

In reality two dangers threaten the cell in the process of reproduction. On the one hand, the conjugation of two cells implies the penetration of one substance by another which remains active and alive and has not, as happens in nutrition, first been rendered innocuous by the digestive juices and its prior death. And, on the other hand, the act of fission involves a disintegration of the substance which if continued would result in its annihilation.

Now I think that the substance is biologically aware of these two dangers, that they are transmitted throughout the whole course of evolution down to man himself and that they thus constitute the most primitive sources both of the perforation complex and the castration complex which we discover at work in women and in men.

The fear of *penetration* of the protoplasm is reflected in the dread of penetration felt by so many virgins and is no doubt at the root of many cases of frigidity in women. It can provide the foundation of the imposing edifice (to which all the accretions of the super-ego contribute) which we know under the form of symptoms.

The fear of *disintegration* of the protoplasm would in turn be found to underlie the castration complex. In order to perpetuate its existence every individual must abandon a part of its substance which becomes detached from it. But the narcissistic integrity of the substance suffers in consequence. And this narcissistic aversion to fission, transferred to the executive and representative organ of procreation, can serve as the foundation of the castration complex, with all the accretions derived from phylogenetic and ontogenetic experiences.

VI. *Libidinal Erotism and Vital Anxiety*

Certainly the erotic impulsion, which prompts the individual to seek biological pleasure—this pleasure being a sign that its vital instincts are satisfied—soon seems to place itself at the disposal of the aspirations of the species. The irruption of one living creature into another of its own species is distinguished by the organism from all other kinds of irruption. Even the cellular protoplasm, in the earliest phases of life as we have imagined them, must feel that it makes a difference whether its substance is penetrated by a kindred substance or (let us say) by a grain of sand. Some part of what it experiences in the course of feeding on other organic substances must play a part here: the primitive pleasure in nutrition invests in some degree the libidinal pleasure derived by the cell from its receptive activities prior to reproduction. But it is no less certain that beneath this process of eroticization something survives of the primitive fears which penetration holds for the substance.

Similarly there can be no denying the erotic pleasure the male obtains from expelling his seminal fluid, especially in the higher ranks of the animal kingdom. Did the first mass of protoplasm experience a biological foretaste of it at the moment of fissiparous division? I do not know. But no less undeniable than this pleasure found in the more advanced forms of animal life is the deep anxiety present in man at the idea of being separated from a part of himself, an anxiety always ready to rise to the surface and to give substance to the ubiquitous castration complex. The sudden fear which often attends the first ejaculation or loss of semen in adolescence would lend colour to these views.

VII. *Fear of Perforation the more General Fear*

If we survey the whole extent of the animal kingdom we shall see that in those species in which fertilization takes place internally, the females all exhibit in varying degrees a fear of the male. The castration complex in human beings seems to have few recognizable prototypes among animals; on the other hand something analogous to the perforation complex in women is found in many female mammals. One has only to observe the domestic animals around us. For example, some bitches actually refuse the male altogether and begin to tremble in what one might describe as a hysterical manner if an attempt is made to force them to submit.

And so in spite of the fact that in the course of cellular evolution certain ovules have developed a micropyle, a kind of primitive cellular "vagina" or channel for reception, and that female mammals have acquired a definitely receptive vagina, sexual penetration by the male continues to be regarded as a formidable irruption even by females which, like the bitch, have no hymen but simply a contraction of the genital canal between the vulva and the vagina.

But here we are concerned with the perforation complex in women, and in them the hymen is fully formed. Accordingly their fear of sexual penetration, which finds expression in the terrifying sadistic form of the perforation complex, does not rest merely upon a palaeobiological cellular foundation but upon a present-day anatomical reality, renewed in every virgin.

The male mammal on the other hand seems to show a more spirited reaction to the disintegration of his substance in sexual discharge than does the female to penetration. Generous and aggressive, he may go so far as to dissipate for a time the major part of his vital energies, as stags will during the rutting season. Doubtless the centrifugal, i.e. male, sexual impulsion is more in accordance with the original direction of life, which aims at expansion and the conquest of ever wider territories in which to find scope for its energies.

We need not be surprised then, when we turn to the human race, if we find that women react with anxiety and terror to their sexuality far more often than do men. And not without reason. Sexuality in mammals quite generally implies for the female an internal violation of her substance, a violation prolonged by reason of gestation and followed by disruption in the process of giving birth. It is therefore more dangerous for her than for the male and really deserves to be feared more.

It would be interesting to discover the relation between sexuality and anxiety in the male of the bee, the praying mantis and the spider, for whom love brings death.

VIII. *Anxiety always a Reaction to Objective Danger*

And this brings me to some reflections on the nature of anxiety in general. The problem, which occupies a central position alike in psychology and in physiology, has already been discussed many times.

Just as the anxiety women feel on account of their sexuality (leaving aside the question of a more repressive attitude on the part of society) seems to be objectively founded, so all anxiety must in the last instance, or rather in the first instance, have been at one time objectively founded.

Anxiety is a signal of vital danger. And, even if we adopt the classification favoured by Anna Freud in her recent book[1] and distinguish three principal types of anxiety, we are nevertheless still able to find a common denominator for all these three types in the organism's reaction to an objective danger.

So far as regards the *objective* anxiety of Anna Freud's classification, it is self-evident that this emanates from an objective danger and that the danger-signal, which is what it really is, is justified. *Moral* anxiety is the internalized anxiety which the child feels before his educator or the criminal before his judge, for very definite objective reasons. Lastly, *instinctual* anxiety seems to have an entirely objective or social basis if we regard it as a reaction to the danger of giving way to crime, with punishment as a corollary.

[1] *The Ego and the Mechanisms of Defence*, (1936).

Even the most manifestly neurotic anxiety can be reduced to a reaction originally inspired by an objective danger. Let us take for example a phobia of spiders. The spiders in our part of the world are not particularly dangerous. But when we reflect that spiders are a more or less widespread symbol of a "bad mother" we shall recognize that the dread experienced by those who suffer from a phobia of spiders had a very real basis in the early history both of the individual and of the race. Bad mothers are a serious danger to their children, as witness even in our own day the cases of illtreated children which are reported in the Press. And this anxiety of a bad mother which was once justified objectively has only become neurotic because it has persisted at a stage when the mother is no longer to be feared and has been displaced and localized where the fear is no longer relevant—thus constituting a dual disorder of the preconscious categories of time and space.

Let us revert, however, to Anna Freud's conception of instinctual anxiety. She treats it as a reaction to the perception of instinct regarded as a danger in itself. But from the palaeobiological standpoint which we are trying to describe, we can also justify it, without denying it its significance as a reaction to an objective danger.

Anna Freud surmises that the topographical ego is afraid of the instincts in the id which threaten to overwhelm it; hence the acute anxiety of childhood and adolescence when the balance of power between the ego and the instincts is weighted in favour of the latter. I think that this view is quite correct, but we may supplement it with the conception derived from our palaeobiological theme.

Bleuler[1] had already spoken, in somewhat confused terms to be sure, of man's fear of his sexuality as such. If it is true then that human beings are afraid of their sexual instincts, quite apart from all social or moral repression, it is no doubt because those instincts interfere with the preservation of the narcissistic integrity of the biological ego, of the individual as such.

Because it threatens the male substance with disintegration and decrees penetration for the female, sexuality acts as a disturber of the peace. And all the erotic feeling that is

[1] "Der Sexualwiderstand" (1913).

associated with this drive of the species against the individual is not always enough to ensure acceptance of its demands. Individual self-preservation rebels against the race-preservative aims of the libido.

IX. Human Anxiety and the Human Brain

Finally, I should like to say a few words concerning the relation between human anxiety and the human brain. Just as the volume of our libido must be connected with the development of our nervous system, it is no doubt to the volume of our brain that we owe our great capacity for anxiety, which is probably incomparably greater than that of the other animals. Fear in the face of vital dangers we have in common with them; but the specific fear, which children in particular feel before the rising tide of their sexuality, is doubtless related to the size of the brain in which the idea of the ego is developing.

More deeply than the other animals, the human child and after him the adult female and even the male must, thanks to the human brain, feel the danger to the individual, to the biological ego, implicit in the claims of the species.

It is because he must die that these claims make themselves heard and it seems as though he understood this from the very first. It seems as though, behind all the blandishments which Nature uses to disguise the sexual trap, he were aware that it lay stretched before him and that he is to remain caught in it while others are to pursue the path.

When the brain is less developed, the animal seems to fall more blindly into the trap. Man, his ego's existence threatened by the claims of his sexuality which involve the expulsion or the violation of his substance, always experiences mingled feelings of attraction and anxiety in varying proportions before the demands of Eros.

IV
NOTES ON EXCISION

NOTES ON EXCISION[1]

THE PRACTICE of excision or clitoridectomy, common to many races, has been reported by explorers, travellers, missionaries and anthropologists. Montaigne found it most surprising and cited "female circumcision" as one of humanity's strangest practices.

Though this custom has been frequently described, its reasons, even rationalized, remain obscure, while those who investigated it seem to have neglected its effects on female psycho-sexuality.

We know that there was a time, during the nineteenth century, when European surgeons, encouraged by the reduced risks of aseptic surgery, resorted to clitoridectomy in the hope of "curing" little girls given to excessive masturbation. We also know that no "cure" generally occurred in such cases and that these stubborn girls went on masturbating. We see this noted in passing, in surgical works of the time, which fact was confirmed by Prof. Pinard when I questioned him on the subject. He could not, however, show me a woman thus mutilated, for the operation had long been given up in Paris.

Then, in Vienna, Freud gave me a book to read which had recently been published in Berlin. It was *Neger Eros*, by Felix Bryk, who had spent some time in East Africa studying the customs of the Nandis, which tribe inhabits the slopes of Mt. Elgon. In this book, Bryk describes the operation which deprives the Nandi girls of the clitoris: at seventeen or eighteen, when fully nubile, the clitoris is cauterised with a red-hot stone by an old woman. Trying to explain the reason for this cruel custom, Bryk claims that the Nandi males, in this way, seek to maximally feminize their females by doing away with this penile vestige, the clitoris, which, he adds, must result in encouraging the transfer of orgastic sensitivity from the girl's infantile erotogenic zone, the clitoris, to the adult erotogenic zone of the woman, which must necessarily be the vagina at puberty.

Freud drew my attention to the fact that Bryk must have

[1] Translated by John Rodker.

been familiar with his own theory of the transfer, at puberty, of erotogenic sensitivity from one zone to the other, and thought Bryk's hypothesis well worth examining, and checking, in the light of the facts. In any case, he said, this operation should not suppress the erotistic or orgasic potentiality in the woman; otherwise the Nandi men would never have allowed a custom which deprived them of mutual participation in voluptuous pleasure, which all men prize in all climes.

Since that time, I have questioned a number of travellers and ethnologists who have had sexual relations with such women, even including Somali women who had undergone the cruel rite of infibulation. They told me that these women seemed capable of experiencing voluptuous pleasure. Apart, however, from the fact that the male, at such times, is hardly capable of observing coldly and realistically, we know to what extent males of all colour may be deluded by women in such matters, helped by their vanity and their indifference. Might not the Nandi males also be capable of being similarly deluded? The problem could not therefore be approached from the point of view of the male partner, since he is the worst observer of all in whatever concerns feminine psycho-sexuality.

Human material for observations was lacking and even, as I write, what I have been able to collect is not ample. But since precise observations on this subject are scarce, and since I do not know when I shall glean others, I thought it worth while to publish what I had, hoping it would inspire other inquirers to fill-out and test, with new material, the correctness of the theories they suggested.

Case I. In the autumn of 1929, when in Berlin with Freud, I was told by a young woman doctor, Dr. Hupfer, there on a visit, of a most interesting case at the Leipzig psychiatric clinic. The subject was a young German woman afflicted with compulsive masturbation who had resorted to every possible form of surgical mutilation for relief, though always unsuccessfully. I therefore decided that, on my way to Vienna to which I was to return with Freud, I would stop at Leipzig to see her, which I did at the psychiatric clinic, in the presence of Dr. Hupfer and Dr. Herbert Weigel.

The patient, at the time, was thirty-six, fair and rather pretty; she looked refined and was of lower middle-class origin.

This woman disclosed that her compulsive masturbation forced her to masturbate up to fifteen times a day. It afflicted her greatly, but she could not resist this compulsion which would seize her at the most inopportune times as, for instance, when preparing the family meal. She would then be forced to interrupt what she was doing, hurry to the next room and masturbate quickly in a crouching position, after which she was able to resume her domestic tasks. An immense shame would then leave her prostrated, but soon the compulsion would reappear.

With her husband, this woman remained totally frigid during coitus, being of exclusively clitoridal type. Only about twice, when slightly tipsy, had she felt any vaginal sensation in coitus.

To end her torturing, humiliating compulsion, she had consulted various doctors, one of whom referred her to a surgeon.

I should have liked to have had the surgical observations but, naturally, I waited for them in vain. It proved impossible for Dr. Weigel to get them for me. All I could obtain were the following details which he sent me later by letter:

Leipzig, May 5th, 1931.

"Madam,

"I am glad to be able to provide more precise details regarding Frau R. (born 1893).

"Since her tenth year, she has suffered from a continual and violent itching of the external genitals and excessive masturbation up to eight, ten and twelve times a day. In 1922 she married. She prefers masturbation to sexual relations. In 1928 she underwent a laparotomy, with resection of the nerves. At the end of 1928, an Alexander-Adam operation. In 1929, resection of the clitoris and castration (ablation of both Fallopians and ovaries). All without the least success. The husband seems to be clumsy in their relations, and carries out coitus without preliminaries. Alleged conscious phantasy while masturbating: *digitatio* by husband.

"After being analysed for four weeks by Dr. Hupfer, she did

not reappear. A surgical clinic had suggested further operative possibilities, to which she probably agreed.

"Worthy of remark among the very sketchy notes we have as to external events in her life are: illegitimate pregnancy in 1918; birth of a legitimate child in 1927, which only, however, lived three days. Since then, she says, greatly increased compulsion to masturbate. The father is epileptic, and two of his sisters are mentally unsound.

"Hoping these meagre details may be helpful,
    I am . . ., etc."

While with Dr. Hupfer, I had been able to observe this woman being gynaecologically examined. Two big lateral cuts were visible where the nerves had been resected. The clitoris had been abraded, as well as the prepuce. The whole vestibular and vulvar region presented a flat scored surface. At my request the patient designated her erotogenic zone to me: it was placed somewhat high, a little over an inch from the orifice of the meatus and precisely on the scar of the *glans clitoris*.

This woman, of high moral principles, seemed truly wretched. Every task was inhibited for her. She would rather have lost all capacity for orgastic pleasure than stay as she was.

In June, 1941, when we were evacuated to Egypt, the Germans having occupied Greece, I resumed my inquiries into excision. In Egypt, most Moslem and Copt girls are excised, generally between their fifth and tenth years. There, I got into touch with Prof. Mahfouz Pasha, gynaecologist to the Coptic Hospital in Cairo. He made it clear that the operation consisted in ablation of the *glans clitoris* and *labia minora*.

It was thought, he told me, that the custom had been brought to Egypt by the Moslems. Yet we know that, from time immemorial, it was special to North-East Africa and has continued from the days of the Pharaohs down to our own times. Egyptian mummies are excised.

At the Copt Hospital, Prof. Mahfouz showed me two excised women he had just delivered. In one, the excised *labia minora* were welded together over the stump of the clitoris which he made me externally palpate. Not much of the clitoris had been abraded in either of these women. He did, however, say he had seen death result.

His opinion was that feminine orgastic sensitivity was in no way affected by the operation, although it was claimed the practice was intended to reduce desire. He had not observed more frigidity among excised Egyptian, than among European women. He had two Frenchwomen and two other Europeans being treated for frigidity at this time. He was giving them pituitary and testicular extracts. (Thus the libido, according to Freud, would be essentially male in both sexes.) He said he had sometimes effected cures (possibly largely due to transference). In one woman, he had restored clitoridal sensitivity only. Other cases, he admitted, could only be treated psychologically.

He had not noticed whether more women of vaginal type occurred among excised women than among other women, and could not therefore reply to my questions on this point.

A psychological investigation, such as I should have liked to undertake in his hospital at Cairo would, he said, be impossible, owing to the scandal it would cause.

To carry out an investigation on these lines, would involve, in fact, a number of difficult conditions:

1. To find an excised woman.
2. An excised woman talking a language familiar to the researcher.
3. An excised woman intelligent and cultured enough to comprehend the scientific interest of such a research.
4. An excised woman who would also consent to reveal her psycho-sexuality and the secrets of her erotic life sincerely. For which reason a woman researcher would stand more chance of success than a man. Women have more trust in each other.

It will be seen therefore how many obstacles, material, linguistic, intellectual and above all, moral, must be overcome for such an inquiry.

Nevertheless, in two different parts of Africa which, for reasons of discretion, I prefer not to state, I did succeed in finding two women who fulfilled the aforesaid conditions.

Case 2. Mrs. A., aged forty; married eight years and mother of one boy and two girls.

She was excised when six. The operation took place in a village, being performed by a sort of witch, a wandering fortune-teller round the villages. She remembered the operation; it was intensely painful. Her four sisters, all older than herself, were also excised. They, too, are all married. Mrs. A. tells me that her own little girls, respectively five and three, will not be excised. The custom, these twenty years, is tending to die out among the educated.

Mrs. A. thinks that the aim of excision is to diminish female sensuality in hot climates. But it does not succeed!

At a second interview, Mrs. A., questioned about her orgastic response, told me it was perfectly normal in coitus. She declared she was always satisfied. But she had needed time to come to it. In any case, her husband was impotent for about three weeks when they first married. He had then seen a doctor, who opined that it was because he had been too chaste. The doctor told him to advise his young wife to help. She did and that very night was deflowered. She bled and suffered a good deal and had to consult a doctor. Then she had to abstain from intercourse for a week. The week over, relations were resumed. The husband suffered from *ejaculatio praecox*. Coitus, with practice, she said, lasted longer, and after about three months she herself reached orgasm. She needs more violence in the act, towards the end.

Mrs. A. began to menstruate at fourteen. She remembers having masturbated in childhood (without reference to the excision) and then resuming the practice after she was twenty. Masturbation was manual, external and not specifically clitoridal.

As a child her mother would harass her for masturbating, but the little girl, nevertheless, did not give it up.

Mrs. A. is very maternal and is constantly surrounded by her children.

In her turn, she harasses her daughter's masturbation. She thinks it endangers the health of the young. I reassure her. Her little boy is clearly in the latency period.

Mrs. A. is evidently of combined clitoridal-vaginal type. Though she masturbated externally in childhood and before marriage, this precocious and obdurate masturbation did not prevent her later, in coitus, from showing herself fully vaginal and adapted to the normal sex-act.

Case 3. Mrs. B., whom I saw at some length, on two occasions, is thirty and highly intelligent.

Her father was a middle-class townsman, her mother of peasant origin. She lost her father as a child and, when she was approaching eleven, her mother and maternal aunt decided to have her excised, despite the objections of the father's brothers. For, said the women, the clitoris grows inordinately at childbirth, and that would disgust a husband!

When she was born, as is the custom, very strong spirit was applied to her clitoris, ostensibly to prevent its growth, a big clitoris being thought ugly and also to indicate excessive sexual desires. As a result or, more likely, constitutionally, she had a very small clitoris. The woman who excised her was a horrible black African woman. Since the clitoris was so small, she had removed more than was necessary. Mrs. B., does not know whether the *labia minora* were involved. In any case, there was haemorrhage, fever and infection of the wound. She was confined to her bed for weeks. The operation has left her with feelings of horror. She remembers her bitterness against her mother for delivering her up to the woman. She hated her for depriving her of something precious, for damaging her in some obscure and unjust way. She began to menstruate at twelve, after the excision. There was no pain and she was not frightened by the sight of blood.

She does not remember ever masturbating clitoridally, neither in childhood nor later, neither before nor after her "circumcision". She only remembers a vague anal masturbation, which gave her about the same pleasure as scratching an itching place, in which she mainly indulged after her excision.

She has now been married three years. She bled very little at defloration. Three months after, she achieved the orgasm in the normal act, but has always been very slow and generally only reaches one orgasm in every three acts. For her, coitus must always be protracted: twenty minutes to half an hour rather than five minutes, but she has never looked at the clock. Her erotogenic sensitivity is still located over the clitoridal scar. If her husband tickles her there, she feels pleasure, but localized on the surface, as it were, even though it may end in orgasm. Her total being, however, remains detached, which unfulfilment she attributes to her mutilation.

Per contra, in coitus with the penis, she experiences complete vaginal satisfaction. When she can reach orgasm, she is entirely happy afterwards: otherwise, she remains ill-humoured. Once the man has had his, she is quite unable to feel any pleasure, whether through him or herself.

If, during coitus, her husband touches her clitoris or rather, its scar, it hinders the development of voluptuous feeling.

She prefers the normal position or that of lying on the man; the sitting position, astraddle the man, gives her no pleasure. She has read Van de Velde's book and tried the methods he advocates.

We see that Mrs. B. must belong constitutionally to the cloacal type (anal masturbation in childhood), which includes a weak phallic clitoridal component, and this explains why the excision mutilation has so little disturbed her erotistic capacities and why it has not affected the internal vaginal zone.

This case seems comparable with that of a non-excised European woman I was able to observe.

This woman, married at eighteen, remained totally frigid with her husband. After a few years, she divorced and remarried. For a long time she remained just as frigid with the second husband, then suddenly achieved a wholly vaginal orgasm. This woman's clitoris had been totally insensitive until she was near her thirtieth year. Clitoridal sensitivity also suddenly and unexpectedly returned. But she was never able to experience full orgastic satisfaction solely through the clitoris. This was because she was mainly vaginal and, in such cases, that is always the clinical picture.

But since this woman had never been excised, she could not blame this clitoridal deficiency on the mutilation of her clitoris, as she might otherwise have done.

We know Freud's theory that erotogenic sensitivity, in girls, is transferred from the clitoris to the vagina. According to him, since *all* little girls masturbate clitoridally, their sensuality thus manifests itself in male mode. Only at puberty does this sensitivity abandon the clitoris and transfer itself to the vagina. The degree in which this transfer is established will determine the woman's more or less successful adaptation to the erotic function in coitus. Disturbances may arise in this evolution of the function. Feminine frigidity is generally only vaginal anaesthesia, the clitoris having unduly retained to itself the whole of the infantile libidinal cathexes.

The categorical nature of this theory has since been contested by various women pupils of Freud, including Karen Horney, Ruth Mack Brunswick and Melanie Klein. According to them, instances of vaginal masturbation may be met with in little girls. Freud, however, thought that these were cases of anal masturbation, later and retrospectively attributed to the vagina which, according to him, is not discovered in childhood, but only when menstrual blood began to pass through it.

Per contra, according to Melanie Klein and, also, Ernest Jones, awareness of the vagina would arise very early in life and the libidinal cathexis of the clitoris would be due less to a persistent infantilism of the erotogenic zones than to a reaction against the vagina. This would be a defence mechanism against the anxiety aroused by the female function, with the talion fear it comprises of being broken into by the mother, whom the child, at one time, wished to disembowel in order to win the phantasied treasures inside her body. This reaction formation is thus conceived by these authors as being essentially psychogenic and only secondarily brought into play.

For my part, I believe that where we meet persistent clitoridalism in women, its causes are far more primitive and innate. All living, all human creatures, are bisexual. The human erotogenic zones reflect the specific psycho-sexuality of each individual. Active, phallic trends express the male; passive cloacal trends the female. The fear of penetration certainly plays its part in the female's refusal of her erotic vaginal function. But this "perforation complex" of the female, as I called it,[1] itself expresses the masculinity complex of the

[1] *See:* "Some Palaeobiological and Biopsychical Reflections" (1936).

girl and woman. Male sexuality is thus centrifugal, convex in its orientation, while that of the female sexuality is centripetal and concave. The vital opposition manifested by every creature, from the amoeba to the elephant, to the penetration, the wounding of its tissue, here, from this vitalistic viewpoint, favours the male. Not for nothing does the child howl when the doctor pushes a spoon into its mouth to look at its throat, or when it has to endure the anal penetration of an enema.

Female sexuality, in fact, implies far more vital danger than male. Apart from castration, to which the male external genital organs are more exposed than the internal genital organs of the female, and venereal diseases which threaten both sexes, the female is far more endangered than the male by her sexuality. The very real dangers of pregnancy and childbirth have no counterpart in the male, without mentioning the pain which accompanies most of her sexual functions: menstruation, defloration, childbirth.

It need not therefore surprise us that the woman accepts her masculinity complex far more easily than does the man his femininity complex. The convex and psycho-sexual engram of the libido is generally more marked in, and better tolerated by, woman than the concave and cloacal psycho-sexual engram of his libido by man. Most highly masculine men detest not only suppositories and enemas, but even having their temperatures taken, per anum, in fever.

On the other hand, if a woman is fully to possess her female erotic function, the erotization of her internal zones must be such that it will neutralize and surmount the vital anxiety aroused by fear of penetration.

Can we identify, early in life, by their different modes of masturbation, one tending outwards, the other inwards, the two feminine types we meet in the adult woman; the cloacal-vaginal and the clitoridal-phallic? And if instances of internal masturbation may be observed or inferred in childhood, to what extent is this masturbation met and, in such cases, is the masturbation anal or vaginal? In any event, it would seem that purely anal masturbation in a little girl, like that practised by Mrs. B. in my Case 3, should of itself enable us to forecast a vaginal sensitivity in the adult; the vagina, as Lou Andreas-Salomè[1] so well said, being merely rented, like the anus, from the primary concave cloaca.

Does infantile vaginal masturbation really exist? Or would the natural barrier of the hymen prevent it, more or less, in each instance? Is a strongly resistive hymen a male stigma (Mrs. A., our Case 2, suffered greatly at her defloration, yet, all the same, was vaginal!)? And with vaginal women, are there some who themselves tore the hymen in childhood with their fingers and not only with foreign bodies, as sometimes occurs in adolescence?

In any case, contrary to what others may think, I do not believe that prenuptial clitoridal masturbation in girls determines later vaginal anaesthesia in coitus. Persistent and solely clitoridal masturbation is far more determined than determinant, more effect than cause. For it seems less the expression of a retarded infantile sexuality than of a strongly masculine innate component. Enduring and exclusive clitoridalism in a woman is far more the expression of an additional, an excessive factor, than of something lacking in her bisexual make-up. The male, as Marañon[2] seems, with justice, to think, having developed further than the female, the woman, in whom everything is smaller than in the male would, apparently, be an inhibited male, arrested in her development by the addition and outgrowth of feminine adjuncts.

If, therefore, a woman is innately of mixed vaginal-clitoridal type, like Mrs. A., in our Case 2, however she may have masturbated in external mode before marriage, she will never become solely clitoridal, "external", for her cloacal, vaginal erotism will duly awake in coitus.

This combined cloacal and phallic type, in any case, seems the most frequently met with among women.

Two types of frigidity occur in woman: total and partial, the latter being that which retains the clitoris as sole erotogenic zone.

The first type of frigidity, where both vagina and clitoris

[1] "Anal" and "Sexual" (1916).
[2] *The Evolution of Sex and Intersexual Conditions* (1930).

remain anaesthetic is hysterogenic; it is an inhibition of psychogenic, neurotic nature. It may suddenly disappear, through events in life, a new sexual partner, or successful psycho-analysis, and what then appears below it is generally an erotic function of feminine, vaginal type. Such was the case with the European woman briefly reported earlier. This need not cause us surprise, since femininity and hysteria are closely related; a certain weakness and lability of the libido, both essentially feminine and not masculine, are needed to create an inhibition so total. Such an inhibition may have been caused by brutal prohibitions of infantile sexuality, masturbation or sexual play with others; basically, it is moral and psychogenic, and psychical causes may equally remove it. The prognosis for total frigidity in women is generally favourable.

Far different are the cases of partial frigidity of clitoridal type. These are almost all founded on an innate, biological bisexuality, obdurate to more or less belated psychical influences. Having found this outlet, the libido tends always to pass and repass the same road, as happens in the various perversions where, by devious routes, it nevertheless succeeds in attaining full satisfaction. Thus, the clitoridal type of woman remains unconsciously proud of her masculinity, despite the conscious suffering it constantly brings and her often intense frustration in normal coitus, which is felt as a sort of infirmity. In extreme cases, the aversion to penetration may be seen to reach such a point, that the otherwise so-sensitive clitoris will suddenly become anaesthetic if, during its excitation, vaginal penetration occurs, and that, whatever position the male may consent to take. Surgical intervention, such as the Halban-Narjani operation[1] which brings the clitoris close to the vaginal entrance, itself changes little in these extreme cases of coital anaesthesia due to such strong aversion to penetration.

We must not, however, think that these women, whom penetration so repels, are therefore inevitably homosexual. Object-choice and libidinal positions occur independently of each other. Solely clitoridal women are often very heterosexual; as worshippers of the phallus, they could never love anyone in whom it was lacking. They desire the male, and

[1] Halban: *Gynäkologische Operationslehre* (1932).

even seek him out with all the activity of their masculine natures yet, in coitus, they present what we might call an unconscious "sword-swallower's psychology". It is as though, each time, they proclaimed: "See, I love my beloved so much that, for him, I expose myself to the fearful danger of penetration! But it does not hurt! I feel nothing! I am intact!"

Such women, though they seek out the male, are often more or less repelled by motherhood.

Can we suppress excessive clitoridalism in woman by ablation of the clitoris? Case 1, which I cited, of the Leipzig woman, appears to answer this question negatively. It may be objected, however, that this was an extreme case by the intensity of its masturbation urge, and also that, at the late age at which clitoridectomy was practised, the nervous engrams were fixed and could no longer be modified, as in the case of eunuchs castrated as adults. Nevertheless, the evidence of Dr. Pinard and others, cited earlier, all tends to invalidate the possibility of inhibiting masturbation in little girls by removing the clitoris as, for a time, was tried in Europe. The case of Mrs. A., our second instance, who was excised at six, testifies in the same direction, this woman having practised an external mode of masturbation, if not solely clitoridal, after excision. This, as we showed, did not, after her somewhat late marriage, prevent her manifesting a normal vaginal orgastic sensitivity which she had constitutionally held in reserve, ready to awake in the normal sex act.

I believe that the ritual sexual mutilations imposed on African women since time immemorial, for Egyptian mummies are excised—as Cleopatra herself must have been—constitute the exact physical counterpart of the psychical intimidations imposed in childhood on the sexuality of European little girls. I also think that, as regards the later sexuality of the woman, they involve the same results.

With the progressive introjection of the child's upbringers and educators, and the concomitant reinforcement of the super-ego or moral conscience, less physical coercion seems necessary than in primitive times, when the archaic instincts were stronger and harder to curb. The same results that were achieved in the past by physical violence are now procured by psychical intimidation. Our penal code no longer comprises the tortures of the past or those still met among primitive tribes. And the intimidation of juvenile sexuality follows the same law of diminishing severity as the penal code, in so far as concerns brutality of repression.

If mutilations, however, work by daunting an individual's psycho-sexuality, more or less, depending on its strength, they seem no more able to make it change its orientation than do our own intimidations of our children. This orientation seems to derive from the innately more or less bisexual nervous centres and that, whatever may occur from an outside source.

Among excised women, clitoridals with a strong convex libidinal orientation must retain the same erotization for the clitoridal scar, like the Leipzig woman of Case 1. Vaginals are naturally, however, not affected in their orgastic potentialities by exclusion of the clitoris. Women of combined vaginal-clitoridal type, the most frequent, retain both zones, as in Cases 2 and 3. Among these, may there be women of a type so indefinite that excising the clitoris might help to internalize the erotogenic zone, and in some degree intensify internal vaginal sensitivity? This was Freud's qualified opinion when, one day, I expressed my objections to Bryk's theory. Nevertheless, I think that the physical intimidation of the girl's sexuality by this cruel excision would not achieve the aim of feminizing, vaginalizing her, any better than the psychical intimidation of the clitoridal masturbation of European little girls. The proportion of clitoridals among European or American women is fairly high, even among girls who were terrified by various threats as to their masturbation in childhood, for doubts of the success of excision to remain on that score.

I know it has been claimed that the excessive clitoridalism of European or American women would be due to the disturbing effects of a civilization which tended to effeminate males as much as masculinize females; in a word, to diminish the difference between the sexes.[1] According to this theory,

[1] Marañon has advanced the opposite view and expressed the hope that among cultured peoples, as a result of continuous progress, males and females would become ever less bisexual or inter-sexual!

uncivilized women should be far more normal! True, we have no sure statistics on this most difficult of all subjects for inquiry; the mysterious psycho-sexuality of woman. But the belief in the absolute normality of the primitive woman must be an offshoot of the Rousseau-ian illusion that man, in a state of Nature, was perfect, but has been spoilt and ruined by civilization, much of which Utopia the Communists have largely resuscitated to-day in their attacks on society as the cause of all evil! Anthropologists, like Géza Róheim, who have drawn attention to this subject, found many cases of clitoridalism among primitive women. In any case, to question it, would be to question the biological foundation of human bisexuality.

Nevertheless, among the African women who belong to the last two categories, the vaginal and combined, there must also be some whose libido, in this similar to that of certain European women, has not the strength to withstand intimidation, the physical and bloody intimidation, here, of excision. Such women must then lose all potentiality for erotic satisfaction. Although I myself have never met any, there must be some African women, as there are European, who are totally frigid, which cases of total frigidity may be capable of being modified by external events, in this, like the European woman I cited at the same time as my African Case 3.

Should we, among these excised women, as regards the narrower, biological aspect of the erotic function, find the three great categories of women so well described and distinguished by Freud in the more general outlook of the total psycho-sexuality of women?

In one of his later papers, *Female Sexuality* (1931), Freud classifies women in three main categories, depending on their reactions to the infantile discovery of the difference between the sexes and the penis envy which results: the *claimers*, the *acceptives* and the *renouncers*.

The *claimers*, having seen the boy's penis, and longing for one, claim it to the point of unconsciously succeeding in phantasying its possession. They over-cathect their clitoris and in their lives tend to assume every psychical and social male attitude. Here we must distinguish, as does Abraham, two sub-types: the revenge type (*Rachetypus*) and the wish type (*Wunschtypus*). In this last, the illusion of possessing the penis may so deny reality as no longer to need the revenge.

Acceptives comprise women as well adapted to their biological function, as to their social role. They have duly replaced the desire for the penis by that for the child and have accepted the substitution, for the male phallic zone, of the vaginal female zone through which the male and the child will pass. In this case, penetration has been erotized successfully and the woman has made the necessary distinction between the penetration-wound to inflict pain and the penetration-caress that gives pleasure and life. A harmoniously combined type of clitoridal-vaginal function is frequent among such women.

The renouncers, finally, are women whom the discovery of the difference between the sexes has so disheartened, discouraged and rebuffed, that they prefer to abandon all use of their sexuality. Thus, biologically outclassed by the male, they abandon all sexual rivalry with him. The totally frigid who, nevertheless, have accepted the male, belong to the class of acceptives, though inhibited for the time being. The true renouncers truly abandon risking the male's embrace and try not to compete with him in his own domain. Mostly, they provide those armies of spinsters given to feminine social functions: mother substitutes, nurses, nursemaids, school teachers, social workers, often desexualized more or less; they are a kind of human counterpart of the worker masses among ants and bees. They must be far rarer among primitives than with us, for the primitive woman cannot so easily evade her child-bearing role.

Finally, we must emphasize that the various ways in which girls react to the discovery of the difference between the sexes must, originally, be determined by the more or less innate bisexuality, and the more or less libidinal make-up of the subject, apart from any psychical contribution deriving from external infantile events. In the same way, every child, when able to observe adult coitus, reacts to this "primal scene" as male or female, and identifies, more or less, with active male or passive female, according to the degree of masculinity or femininity inherent in its constitution.

Generally, it is primitive communities with patriarchal structures which impose ritual sexual mutilations on their children. It seems it would be the "fathers", the tribal ancients, successors of the father of the primal horde, who thus seek to intimidate the child's sexuality; that of the sons, their rivals, and of the daughters, their mates.

But now we must ask to what extent a wish to maximally feminize the girls enters into this intimidating excision ritual of the tribal ancients, which mutilations, be it said, are delegated to the old women who doubtless enjoy thus revenging their age on the young?

That such a wish exists, as Bryk supposed, is not indeed impossible. It seems, in effect, that two kinds of men may be met in all communities, from the most primitive to the most civilized. These might be called the enemies or friends of the clitoris.

When, as the supreme insult, Egyptian Moslems cry "Mother of the clitoris" to European women, they express the former of these attitudes. Bryk also reports that Nandi men have a deep repugnance to speaking of "what hangs" between a woman's legs, in allusion to the clitoris, and I have already cited Mrs. B., on the disgust that would seize a husband if, as was feared, his mate's clitoris were to lengthen after a confinement.

Very masculine men do, in fact, seem repelled by anything not feminine in women, and this attitude is also met among many Europeans.

On the other hand, there are men with more bisexual, more feminoid natures, who seek the missing complement of their own masculinity in women. In their unconscious, such men continue fixated on the "phallic mother" of their infantile phantasies, and compose what might be called the class of "friends of the clitoris". Such men find pleasure in the female's minute penis, they like to play with it, and I have even known an extreme case where the man, a European, reversing the normal relation of the sexes, experienced great pleasure in introducing his mate's clitoris into his own urethral aperture!

It is in this category of devotees of the phallic mother that we must class the males of such African tribes as the Bapedi of Northern Transvaal who, far different from those who practise excision, like to lengthen the nymphea of their girls so that they come to mimic a penis.

These various practices, however, seem only to gratify the phantasies of those who impose them on the girls. They, doubtless, change little in the girl's innate bisexuality, which outside influences, in any case, could only slightly modify.

But even though the nymphea of Bantu women were to reach several inches, they would still, nevertheless, not be a penis. Nor will the mere ablation of a woman's clitoris suffice to internalize her sexuality, as we showed in our Leipzig case, or even in that of Mrs. A, our second instance, who continued her external masturbation despite her excision.

Given the example of European women who are subjected to a psychical, sexual intimidation from childhood, as well as that of African women exposed to physical sexual intimidation through ritual mutilations, it appears that female sexuality opposes any change in its individual natural orientation, more or less bisexual in each case.

Educative influence may be very powerful as regards moral inhibitions. I knew a little girl in whom excessive repression of infantile masturbation, (for many months her arms were cruelly tied to the bars of her bed at night), proved truly catastrophic to her sexuality, determining so obdurate a total frigidity that nothing, neither new lovers, nor even psycho-analysis, was able to remove it.

The degree of a woman's erotistic masculinity, however, does not seem able to be modified so easily. Fierce though the threats which menace a girl's infantile clitoridal masturbation may be, including even ablation of the clitoris, they will not, for that, succeed in modifying her innate degree of bisexuality.

In the conflict between social morality and human instinct, education and re-education often reveal themselves very powerful. In the conflict, within our instincts, between the male and female that dwells in each of us, the power of education and re-education remains but small. Here, Nature holds the last word.

LIST OF WORKS REFERRED TO IN THE TEXT

Abbreviations.

Coll. Papers. FREUD, SIGMUND. *Collected Papers*, 5 vols. Institute of Psycho-Analysis and The Hogarth Press, London.
Ges. Werke. FREUD, SIGMUND. *Gesammelte Werke*, 18 vols. Imago Publishing Co. Ltd., London.
Int. J. Psycho-Anal. *The International Journal of Psycho-Analysis*, London.
J.N.M.D. *The Journal of Nervous and Mental Disease*, New York.
Ps-a Q. Inc. *The Psycho-analytic Quarterly Incorporated*, New York.

* * *

ABRAHAM, K. (1917). "Ejaculatio Praecox". *Int. Z. ärztl. Psychoanal.*, **4**.
(*Trans.:* "Ejaculatio Praecox", in: *Selected Papers*, London, 1927.)
ABRAHAM, K. (1921). "Ausserungsformen des weiblichen Kastrationskomplex", *Int. Z. Psychoanal.*, **7**.
(*Trans.:* "Manifestations of the Female Castration Complex", in: *Selected Papers*, London, 1927.)
ABRAHAM, K. (1924). "Versuch einer Entwicklungsgeschichte der Libido", Vienna.
(*Trans.:* "A Short Study of the Development of the Libido", in: *Selected Papers*, London, 1927.)
ANDREAS-SALOMÉ, L. (1916). " 'Anal' und 'Sexual' ", *Imago*, **4**.
BLEULER, E. (1913). "Der Sexualwiderstand", *Jb. psychoanal. psychopath. Forsch.*, **5**.
BONAPARTE, M. (1933). *Edgar Poe, Etude Psychanalytique*, Paris.
(*Trans.: The Life and Works of Edgar Allan Poe*, London, 1949.)
BRYK, F. (1928). *Neger Eros*, Berlin.

CERULLI, —. (1930–33). *Etiopia Occidentale,*
DEUTSCH, H. (1925). *Psychoanalyse der weiblichen Sexualfunktionen,* Vienna.
DEUTSCH, H. (1925). "Psychologie des Weibes in den Funktionen der Fortpflanzung", *Int. Z. Psychoanal.,* **11**.
(*Trans.:* "The Psychology of Women in Relation to the Functions of Reproduction", *Int. J. Psycho-Anal.,* **6**.)
DEUTSCH, H. (1930). "Der Feminine Masochismus und seine Beziehung zur Frigidität", *Int. Z. Psychoanal.,* **16**.
(*Trans.:* "The Significance of Masochism in the Mental Life of Women", in: *The Psycho-Analytic Reader,* London, 1950.)
DEUTSCH, H. (1932). "Über die weibliche Homosexualität", *Int. J. Psycho-Anal.,* **18**.
(*Trans.:* "On Female Homosexuality", in: *The Psycho-Analytic Reader,* London, 1950.)
FENICHEL, O. (1929). "Zur prägenitalen Vorgeschichte des Ödipuskomplexes", *Int. Z. Psychoanal.,* **15**.
(*Trans.:* "The Pregenital Antecedents of the Oedipus Complex", *Int. J. Psycho-Anal.,* **12**.)
FERENCZI, S. (1924). *Versuch einer Genitaltheorie,* Vienna.
(*Trans.: Thalassa, A Theory of Genitality,* New York, 1938.)
FREUD, A. (1936). *Das Ich und die Abwehrmechanismen,* London, 1946.
(*Trans.: The Ego and the Mechanisms of Defence,* London, 1937.)
FREUD, S. (1905). *Drei Abhandlungen zur Sexualtheorie,* Vienna. (*Ges. Werke,* V, London, 1949.)
(*Trans.: Three Essays on the Theory of Sexuality,* London, 1949.)
FREUD, S. (1908). "Über infantile Sexualtheorien", *Sexualprobleme,* new issue of the periodical *Mutterschutz,* **4**. (*Ges. Werke* VII, London, 1941.)
(*Trans.:* "On the Sexual Theories of Children", *Coll. Papers,* II, London, 1924.)
FREUD, S. (1912). "Zur Einleitung der Onaniediskussion—Schlusswort". In: *Diskussionen der Wiener psychoanalytischen Vereinigung,* Wiesbaden. (*Ges. Werke,* VIII, London, 1943.)

FREUD, S. (1913). *Totem und Tabu*, Vienna. (*Ges. Werke*, IX, London, 1940).
(*Trans.: Totem and Taboo*, London, 1919.)

FREUD, S. (1916). "Über Triebumsetzungen, insbesondere der Analerotik", *Int. Z. Psychoanal.*, **4**. (*Ges. Werke* X, London, 1949.)
(*Trans.:* "On the Transformation of Instincts with Special Reference to Anal Erotism", *Coll. Papers*, II, London, 1924.)

FREUD, S. (1917). *Vorlesungen zur Einführung in die Psychoanalyse*, Vienna. (*Ges. Werke* XI, London, 1940.)
(*Trans.:* *Introductory Lectures on Psycho-Analysis*, London, revised ed. 1929.)

FREUD, S. (1918). "Beiträge zur Psychologie des Liebeslebens: (iii) Das Tabu der Virginität", *Sammlung*, **4**. (*Ges. Werke* XII, London, 1947.)
(*Trans.:* "Contributions to the Psychology of Love. The Taboo of Virginity". *Coll. Papers* IV, London, 1925.)

FREUD, S. (1919). "'Ein Kind wird geschlagen'", *Int. Z. Psychoanal.*, **5**. (*Ges. Werke* XII, London, 1947.)
(*Trans.:* "'A Child is being Beaten'. A Contribution to the Study of the Origin of Sexual Perversions." *Coll. Papers* II, London, 1924.)

FREUD, S. (1923). *Das Ich und das Es*, Vienna. (*Ges. Werke* XIII, London, 1940.)
(*Trans.: The Ego and the Id*, London, 1927.)

FREUD, S. (1923). "Die infantile Genitalorganization", *Int. Z. Psychoanal.*, **9**. (*Ges. Werke*. XIII, London, 1940.)
(*Trans.:* "The Infantile Genital Organization of the Libido", *Coll. Papers* II, London, 1924.)

FREUD, S. (1924). "Das ökonomische Problem des Masochismus", *Int. Z. Psychoanal.*, **10**. (*Ges. Werke* XIII, London, 1940.)
(*Trans.:* "The Economic Problem in Masochism", *Coll. Papers* II, London, 1924.)

FREUD, S. (1924). "Der Untergang des Ödipuskomplexes", *Int. Z. Psychoanal.*, **10**. (*Ges. Werke* XIII, London, 1940.)
(*Trans.:* "The Passing of the Oedipus Complex, *Coll. Papers* II, London, 1924.)

Freud, S. (1925). "Einige psychische Folgen des anatomischen Geschlechtsunterschieds", *Int. Z. Psychoanal.*, **11**. (*Ges. Werke* XIV, London, 1948.)
(*Trans.:* "Some Psychological Consequences of the Anatomical Distinction between the Sexes", *Coll. Papers* V, London, 1950.)
Freud, S. (1926). *Die Frage der Laienanalyse*, Vienna. (*Ges. Werke* XIV, London, 1948.)
(*Trans:.* *The Question of Lay-Analysis*, London, 1948.)
Freud, S. (1930). *Das Unbehagen in der Kultur*, Vienna. (*Ges. Werke* XIV, London, 1948.)
(*Trans.:* *Civilization and its Discontents*, London, 1930.)
Freud, S. (1931). "Über die weibliche Sexualität", *Int. Z. Psychoanal.*, **17**. (*Ges. Werke* XIV, London, 1948.)
(*Trans.:* "Female Sexuality", *Coll. Papers* V, London, 1950.)
Freud, S. (1932). *Neue Folge der Vorlesungen zur Einführung in die Psychoanalyse*, Vienna. (*Ges. Werke* XV, London, 1950.)
(*Trans.:* *New Introductory Lectures on Psycho-Analysis*, London, 1933.)
Halban, J. (1932). *Gynäkologische Operationslehre*, Berlin.
Horney, K. (1923). "Zur Genese des weiblichen Kastrationskomplexes", *Int. Z. Psychoanal.*, **9**.
(*Trans.:* "On the Genesis of the Castration Complex in Women", *Int. J. Psycho-Anal.*, **5**.)
Horney, K. (1926). "Flucht aus der Weiblichkeit", *Int. Z. Psychoanal.*, **12**.
(*Trans.:* "The Flight from Womanhood", *Int. J. Psycho-Anal*, **7**.)
Horney, K. (1932). "Die Angst vor der Frau", *Int. Z. Psychoanal.*, **18**.
(*Trans.:* "The Dread of Woman", *Int. J. Psycho-Anal.*, **13**.)
Horney, K. (1933). "Die Verleugnung der Vagina", *Int. Z. Psychoanal.*, **19**.
(*Trans.:* "The Denial of the Vagina", *Int. J. Psycho-Anal.*, **14**).
Jones, E. (1927). "The Early Development of Female Sexuality", *Int. J. Psycho-Anal.*, **8**.
In: *Papers on Psycho-Analysis*, London, 1938.

JONES, E. (1933). "The Phallic Phase". *Int. J. Psycho-Anal.*, **14**.
KINSEY, A., POMEROY, W. B., MARTIN, C. E. (1948). *Sexual Behavior in the Human Male*. Philadelphia and London.
KLEIN, M. (1927). "Early Stages of the Oedipus Conflict", *Int. J. Psycho-Anal.*, **9**.
KLEIN, M. (1932). *The Psycho-Analysis of Children*, London.
LAMPL-de GROOT, J. (1927). "Zur Entwicklungsgeschichte des Ödipuskomplexes der Frau", *Int. Z. Psychoanal.*, **8**.
(*Trans.*: "The Evolution of the Oedipus Complex in Women", in: *The Psycho-Analytic Reader*, London, 1950.)
MACK BRUNSWICK, R. (1928). "Die Analyse eines Eifersuchtwahnes", *Int. Z. Psychoanal.*, **14**.
(*Trans.*: "The Analysis of a Case of Paranoia", *J. Nerv. & Ment. Dis.*, **70**.)
MARAÑON, G. (1930). *La Evolucion de la Sexualidad y los Estados Intersexuales*, Madrid.
(*Trans.*: *The Evolution of Sex and Intersexual Conditions*, London, 1932.)
MEISENHEIMER, J. (1921). *Geschlecht und Geschlechter*, Jena.
MICHELET, J. (1858). *L'Amour*, Paris.
MUELLER, J. (1931). "Ein Beitrag zur Frage der Libidoentwicklung des Mädchens in der genitalen Phase", *Int. Z. Psychoanal.*, **17**.
(*Trans.*: "A Contribution to the Problem of Libidinal Development in the Genital Phase in Girls", *Int. J. Psycho-Anal.*, **13**.)
OPHUIJSEN, J. H. W. VAN (1916–18). "Beiträge zum Männlichkeitskomplex der Frau", *Int. Z. ärztl. Psychoanal.*, **4**.
(*Trans.*: "Contributions to the Masculinity Complex in Women", *Int. J. Psycho-Anal.*, **5**.)
PLOSS, H. & BARTELS, M. (1884). *Das Weib*, Leipzig.
(*Trans.*: *Woman*, London, 1935.)
RADÓ, S. (1933). "Fear of Castration in Women". *Psychoanal. Quart.*, **2**.

INDEX

Abraham, K., 5, 13, 15, 16, 18, 19, 23, 25, 33, 35, 46, 148, 164, 176n., 205
Abyssinians, circumcision and excision among, 160
Acceptives, 2, 145, 158, 162, 205, 206
Active mother phantasy, 46, 88
Active (primary) Oedipus complex, 20, 21, 22n., 76, 79–81, 94, 96, 107
Activity and passivity, 16, 21, 24, 32, 59, 78, 109–14; Table of developmental stages, 26–7
Adaptation, sexual, to environment, 145–52
Adler, A., 95
Adolescence, 185, 187, 201
Adult sexuality, and Oedipus complex, 73–5, 90; of man, 126; see Male sexuality, Sexuality; of woman, 77, 90, 129–39, 140; see Female sexuality, Sexuality, Woman
Adults, role of, in girl's sexual development, 140–1
Aggression, 17, 29, 52, 79–82, 172; against frustrating father in girl, 133–4; and libido, 81; and object love, 80; centrifugal=masculine, 53, 172; centripetal=feminine, 53, 172; desexualization of, 79–82; in feminine masochism, 86, 174; in oral phase, 31, 79; in phallic phase, 79; in sadistic-anal phase, 79
Aggressive and libidinal urges in infancy, 78–82, 86
Alloplastic adaptation, 146–7
Ambivalence, 26
Amnesia, infantile, 87, 89, 95, 132, 135
Anal-erotic stage, and male masochism, 46
Anal erotism, 182; passive, primary, 24, 25, 29
Analyst, substituted for prohibitive mother, 135
Anatomical factors in clitoridal and frigid women, 150–2
Animals, castration and perforation fear in, 185, 200
Antagonism, between individual and species, 182–3; between libido and self-preservation, 187–8
Anus, digestive and erotogenic, 28
Anxiety, 184–8; about masturbation, 37, 39; and incestuous wishes, 31; neutralized by masochism, 51: types of, 186–8; vital, 184–5, 200

Ashheim; 15
Autoerotism, 26–7
Autoplastic adaptation, 146, 148, 150–2; and psycho-analysis, 148–9

Beaten child = (phallic) clitoris of girl, 83–4, 88, 90
Beating phantasies, 83–96; as conservation of infantile perversion, 87, 97
Beating rites, 96n
Beer, G. R. de, 13n.
Behaviourist substantiation of infantile sexuality, 57n.
Biogenetic principle, 13
Biological, borderline, 149; castration of the female, 153, 158, 159; ego defends body integrity, 102, 187–8; predetermination, 39, 59; regression in woman, 44
Bisexual identification, 49
Bisexuality, 5, 7, 35, 38, 49–50, 53, 59, 86, 108, 114, 121, 130, 137, 146, 149, 150, 156, 159, 163, 170, 175, 199, 205; and femininity in man, 95, 146, 207–8; and masculinity in girl, 55, 57, 58, 59, 174, 208; biological theory of, 7–12; embryological hypotheses, 13–15; innate, and partial frigidity, 202; innate, of girl, not modifiable, 206, 208; prefigured in sadistic-anal stage, 16–7; syndromes of, 9
Bleuler, E., 91, 187
Boy, active and passive tendencies, 24, 25, 26–7, 28, 42–5; and concept of vagina, 36; castration complex of, 28, 29, 42, 153, 159, 164; desire for and fear of passive penetration, 50; libidinal development, 26–7, 41–2, 96; masturbation an early training, 58; narcissistic libido for own penis of, 126; Oedipus complex, 26–7, 28, 41, 42, 43, 79–82, 125, 126; passive stage, 139; pathogenic consequences of seduction, 133; phallic stage should persist in, 140; pre-feminine, 29; sister as substitute oedipal love object for, 136; stages of object-love, 21, 22, 24, 25, 41
Brain and anxiety, 188
Brother, role of, for girl, 130, 132–7, 141
Bryk, F., 154, 191, 192, 204, 207

Cannibalistic, oral phase, 16; urges of little girl, 52

Caresses and masochism, 170
Castration, fear and concept of vagina, 50; phantasy of girl, 76, 172; threats, 73; 126
Castration-complex, 5, 21, 22, 26–7, 28, 29, 35, 41, 44, 81, 87, 89, 93, 126, 148, 158, 159, 172, 177, 181; feminine, dual nature of, 159; girl's reaction to, predetermined, 39; in male mainly cultural, 153, 159; internal, of small girl, 52; mother's, and son, 164; of girl earlier than boy's, 42; patriarchal morality and, 29; primitive sources of, 183, 184
Castration-violation-childbirth, 29, 48
Cerulli; 153n
Chastity, male wants partner chaste, 158
Child, wish for, 48, 206
Childhood, instinctual anxiety in, 187
Choice of sexual partner, 146, 147–8
Circumcision, 153, 160; "female", 191
Civilization, effeminates males, masculinizes females, 204
Claimers, 1, 145–8, 151, 159, 162, 205
Clitoridal, anaesthesia, 3, 111, 198, 202; caresses, 45, 59, 111, 120, 137, 198, 202, 207; fixation, predisposing factors in, 57–8; masturbation, persistent, due to masculine component, 201; phallic type of woman, 200; seduction, 141; sensitivity, secondarily developed by girl, 31, 40; sensitivity, variations in, 105–6; -vaginal function, 177; vaginal type of woman, 196, 201, 204, 206; women, 2–4, 5, 10, 11, 37, 39, 47, 48, 55–6, 57–8, 59–61, 76, 86, 94, 104, 109–10, 113, 114, 115, 120, 137, 146–9, 150, 159, 177, 193, 199, 201, 202, 203, 204, 205
Clitoridalism, and ablation of clitoris, 203–5
Clitoridectomy, cases of, 157, 192–209; in Nandi tribe, 191–2
Clitoris, 29, 43, 59, 76–7, 82–3, 100, 107–9, 110, 126, 130, 139, 151, 175, 177; affirmation of, 103–9; attitude of men to, 207–8; big clitoris thought ugly, 197; enemies of, 207; excision of, 153–61, 162, 191–7, 203–5; friends of, 207–8; Halban-Narjani operation, 151–2; libidinal fixation on, 54, 57, 77, 148–9, 151; loved in woman by feminoid men, 147, 207–8; over cathected, 199, 205
Cloaca, "active", 107; and oral erotism, 31; and phallus, in woman, 175–8; both active and passive, 17; dentated, 24; dominance of, in girl, 36; exclusion of, 26–7, 35; passive, 23, 24; recathected in feminine males, 40; supremacy of, in sadistic-anal stage, 34
Cloacal, castration complex in girl (M. Klein), 31; child, girl's wish for, 29; passivity, 26–7, 28; stages in girl, 36, 44, 54, 89, 140; type of woman, 198; -vaginal type of woman, 200
Cloacal erotism, 25; of girl, 29, 35, 108, 140, 176; of men, 46, 146
Coitus, 41, 48, 85, 111, 169, 175; and time, 138; child's reaction to observation of, 206; in clitoridal women, 59–61, 105–6, 137, 148, 149, 157; in feminoid men, 147; in masochistic perverts, 92; observed by child, 31, 42, 49, 52, 55, 71–2, 171–2, 174, 176; of man=masturbation, 59; positions in, 202; prototypes for; in girl, 108; sadistic concept of, in child, 171
Compulsive masturbation, 157, 192–4
Concave, mental representation of sexual pleasure, 105–7, 112, 177
Conflicting drives in feminine sexual development, 103, 112–13, 208
Conscience, 80, 160, 203
Conservation of infantile (beating) perversion, 87, 97
Constitution, role in femininity and masculinity, 206–7
Constitutional, cathexes of erotogenic zones, 54–6, 113, 120–2, 140, 176; factors in masculine girls, 55, 177
Convex mental representation of sexual pleasure, 105, 112, 177
Cultural, castration, 153, 154; morality and woman, 67, 103, 133–5, 162

Death wish and moral inhibitions, 122–3
Defence, against masochism, 175, 176, 178; of "sacred frontiers of body", 182
Defloration, 170, 196, 201; artificial, 137; by ritual figures, 137
Deflorator, role of, 136–9
Defusion of aggression and libido, 79–82, 86, 172
Denial of reality, 206
Deuterophallic phase, 20n.
Deutsch, H., 3, 5, 10n., 29, 39, 48, 58, 77, 86, 109n., 115, 169
Devouring implies aggression and love, 52
Displacement, 51, 88, 125; in spider phobia, 187; principles of total, in girl, 99–100

INDEX

Dohrn; 15
Dreams, female, echoing discovery of vagina, 37, 38; of clitoridal women, 60; of falling, 38
Dual erotogenic zones in women, 56, 57
Dynamic stereotype (Pavlov's), 58, 152, 157

Earliest experiences in primitives less determinant, 156
Education, and social morality, 208; and bisexuality, 209
Ego, and homosexuality, 145; and instinctual anxiety, 187; and masochism, 175; and passivity, 175, 178
Egypt, excision in, 194
Ejaculatio praecox, 46
Embryology of sexes, 13–5
End-pleasure (*see* Orgasm), 56, 116, 121, 123, 135, 138, 158
Enemas, 108, 173n., 200
Engrams, 200, 203; of oedipal phantasies, and adult erotic function, 123–5, 141
Erection, 43
Erotic behaviour, of man, 147, of woman, 59, 109–15; function, hereditary transmission of, 67; selection, 67
Erotogenic factors, innate, 116, in masculine girls, 55, 177; *see* Bisexuality
Erotogenic zones, constitutional cathexes of, 54–6, 113, 120–2, 140, 176; dual, in women, 56, 57; in feminine development, 100–9, 120, 121, 137, 140, 175–8, 192, 198–9; may replace each other, 140; reflect individual's psycho-sexuality, 199
Excision of clitoris, 153–61, 162, 191–7, 203–5, 207; and vaginal sensitivity, 204; delegated to old women, 158, 207; effect on types of women, 204, 205, 208; psychological investigation into, 195

Father, libidinal object for both sexes in second, passive, oedipal phase, 21; role of, for girl, 125–32, 133–4, 141
Father-love of girl, 29, 125–32
"Fathers", tribal, and sexual mutilation, 207
Fear, of body disintegration, 183–4, 187; of castration "wound", in children, 38, 39, 40, 50; of first ejaculation, 184–5; of man, in woman, 49n.; of mother, in girl, 51–3, 199; of motherhood, 49, 50–1; of penetration, 173, 175, 176, 178, 181, 183, 185, 199, 200; of sexuality, 187; of the male, 185; of vagina, in little girl, 37–8, 50; of woman, in man, 49n.; retaliatory, 52–3, 199
Fellatio, 43
Female, feminizing of the, 152, 153, 154, 158, 159, 191, 204, 207
Female sexuality, conflicting drives in development of, 103, 112–13, 208; disturbances in, attributable to Nature or Culture, 162–5, 208; divergent analytic theories of, 30–9, 51–3, 199; factors which determine adult, 118–25, 139–141, 163, 207; opposes change, 208; outline of development, 139–41; types of, 1, 69–70, 109–15, 135, 141, 145, 148, 195, 200–6
Feminine, -homosexual woman, 110; masochistic drives, ideal vicissitude of, 98; woman, partly masculine, 148, 152
Femininity, and hysteria, 202; -complex of man, 200; constitutional, 176, 207; factors disturbing development, 46–61, 65–70, 96–103; normal development of, 41–2, 56, 77, 98, 100, 107, 136, 139–41, 175; prejudiced by aggression directed outward, 52–3; primary nature of woman's, 32–3; protest against, in woman, 86; risks and dangers of, 136, 186, 200
Feminoid component in boys and men, 139, 146, 207–8
Fenichel, O., 16, 44
Ferenczi, S., 24, 61
Fidelity, to oedipal love-objects, 129–30
Fixation, anal or cloacal on mother in girl, 108; at cloacal-phallic stage in men, 146; at phallic stage in clitoridal women, 56–7, 58; clitoridal, 54, 57, 77, 148–9, 164, 199; on father, 47, 129, 134; on mother, 47, 48, 107, 108, 137, 149; on "phallic mother" in men, 207–8
Flagellants, 46
Fliess, W., 95
Foot crushing, in China, 154
Fore-pleasure, 56, 74, 98, 116, 120–1, 138, 140, 147
Freud, A., 186, 187
Freud, S., 1, 6, 7, 9, 15, 16, 19n., 20, 22n., 29, 30, 32, 34, 36, 38, 39, 44, 46, 49, 51, 53n., 64, 77, 79n., 80, 83, 84, 86–96, 97, 98, 99, 100, 101, 112, 116, 117, 118, 119, 124, 125, 126, 130, 137, 145, 153, 154, 156, 158, 165, 169, 170, 173n., 176n., 191, 192, 195, 198, 199, 204, 205

Frigidity, 1, 10, 23, 58, 60, 70, 103, 104, 118, 138, 146, 148, 160, 162, 183, 185, 199; aetiologies and types of, 148-9, 201-3; analytic cure of, 2, 3, 135, 148-9, 152, 208; and perversion, 149; female condition of, 70; hormonal treatment of, 195; partial (*see* Clitoridal women), 3, 113-15, 201-2; prognosis in total, 202; surgical treatment, cases of, 151-2; total, 3, 111, 114, 158, 177, 193, 198, 201-2, 205, 206, 208

Functional sexual disturbances, 160, 162

Genital stage, 26-7, 28, 33, 35
Genital zone, primacy of, 98
Genitals, excluded, 21, 22, 23, 26-7, 33, 35
Girl, active phallic stage of, 44, 139; aggression of, 133-4; attitudes towards object, 26-7, 28, 41, 44, 127, 130, 137; attitudes towards pain, 39, 49n., 129, 176; beneficial consequences of seduction, 119, 134, 136; brother as substitute oedipal love object, 130, 134, 136; castration complex in, 20, 21, 28, 29, 38, 41, 42, 126, 148, 158, 177, in M. Klein's view, 31-2; concept of coitus, 171-5, 176; concept of vagina in, 36, 38, 50, 127, 139; denial of vagina in, 38, 39, 49n., 137; discovery of vagina, 199; father (oedipal) substitutes, 136; fear of being wounded, 31, 49, 102, 103n., 129, 173, 176; fear of being robbed of body contents, 31, 52, 199; frustrated by father, 130-2, 133-4; libidinal cathexis of clitoris a reaction-formation, 199; libidinal development, 26-7, 28, 41-2, 56, 99-103, 139-41, 176, 199; masturbation of, 3, 4, 5, 20-1, 30, 33, 36, 38, 39, 42, 54-7, 58, 72-3, 99, 100, 101, 139-40, 156, 176, 196, 197, 198, 199, 200; oedipal fear of mother-rival, 51; Oedipus complex, 26-7, 28, 41, 42, 48, 74-5, 107-8, 109, 126-7, 130, 131, 136, 140; passive cloacal stages, 44, 139; passive phallic stages, 44, 139; passive tendencies, 24, 26-7, 28, 44-5; pathogenicity of seduction, 133, 135; phallic strivings towards mother, 44, 50, 107; pre-masculine, 29; reaction to sex difference, 206; reactions to primal scene, 172-5, 176, 206-7; refusal of feminine role, 102, 176; repression of phallic masturbation, 21, 38, 54-5, 58; repression of vaginal sensitivity, 31; role of father, 127-32; stages of object-love, 21, 22, 24, 26-7, 41, 99-101, 126-7; super-ego in baby girl, 31, 52-3
Guilt, sense of, and masochism, 89, 91; and sexual function, 119; for oedipal wishes, 122

Haeckel, E., 13
Halban, J., 151, 202n.
Halban-Narjani, operation, 150-2, 153, 202
Health and normality, 145-6
Hereditary transmission of erotic function, 67
Hermaphroditism, 163; larval, in clitoridal women, 114; to gonochorism, 163
Heterosexual women, 76; types of, 110-13, 146
Heterosexuality, of clitoridal women, 202-3; of girl, saved by brother, 130
Hirsh; 15
Homosexual, men, 46, 139; women, 2, 47, 109-10, 131, 145, 149
Homosexuality, female, and clitoridal, 202-3; in heterosexual women, 113
Hormones, 15, 152
Horney, K., 5, 30, 32, 36, 37, 39, 49, 76n., 102n., 173n., 199
Hupfer; 157, 192, 193, 194
Hymen, 38, 106, 137, 185, 201
Hymenoptera, sexual repression in, 163
Hysteria, genital-phallic foundation of, 19, 21, 23
Hysterical, frigidity, 148-9, 202; inhibition, case of, 135-6; inhibition and vaginal anaesthesia, 114, 202; repression and orgasm, 58

Id, 119
Identification, 47, 48, 49, 51, 55; in observation of adult coitus, 206; with the active mother, 109-10; with the father, in homosexual women, 110
Imagination, infantile, and adult sexuality, 122-5
Impotence, 23, 24, 43, 92, 95, 160
Incest, 80; cases of, 117; prohibition overcome, 126; wishes, transferred to mother-in-law, 24n.
Incestuous, sex play between brother and sister, 132-6; wishes of girl, 31, 122, 131; wishes of boy, 96, 153
Inertia, of instincts, 124-5; relative dynamic of female, 69
Infibulation, 153, 192
Inhibition, 113, 114, 115, 118, 123, 125, 202-4, 208; hysterical, 114, 136, 202; through frustration, 129

Inner voice, critical, 91
Innate erotogenic factors, 116, 206 see Bisexuality, constitutional hereditary
Instinctual, anxiety, 186–7; urges in feminine development, 99–103
Introjection of educators, 203
Isolation of masochistic drive, 97

Jealousy, in older women of the young, 158, 207; little girl's, 52, 127–8; of rival sibling, 83, 88, 93
Jews, circumcision among, 160
Jones, E., 6, 30, 32, 39, 199

Kinsey, A., 57n.
Klein, M., 6, 17n., 30–1, 32, 51, 52, 76n., 173n., 181, 199
Kleptomania, 19
Krabbe, 15

Lactation, 169
Lamarck, J.-B., 106
Lampl-de Groot, J., 2, 5, 44
Latency period, 26–7, 28, 34, 44, 77, 160; cloaca dormant in, 36; masturbation in, 54–7, 76
Libidinal, cathexis, 30; development, feminine before masculine, 34; development, ideally normal, 41–2, 56, 77; make-up, determines girl's reactions, 206
Libido, and self-preservation, 173, 187–8; centrifugal=masculine, 53, 177, 185; centripetal=feminine, 53; developmental stages of, 15–23, 24, 25, 84, 176, Tables of, 18, 26–7; essentially masculine, 54, 195; genital, in childhood, 24; labile in infancy, 140; of woman, 66–7, 69, 84, 202, 205; phallic into vaginal, 30; positions, aims and objects, of, 107–9; "sticky", 130; sublimated, 145
Lipschütz, A., 15
Loewenstein, R., 42, 164
Love, in man and woman, 67–9; see Partial love, Object love
Love object, change of, 136
Lust murderers, 79

Mack Brunswick, R., 6, 22n., 24, 173n., 199
Mahfouz Pasha, 194
Male, as a mirror, 146–7; attitude in women, 205; "civilized", 147; condition of feminine frigidity; 70; narcissism of girl, 102; sexuality, 116
Male and female compared, activity and passivity, 16, 28; aggression, 52–3; attitude towards pain, 39; biologically, 8–12; libidinal development, 13–5, 41, 52–3; Table of developmental stages, 26–7
Malinowski, B., 160
Marañon, G., 8–12, 14, 34, 110n., 163–5, 170, 175, 201, 204n.
Martin, C. E., 57n.
Masculine, -homosexual woman, 110; men, 207; protest (biologically bisexual), 86, 90, 102, 103n., 140, 145, Adler's theory, 95–6
Masculinity, constitutional, 177, 201; favoured by aggression directed outward, 52–3, 130; innate, of little girl, 39, 55, 102, 174, 201, 208; woman's, not easily modifiable, 208
Masculinity complex, 3, 5–7, 83, 130, 146, 151, 159, 162, 199, 200; Freud's view, 32–3
Masculinization of woman, 164
Masochism, and activity, 173–5; and clitoridal masturbation, 77–82, 176; and passivity, 77, 81, 174, 175, 176, 177; as perversion, 92–5, 175; defences against, 175–8; erotogenic, in girl, 51, 89, 91, 103, 137; feminine, 38–9, 76–115, 129, 146, 151, 169, 175–8; genesis of, 90–1; girl's, 29, 81, 176; masculine, 46, 81; moral, 89, 91, 92, 97, 103; protest against, in women, 86; prototypal cellular, 78
Masochistic, instinctual drives, vicissitudes of, 96–103; -phallic stage of girl, 84; phantasies of men and women, 83–95, 96, 98
Masturbation, 20–1, 43, 54–7, 71–5, 77, 195; anal, 197, 199, 200; and orgasm, 156; and prohibition, 54, 72–3, 123, 160, 196, 202, 204, 208; clitoridal, 4, 5, 36, 42, 54, 58, 76–7, 84–5, 98, 129, 135, 176, by adult seducer, 120, 121; compulsive, case of, 157, 192–4; excessive, and clitoridectomy, 156, 191, 192–4, 203; infantile, 54–8, 71, 123, 124, 139–40, 156, 163, 176, 196; infantile, and sense of guilt, 91–2, 123; its male character in little girl, 33, 55, 199; modes of, and feminine types, 200–1; obsessional symptom substituted for, in latency girl, 55–6; persistent clitoridal, more effect than cause, 201; phantasies, 55, 73–4, 83, 84, 87, 92, 93, 94, 96, 123; threats, 73, 204; vaginal, in little girl, 30, 176, 199, 200–1
Maternal instinct, 47–8
Maturation, precocious erotic, 56–7
Meisenheimer, J., 68n.

Men, types of, 207–8
Menopause, 8, 10–11n.
Menstrual blood, observation of, by girl, 173
Menstruation, 57, 169, 170; after excision, 196, 197; and beating rites, 96n.; and vaginal erotization, 29, 140
Michelet, J., 169
Montaigne, M., 191
Moral, anxiety, 186; condemnation, pathogenic, 117–18, 123, 131–2, 133, 135; condition of feminine frigidity, 70; inhibitions and education, 208; repression, 177
Morality, 79, 160, 208; development in the child, 71–5, 80, 131, 132
Mother, first libidinal object, 16, 43–5, 48; first oedipal object for both sexes, 20, 21; girl's aggression against, 29, 51–3, 127, repressed, 131; -in-law, 24n.; substitutes, 206
Motherhood, and woman's virility, 170; fear of, 49, 69–70; rejection of, 48, 203
Mouth, active and passive, 17; passive, 24
Mucosae, passive anal erotism of, 16, 24
Mueller, J., 5
Muscular, drives, 29; system, active character of, 16, 24, 27; system, and aggression, 79

Narcissism, 16, 26–7, 48, 49n.
Narjani, A. E., 150
Nature and culture in female sexuality, 162–5, 208
Negative Oedipus complex, 20
Nervous functions irreversible, 115
Neuroses and civilization, 160
Neurosis, and repression, 97; resulting from renunciation, 145
Neurotic, anxiety, 187; symptom substituted for masturbation in latency girl, 55–6
Normal, development, 41–2, 56, 98; sexual function, 137, 199
Normality, and health, 145–6; through seduction, 116
Nurses and nursemaids, 206
Nursing-mother, 69
Nymphea, of girl, lengthened by Bapedi, 207
Nymphomania, 157

Object, choice, 43, 135, 136, 145, 146, 202; -love, stages of, 18, 21, 22, 24, 41–4, 47, 78–82, 85, Table of stages, 26–7; -relationships, in feminine development, 99, 100–1, 107–8, 109–10, 111–14

Objective, anxiety, 186, 187; danger as foundation for all anxiety, 186, 187
Obsessional symptom substituted for masturbation in latency girl, 55–6
Odier, C., 19n., 36n.
Oedipal, aggression, 133; defusion of urges, 80, 86; frustration, effects of, in boy and girl, 125–30, 133–4, 136; phantasies, role in psychosexual development, 122–5; phase, masturbation in, 74–5; rejection of daughter by father, 131–2, 133–4, 135
Oedipus complex, beginning of, 31; dominance of excitations or inhibitions, 125; in boy, 26–7, 28, 41–2, 43, 79–82, 125; in girl, 26–7, 28, 41, 42, 47–8, 52, 74–5, 76, 80–2, 90, 108, 125–30, 136, 140, 177; passing of, 22n., 29, 41–2, 75, 124, 126; psychosexual preparation for adult life, 123; vicissitudes of, 111–15, 137; see Active, Passive
Ogresses, eating children, 52
Ophuijsen, J. H. W. van, 5
Oral, activity, 26–7; concept of coitus, 171; erotism, 16, 31, 182; passivity, 26–7; phases, 16, 26–7, 176
Orgasm, after menopause, 11n.; clitoridal, in pre-puberty, 56–7, 58, 59, 77; first occurrence fixates libido to stage and zone, 56, 116, 120–1; in excised women, 196, 197–8; in masturbation, 20, 56–7, 58, 157; in nymphomania, 157; initiation of girl to, 116–25, 141; of man, 9, without erection, 43; of woman, 9–11, 58, 59, 69, 85, 106–7, 111, 151, 155, 192; see End-pleasure
Orgastic sensitivity, and excision, 195; transfer from clitoris to vagina, 191–2, 198–9, 203

Pain, 38, 39, 49, 91, 129, 137, 169–71, 176, 200
Paranoia, in woman, 24
Parental intercourse, 31, 42
Parricide, 80
Partial, love, 26–7; object- (organ-)— cathexes of child, 172
Parturition, 170, 186
Passive, fixation to mother, in men, 94, in women, 47; (secondary) Oedipus complex, 21–3, 41–2, 87, 94, 96, of girl, 77, 81–2, 90, 93, 100, 126, 136, 140; phallic stage, in boy, 42, 78, in girl, 42, 44–5, 78, 140; phallus, 42–5, in male masochists, 46, 94
Passivity, and pain=masochism, 91; development of, 24–30, 42–5; protest against, in women, 86; see Inertia

Patience, erotized, of male, 138
Patriarchal morality and castration complex, 29
Pavlov, I. P., 58, 118, 129n.
Pederasty, 139
Penetration, 43, 47, 50, 60–1, 84, 102, 105, 129, 141, 173, 175, 184; anal, 82; aversion to, in clitoridal women, 202; biological, 181–4; erotized, 206; opposition to, 200
Penis desire, 1, 3, 48, 82, 151, 176, 205–6; and basic bisexuality, 7; and ultimate femininity, 2, 29
Penis envy, 3, 23, 31, 32, 181; divergent theories, 31–3, 103n.; *see* Phallus
Perforation complex, 183, 185, 199
Perversion, 97–8, 202; infantile, 87, 90; through seduction, of women and children, 116
Phallic, activity, 26–7, 55, 56, 78–9, 140; mother, 207; passivity, 26–7, 42–5, 89, 140; zone, fixation to, 3, 5, 7
Phallic phase, earlier, positive, 18–9, 35; beginning of, 28, 78, in girl, 20n., 26–7, 35–6, 89, in M. Klein's view, 32; later phase, with exclusion of genitals, 21, 22, 23, 26–7, 35, 89, 91, 146
Phallus, active, 24, 43, 44, 91; exclusion of, 21, 22, 23, 26–7, 29, 35, 57, 146; passive, 42–5, 46, 107, 177; passive pre-history of, 41–5, 82, 89; primarily passive in woman, 44, 177
Phantasies, consciously remembered, 87–90, 92, 95, 98; in clitoridal masturbation, 77, 129, 193; in phallic masturbation, 43; masochistic, 83–96, 98–9, 101; masturbatory, in oedipal phase, 74–5, 123; masturbatory of male masochists, 46; of active castration of the male, 107; of active male phallus, in women, 47, 60, 206; of being beaten, 83–96; of being ripped open, 181; of cannibalistic mother, 52; of castration, 76, 79; of clitoridal women, 60, 193; of cloacal baby, 51; of demons and fairies, 74; of penis caressed or beaten, 46–7; of phallic woman, in men, 146–7; of seduction by mother, 43; sado-masochistic, of child, 172, 174; vicissitudes of infantile phantasies, 96, 99; with passive aim, in man, 94
Phantasies of girl, of anal penetration, 82; of devouring mother's body contents, 31, 52; of father's assault on clitoris, 82, 83, 84; of oral incorporation of penis, 32; of sadistic coitus, 29; phallic sadistic, 99, 101, 112; phylogenetic, 31; with passive aim, 76

Phobia of spiders, 187
Pinard; 191, 203
Play, nature of, 124
Pleasure, erotic, and fear, 184; in woman, 170–1
Pleasure principle, 60
Pomeroy, W. B., 57n.
Positive Oedipus complex, 20, 52, 81
Potency, and reproduction, 67; disturbances, 42, 43, 146, 162, 164
Predisposition, 122; to clitoridal fixation, 57–8
Pregenital, 44
Pregnancy, 170, 186
Pre-oedipal, 44
Pre-pubertal sexuality of girl, 76–7
Primitives, ablation of clitoris, 153; ablation of male nipples, 153–4n.; excision of clitoris, 153–61
Prohibition of infantile sexuality, and inhibition, 202–4, 208
Prostitution complex, 130
Protophallic phase, 20n.
Pseudologia, 19
Psychic reality of oedipal emotions and wishes, 122–5
Psychical, intimidation, 203–4; "mutilations", 160, 203
Psycho-analysis, a corrective, 164–5; and autoplastic adaptation, 148–9; of female homosexual, 145; of frigidity, 148–9, 152, 202; of neurotic renouncer, 145; of perversions, 149; termination of, 149
Psycho-analytic therapy, of vaginal anaesthesia, 114–15, 135, 148; quantitative basis of, 119
Psychology and biology, 78
Psychosexual development, 13; influence of seduction on, 117–25; and normality, 23, 117, 205
Psychosexuality, determining conditions of, 120, 123–5, 204–5
Puberty, 26–7, 28, 29, 44, 54, 98, 100, 160, 192, 199; rites, 153

Quantitative relation of excitation and inhibition, 118–25

Radó, S., 6n.
Reaction-formation, 32, 35, 87, 97, 199
Reality, denial of, 206; maladaptation to, 125
Rebellion against father in boy and girl, 130–1, 133, 134, 137
Regression, 82, 84, 89, 90, 100, 177; to cloacal organization, 35, 91, in males, 40; to earlier love-object, 130; to phallic stage, 19, 32

INDEX

Rejection, father's of little girl, 131–2, 133–4, 135
Renouncers, 1, 145, 158, 162, 163, 206
Repetition compulsion, 116, 125, 135
Repression, 74, 87, 91, 95, 96, 97, 113, 148; anal, and vaginal function, 108–9; and "apparent" ignorance, 39; excessive, 125, 208; in seduced girls, 118, 133, 136; moral, 177; of active phallic sexuality of woman, 44, 112; of earlier phallic stage, 19, 34, 40; of masochistic drives in feminine development, 102–3; sexual, from without, 159, 160, 208; successful, 124; unsuccessful, 125
Reproduction and narcissism, 183, 184
Revenge, reaction to castration complex in woman, 148; type of women, 206
Ritual mutilation, 160, 203, 204, 207
Rod in girl's beating phantasies, 84–5, 86, 89
Róheim, G., 17n., 205

Sadism, and activity, 172; erotogenic, and sex instinct, 79; essentially male, 53; native, of infant, 53; of child, 78, 79; of girl, 84, 101, 107; primary, towards mother, 52, 99, 107; transformed into masochism, 107–8, 112, 140; turned upon self, 84, 91
Sadistic-anal stages, 16, 24, 26–7, 34, 78, 176; and bi-sexuality, 17
Sadistic-cloacal phase, 176
Sadistic concept of coitus, 171, 175, 176, 178
Sado-masochism, 77, 89
School teachers, 206
Schopenhauer, F., 122
Seduction, first, of girl, 116–25, 141; homosexual in adolescence, 109; infantile, 55, 57, 58, 71–2, 116–21, 132–6, 141, 163; of little girls, cases of, 117–18, 133–6; "unsuccessful", 121, 141
Self-preservation, 38, 173, 187–8
Sex difference, 172; and observation of coitus, 42; trauma of, 1, 81, 87, 206
Sexes, male and female, biologically progressive and regressive, 8–12; libidinal development compared, 13–15, 26–7, 66–7, 126–7, 130
Sexual, attitudes conditioned by Oedipus complexes, 75, 125–30, 136; differentiation, 68, 163–4, 204–5; functions divorced in woman, 67; games of children, 72, 132, 133–4; hormones, 15, 152, 195; ideation of child, 73–5; instincts interfere with narcissistic integrity, 187; investigation, infantile, 124; mutilations, and psychical intimidations, 203–4, 208; partner, choice of, 146, 147–8; theories, infantile, 50–1.
Sexual pleasure, *concave* representation, 105–7, 112, 177; *convex* representation, 105, 112, 177
Sexuality, adult, of man, 126; and anxiety, 185–6, 199; dangers and risks for female, 136, 186; infantile, prohibition and inhibition of, 202–4, 208; male and female, 200; man's fear of, 187; of child, role of adults, 71–2, 117–18, 133–6, 140–1, 202; of girl, changes in, 127; prepubertal of girl, 76–7
Sister, role of, for boy, 136
Skin, excitations of, 24
Sleeping Beauty, 54, 56, 76, 136
Social, activity, 145; workers, 206
Sollier, P., 148n.
Somatic compliance, 139
"Sphincter-morals", 25
Spiders, symbol of "bad mother", 187
Spinsters, and social functions, 206
Sterility, 1
Sublimation, 80, 87, 97
Sucking oral phase, 16
Superego, and primary aggression, 31, 52–3; of boy, 79–81; of girl, 81, 91, 119, 131–2, 173n., 177, 181, 203
Surgeon-father, 151
Symbols for vagina, 37
Symptom formation, 96, 183

Tamm, A., 86n.
Therapeutic surprises, 149
Tomboy, latency girl, 55
Trauma of coitus observation, 174
Traumata and predisposition, 122
Trobrianders and latency period, 160

Urethral erotism, 182

Vagina, 29–30; as adjunct to anus, 34; affirmed, 28, 41, 48, 141, 145, 206; and clitoris, erotogenic, 111, 114, 115, 137–8, 140, 141, 177, 191–2, 198–9; and cloaca, 108–9, 113; and girl's oral erotism, 31; and penis, 33; boy's and girl's concept of, 36, 38, 40, 50, 140; denial of, 38, 39, 40, 49n., 102n., 103–9, 137; dentata, 24n., 53n.;= "hollow penis", 85, 105; little girl's fears of, 37–8, 50, 140; not discovered in childhood, 199; opened by Chinese mother, 154; -pleasure and -anxiety, 39, 140; role in little girl, 36, 38, 50, 54, 130, 140; sealing of, 153; symbolic representations of, 37

Vaginal, anaesthesia, 3, 31, 38, 104, 108, 113, 114, 115, 135, 170, 199, 201, 202; masturbation, 30, 176, 199, 200–1; seduction, 141
Vaginal-clitoridal type of women (combined cloacal and phallic), 196, 201, 204, 205, 206
Vaginal function, 47–9, 54, 66–70, 77, 84–6, 121, 134, 135, 151, 155, 178, 199; and infantile masturbation, 196; refusal of, 199
Vaginal sensitivity, 2, 5, 10, 23, 85, 109–15, 121, 149, 151; after menopause, 10–1n., 115; and excision, 204; and infantile anal masturbation, 200–1; early, 31, 39, 140; in puberty, 5, 29
Vaginal type of woman, 195, 204, 205
Vaginismus, 106
Virgins, fear of penetration in, 183; in China, 154; sublimated libido of, 145; *see* Spinsters

Viriloid, factors in girls, 55, 113; function in clitoridal women, 111; phase after menopause, 8, 10n.
Vital, anxiety, 184–5, 200; ego, 173n., 175, 178; protest, 103n., 140
Vitellinism of female cell, 67–70

Waiting, the female role, 54, 57
Wars and homicidal inhibition, 80
Weigel, H., 157, 192, 193
Woman's, libido, 66–70, 202; erotic function, 59, 65–7, 77, 98–9, 121, 134, 135, 178; protest against masochism, passivity, femininity, 86; psychosexuality, 205; common principle in, 115; vitellinism, 67–70
Womb, return to, 61
Women, types of, 1, 109–15, 135, 141, 145, 148, 195, 200–6

Zawandoski; 15